LABOUR
OF
LOVE

LABOUR OF LOVE

A personal history of
midwifery in Aotearoa

JOAN SKINNER

MASSEY UNIVERSITY PRESS

For Pat and Ro

Prologue

I stood in the far corner of the bright room, holding my breath, trying to be neither seen nor heard. The woman opposite me was lying flat on her back on the high, narrow bed, her eyes squeezed shut, her right hand gripping her husband's. Crushing it, white-hot. Her other arm was strapped down, and a plastic tube emerged from the bandages, connected to a glass bottle suspended from a metal pole. Her legs were pulled far apart and hung in two straps, from two more poles, swaying. She tried to roll from side to side, agitated and in pain. The bottle clanged against the pole. An overhead light, a metre wide, was focused, full-beam, on her exposed perineum. Her bottom was at the very edge of the bed. It looked precarious and I worried about the baby landing on the floor.

'Give us a nice big push, love. We can nearly see the head.' The midwife's voice and movements were brusque and insensitive. She had spread sterile drapes along the woman's legs and across her stomach, seeming to separate the woman from her birth. The midwife wore a mask, and her hair was covered in a cap. A white gown, nearly to the ground, and sterile gloves completed her attire. She, too, seemed to have become removed from what was happening.

Yet here were two women, connected in their work.

The door burst open beside me and the doctor, also dressed in white, strode in. He was wearing a floor-length plastic apron and, for some reason, white gumboots, as if in an abattoir.

'Thank you, nurse,' he said to the midwife, who stepped aside, saying nothing.

'Now, Mrs Smith, give us another good push,' he said as he snapped on his gloves, not looking at her.

The woman's eyes snapped open as another wave of pain took over her body. 'No. I can't do it. Get it out, get it out.'

The doctor turned away, impassively, and sorted out his instruments. 'Just a couple more contractions, dear. You're nearly there.'

By now, the woman's vagina and then her anus were stretched to an extent that seemed impossible to me, and a sort of wrinkled, hairy flesh could be seen in the gap opening up.

The woman screamed, and the doctor ordered her to stop pushing.

He moved between the woman's legs to take control of the delivery of what was presumably the baby's head. But he had blocked my view. Some tense moments followed, with calls from both the doctor and the midwife to either stop or start pushing. Despite the doctor's bulk I had a glimpse of the blue, shiny baby as he put her roughly on the trolley, to cut her cord and check her over. The baby roared, every limb tense and taut. I was spellbound. It was the most incredible thing I had ever seen (or partly seen). There seemed something supernatural about the power of that woman to push a new human being out of her body. But no one else in the room seemed to be as awed by this as I was.

The midwife took the baby away to a cot on the other side of the room, and called me over to watch as she weighed and dressed her.

'This is how you wrap a baby so it doesn't get cold and can't wriggle about,' she said, proceeding to swaddle her tightly into a bundle, like some sort of Egyptian mummy. I could not imagine a time when I would ever feel competent enough to handle a baby like that. Then she left the baby alone in the cot at the edge of the room. All I could see was her pink squished-up face and her tiny eyes. She blinked in the too-bright light and looked worried. It was not until the doctor had finished stitching the large cut in her mother's perineum (a sight I could barely look at) that she was reconnected with her mother.

This was my first birth. I had been so overwhelmed and astonished at watching a baby being born that I was unable to critique either the processes or the context of the work of these two women, let alone the power of the doctor and all that he represented. I look back at my naivety with some sense of forgiveness. I was young, a 19-year-old student nurse. There would be time enough to understand what had been going on here.

My daughter Kena had been labouring all day and most of the night, and despite decades of midwifery I became sick with worry, and I wanted to escape. I should've known better, but I'd never felt like this at a birth before. She was managing so well, much better than I ever did in labour. I was in awe. She rested between contractions in the pool of water. It was the middle of the night, and her lounge room was warm, dark and quiet. The student midwife wiped Kena's face with a cool cloth between the pains and looked amazed at what she was being part of. I made tea constantly and fetched endless glasses of iced water. I sometimes relieved her partner, Tavis, by taking over the massage and the quiet affirmations he had been murmuring in her ear. It took a mammoth effort to stay calm and I felt drained of energy. It surprised me. At long last, she started to grunt and push. The midwife, close by but almost invisible, whispered, 'You catch the baby, Joan.'

I moved closer, summoning some energy from somewhere unknown.

'Just a few more gentle pushes, sweetheart. Your baby is nearly here.'

She squeezed both her partner's hands. The flock of birds tattooed across her shoulder seemed to fly as she breathed and grunted her baby boy out into the warm water. I leant down to lift him to the surface. Fresh-born, a gasp and a cough, eyes wide open. My whole body relaxed. Kena reached out, and I scooped his slippery, wriggly body into her arms. Kahurangi stayed connected to her for hours, through the exit from the pool, the delivery of the placenta, the cutting of the cord, the glass of Moët, and his long first breastfeed. Eventually we needed to get Kena up for her to empty her bladder to prevent bleeding, so Tavis held Kahurangi on his chest, skin on skin. While he lay there, contentedly, the midwife gently checked the baby over. Then it was time for her to leave. She would be back in the morning. Kena and Tavis dressed Kahu warmly, and Kena fed him some more. Three years later he still loves eating. Especially chocolate.

The four decades between that first and last birth crossed over into a new millennium. Nothing in the world seems the same now as it was then. The shape of my work has changed, too. I have watched and wondered, faulted and fought, learnt and unlearnt, and then learnt some more. As my understanding has deepened, I have come to recognise that midwifery is not just a skill to make birth safe; it is also a countercultural force capable of modelling connection with each other and with the natural world. I became steadfast in protecting it. I have taught, managed, studied, advised, critiqued; I've been a consultant, an activist and a researcher. Now I am a writer. The stories in this book talk about the life of this midwife. Along the way there is some herstory for context and some reflections on what I think was happening.

This is also the story of my work: from that young 19-year-old, overwhelmed by what she was seeing, through the challenges of becoming a wife and mother myself, to the satisfaction of becoming skilled and confident. The space between work and home has never existed for me. Midwifery has been my life. It has been uncertain, thrilling, terrifying and exhausting, sometimes all at the same time.

I stretched my understanding of birth and midwifery when working as a consultant in the Asia/Pacific region for the World Health Organization and the United Nations. Midwifery became understood globally as a focal point from which high rates of maternal death should be tackled, and I was lucky to be able to support midwifery education and practice in low-income countries. I struggled to make sense of the complex mess of colonisation, inequity, misogyny, development, science and technology; I'm not sure I came to any stable position. My stories illustrate the tussle.

The social and cultural forms in which midwifery exists have shifted. This is reflected in the language used through the book. For example, in the beginning of my working life, the woman giving birth, the people we 'midwifed', were called patients. Then we progressed to the terms client, consumer, service user, mother, partner and birthing woman. More recently, some have promoted using the gender-neutral terms pregnant person or parent. Current modifications to Aotearoa New Zealand's official Midwifery Scope of Practice have recommended that the whānau should be the focus of the kaiwhakawhānau midwife's care, not the individual woman. The word 'woman' is absent.

We used to talk about delivering women (of their babies), but we struggled with the passivity of this term. So, we began to talk about catching babies, birthing women, or supporting and assisting women to birth. Two words have not changed, though. They are *birth* and *midwife*.

They are universal words, translatable into any language.

Everything in this book did happen, but some of the stories are reconfigured for effect or to protect anonymity. I was unable to contact all the women I wrote about, and although pseudonyms have been used, I did not want any reader to recognise their birth without prior knowledge of it being here. Where I have been able to contact women, stories are more complete. Some have wanted their own names used.

I have written this story, my story of birth and midwifery, to honour these women and all the women who trusted me and showed me how to 'be with' them.

PART ONE

BECOMING

1
—
Nature and nurture

There is steam belching from a window of the maternity hospital. I roll the car window down and hear hissing and clanging as a nurse opens a steriliser lid and drops bedpans from long metal forceps onto the bench behind her. I am riveted to the views and sounds behind the sash windows, all half-open despite the winter morning. I can hear talking, although not the words, and I can hear a baby crying. Maybe I might see one.

I am in the back of a Zephyr with my little brother, Mark. Dad has parked in a hurry in the doctors' parking space. He leaps out of the car with a backwards warning for us to 'stay in the car, you two' and disappears into the hospital's grey walls. The car is right up beside the building, and in the shade.

My eyes follow a different nurse, this time one with a crisp white veil. She strides from window to window. When she gets to the fourth one, my father appears, now in his white coat. They pause briefly to talk, looking worried. Then they turn and walk away together. Dad doesn't look at us. Mark and I wait and wait, but despite being used to it when we go with Dad on his calls, this wait seems too long. Maybe something is going wrong with a baby. I watch the windows intensely for a glimpse of Dad. Then, relief. He appears, striding towards us, smiling. 'How about we get a milkshake on the way home?' I decide to have a lime one. As we drive away, the car fills with his cigarette smoke, all worries for babies gone. I am ten, so Mark must be seven. It's 1964.

Mark and I were the miracle babies of our family. Our mother, Ro, singing for the recovering troops and the off-duty staff at this same hospital 20 years earlier, had entranced Pat, a young house surgeon. She was, my Aunty Jo used to tell me, a sexy performer with a beautiful voice and a flair for an audience. Her singing teacher said she was destined for Covent Garden. Dad told us he held his breath watching her. Despite being tone-deaf, the young doctor was thought to be a catch, and would eventually be welcomed into Ro's outrageous and musical Irish family. They married in war and in sepia. Their wedding photo shows a smiling couple, Dad in his pinstriped suit, looking very young, and Mum in a dark dress with her hat right at the back of her head, at a jaunty angle, a corsage of flowers on her lapel. Rosary beads in her hand. They borrowed an old Ford and headed north on honeymoon. Mum returned pregnant and her life's direction veered. Her singing lessons stopped.

She went on to have three babies in three years, Catherine, Lewis and Christopher, while Dad worked every day and every night, setting up his medical practice in Thorndon. Mum's life wound tighter around these three. She would see Dad only briefly each morning and for dinner. Then he would leave again to do his evening calls or to deliver a baby. She talked of having three in nappies, and of draping wet, handwashed naps over every free space in the lounge of their rented house. The small coal fire made some pathetic attempt to dry them. 'This place looks like a Chinese laundry' became a family meme. Such were the 1940s.

In the next four years, Ro birthed Patricia, Phillip, Carmel and Rita. None survived. Patricia was stillborn. She was full-term and perfectly formed, but swollen and yellow. It was a terrible shock, made worse by the fact that the baby had not been baptised so was destined for eternal Limbo, never allowed into Heaven. It seemed to me later that this caused Mum more pain than the death itself. On the rare occasions when we talked about her babies, she always mentioned it. It has stuck in my mind, too. Despite being told by the local Irish cleric, 'For sure now Ro, Jesus would never do that to wee babies', I don't think she ever believed him. Limbo was a Catholic truth.

Phillip, Carmel and Rita were born alive, a year apart, critically ill. All had that same swollen, yellow look. Dad made sure he was there to baptise them as they died, sprinkling a drop of water and making the sign of the cross on their still-wet foreheads. This action was apparently enough to open the gates of Heaven for them. (I've decided to go and keep Patricia company in Limbo.) Mum, of course, was not allowed to hold or see any of these babies, lest she get upset. The wisdom of the day. But she did hold Rita, after demanding to. She seemed proud of herself when she told us

Above: Mum and Dad on their wedding day in 1945, both 24 years old.

Below: Mum and me in 1954. I was a precious live baby after the four who had died.

this. Apparently, the doctor, a friend of Mum and Dad's, came in for his visit and was horrified. 'What on earth are you doing that for, Ro?'

In those days, women had to stay in hospital for two weeks and were not allowed out of bed for days. Dad arranged for Mum to have a bed at Calvary Hospital where she had some space to retreat into her grief away from the sound of crying babies, and where the nuns could care for her. When we asked her how she coped with all this sadness, she talked of turning away from her grief to focus on the 'three left at home'. Once home she would soldier on, seeing Dad off again and again, day and night, to deliver healthy babies to other men's wives.

The cause of the babies' deaths was unclear, although a blood reaction was suspected. Dad told the story of flipping through the ever-present pile of medical journals by his bed and reading an article describing a disorder called neonatal Rhesus disease. Doctors had discovered that antibodies produced in a mother sensitised by cells from a previous baby were able to cross the placenta and attack subsequent babies' red blood cells.

Going back to the research today, I discovered that this disease had been first identified 10 years earlier and a potential treatment had been found as far back as 1945, five years before our babies started dying. To Dad's horror, the article also said (wrongly, as it turned out) that babies were increasingly affected. At some stage he would have told Mum this. I wonder how he did it; I never asked him.

This was the age of modernity, a time when science tried to outwit religion. In 1954, just as my mother was about to give birth to her eighth baby, the treatment at last reached New Zealand. A pathologist arrived from England with a fine plastic tube, small enough to put in a baby's vein to replace the failing blood cells. But by then my mother had accepted that she would never have another live baby. Being forbidden contraception by the Catholic Church, she had resigned herself, with an inner fury but an outer stoicism, to more babies and more deaths. She dared not hope. Labouring hard to give birth to this baby, she yelled at the pathologist who was pacing at the end of her bed, waiting to seize me, 'Get out, get out!'

It was the only bit of my birth story she remembered. Twilight sleep, a potent mix of narcotic and amnesic given to all birthing women, erased the memory of my birth for her.

'They put me out before you were born.'

She slept, but with no dreams, as I was born, jaundiced and anaemic. They whisked me away to cut me open, to find a vein big enough to exchange my bad blood for good. Meanwhile, so I was told, my mother still dared not hope, again turning to her three at home, now all big enough to know something of death.

The Catholic Church had rallied, too. The local parish priest came to the hospital to await my birth, bringing triple sacraments: baptism, confirmation and extreme unction. There would be no Limbo for me. Every priest and nun, most of whom seemed to be Dad's patients, put me on their prayer list. Masses were said daily throughout New Zealand for my rescue. Saint Pius X, newly canonised, was asked to intercede on my behalf. And thus, the job was done: science and religion, joint winners on the day.

Joan Pius Marion Skinner, forever the miracle baby, was taken home by an overwhelmed and unprepared mother to excited and joyful siblings. My mother's attachment to me became as deep and as layered as her grief. My father's joy was unsurpassed. Not long before his death, as an old man, he got down on his hands and knees to lay a kiss on my ankle where my transfusion scar had grown with me.

And then there was Mark. In the three years since my birth, the techniques of exchange transfusion had improved. His birth in 1957 was joyful and less fraught than mine. He was a bonny armful of baby, always full of life. He soon needed an egg added to his bottle to satisfy his appetite.

There was just one more baby. Anastasia, born in 1958, did not survive her exchange transfusion, despite being born less affected than Mark or I. Dad was there and overheard the paediatrician saying, 'I'm not sure this blood is fresh enough.' Guilt and grief returned for us all.

At 38 years old and after 10 full-term pregnancies, my mother's periods stopped. She did not conceive again.

—◦—

This is our family story. It was told to me without drama, coming up naturally, though not often, in conversation. And then it was let go. Nothing was expected of me. It held enough death and fear to make it seem a fairy tale, with me as the happy ending. As I got older it was my aunts who filled in some of the gaps, providing gentle glimpses of

Mark, Dad and I visiting the sisters at the convent on one of Dad's calls.
They loved seeing the 'miracle babies'.

the grief. As an adult, the details became clearer to me. My mother was more able to share, but not too deeply, and Dad let me see through a small gap into his grief and shame. But the birthdays-deathdays were not remembered, and although we would sometimes make visits to our grandparents' graves, the babies' burial site was never even mentioned.

As an adult, dealing with her own psychological aftermath of the births, my sister Catherine looked for their burial place. She searched through the sexton's old records and found it. Miraculously, all five were buried in the same piece of land, land shared with other stillborn babies of the time. She hunted for the spot and found it in a triangle of shrubbery where two paths met. It was ground that wasn't good enough for a real grave.

Unbeknown to Mum, and to us, Dad had kept an old scrap of paper in his top drawer with the coordinates of this burial place. He never told Mum. She, in turn, unbeknownst to Dad, thought that the babies' bodies had been put into the coffins of whoever the undertaker was burying at the time. Apparently, that used to happen.

Before Dad died, he had a plaque made. Much later, we took Mum to visit. She was silent and showed no emotion as she bent down to read the names.

With age, all of us remaining siblings have had the time and distance to gain some understanding of the impact of that time on our parents, our family life and our own lives. We have all had various amounts and types of therapy, for the usual vagaries and traumas of being human. Around the dinner table, we've laughed at the reactions of therapists to our story, a touch of sympathetic glee on their faces. So much material to work with. Despite being funny, the 'here-we-go-again' sort of funny, it can be distracting and take up more sessions than we've been prepared to pay for. Depending on the type of therapy we've chosen, we've been variously diagnosed with intergenerational trauma, attachment deficit disorder, familial dysphoria, addictive personality, Asperger's, depression, anxiety and denial. As many families have at some point. But despite that, we have our own take on the experience of being a Skinner: we all remember being loved, being happy and being safe. As much as they could, Mum and Dad protected us and maybe themselves, too, from the horror of their story.

When we tell the story to other people, it shocks. So much so that I've sometimes found myself comforting the person who's just heard it.

Above: Fifty years after the births of her five babies who had died,
Mum visits the plaque which marks where they are buried.

Below: The Skinner family setting off for Mass.

'No, it's okay now. We're all fine. We had a very happy family.' (Are we? Did we?)

'Really? But how did your mother manage?'

'I have no idea.'

—o—

Hints of Mum can be found in the layers of her backstory. Her Irish side of the family contained generations of loss and trauma: seven centuries of colonisation by the English. The Irish were disenfranchised, evicted from their land, starved and forced into emigration; their whakapapa erased in a single boat trip. In New Zealand, right up to the mid-twentieth century they were still subject to racist oppression and explicit exclusion from many jobs. 'No Irish need apply.' My family holds this story. There were no tales of their Irish ancestors, except that two or three generations back some might have come via Australia. I've wondered whether it might have been via a penal institution. They would never have considered that, out loud at least.

Once in New Zealand, they focused on the present and hoped for the future, eventually identifying with their English oppressors, not with Māori, their co-colonised. When I later visited Ireland, there was no romantic search through ancient baptismal records for me, no relatives to be found, no link with that land. Just a couple of overgrown headstones, possibly related to us, in Toomevara, a bleak village in County Tipperary.

The next layer of her story was her Catholicism, a medieval faith based on guilt and fear. It created a particularly Irish brand of stoicism. 'Offer it up!' Then there was misogyny, of course. It was the deep undercurrent for women, whose dreams were lost somewhere between the bedroom and the kitchen.

Mum's voice was her dream. All of us children, and some of her grandchildren, have powerful memories of her glorious voice as she sang along to arias and operas on the radio, over the kitchen sink. Her identity became built on being Dr Skinner's wife, a role she embraced with a complex mix of enthusiasm and resentment. Yet even that role was fraught. She told us of the time she overheard some doctors' wives, the non-Catholic ones, saying: 'Oh God, she's pregnant again. Why doesn't he leave her alone?'

Mum and Dad's social life was centred on family. I have childhood memories of raucous parties with Mum's four siblings and any local clergy who wanted a night out (one of Mum's brothers was a priest). The singing around the piano, in at least three-part harmony, used to keep Mark and me awake. On our regular trips of complaint down to the front room we were firmly told to 'Get back to bed, you two'. I could see they were having fun, but it was a bit scary. My aunts and uncles would all have a tumbler of whiskey or brandy on the go. Some added milk, in a vain attempt to protect their stomach linings.

Our generation of cousins never had the stamina to replicate these nights. All Mum's siblings, including her at the end, either became alcoholics or married one. There is something unique about this Irish ability to put the fun into dysfunctional while retaining an undercurrent of melancholy. Mum's family perfected this, living at the edge of wickedness, disrespect and self-deprecation. Nothing was taken too seriously — even, strangely, the church itself. Paradox made sense. Life was to be enjoyed, yet life was to be mourned. Even the most challenging things were to be relished. Mum would remind us kids of this anytime we had to do something hard. For anything from a School Certificate English exam to a job interview, we would be encouraged to 'summon your mad McGrath and have fun'. I say this to my own children, and now to my grandchildren.

My memory of Dad at these parties is of him not drinking so much and never singing. But he loved them. He could be seen smiling, humming along (badly), and making sure everyone's glasses were full. It may have been because he was always on call, or possibly his Scottish background on his father's side, which was dour in comparison.

Dad worked very hard, often having evening calls to make or paperwork to do at the surgery. And then there were the thousands of babies being born at every hour of the day and night. He always had to stay close to a phone. If he was out on calls, Mum had to have all the phone numbers of the patients he was visiting at hand so she could track him down.

'Bethany is trying to get hold of you, Pat. Mrs Bloom is in labour, and they think she won't be long.'

We knew the telephone was important. Long conversations with our friends could result in a midwife somewhere getting stressed about being unable to contact Dr Skinner. One night the local Thorndon policeman, probably also one of Dad's patients, knocked at the door to let him know he was needed at Ward 21. In that instance it was another doctor needing his help to provide an anaesthetic for a difficult forceps delivery. In the 1960s, not only was he managing a busy general practice and hundreds of deliveries a year, but he was also providing obstetric anaesthetics. I can't remember who the telephone culprit was that time. Certainly not me.

One evening when Mum was out, and we were still little, Dad called the police to come and look after Mark and me so he could go to a delivery. I remember being terrified when two young policemen arrived. I headed straight to bed, not sleeping till I heard his car returning and the slam of the garage door.

He could never escape work. Even at Mass he would sometimes get a tap on the shoulder. Some midwife or doctor, knowing where the Skinner family could be found every Sunday morning, would have rung the Presbytery looking for him. The priests' housekeeper would come up to the third pew on the left, where we always resided. I was usually unsettled by these happenings. All eyes of the congregation would follow Dad as he walked out of Mass; even the eyes of Jesus himself, hanging just in front of us on a giant cross, blood pouring from his hands and feet.

Was a baby being born or was someone dying? When would he be back?

Everyone in the church knew him, as most were his patients and he'd delivered all their babies. Eventually he developed the habit of leaving Mass before the final blessing, waiting for us in the car. It was his attempt to avoid the inevitable consultations at the church door. People used to queue up for 'just one quick question, Doctor'.

The front four rows on the other side of the church were for the nuns. They would parade down Guildford Terrace from the convent in pairs, just as Mass was about to start. They were all his patients, as were all the priests. By the mid-1960s, in an attempt to modernise Catholicism, the Vatican had issued edicts requiring priests to say Mass facing us and to use English instead of Latin. And then one Sunday morning, there was no parade of nuns. Instead, they arrived as if part of the ordinary congregation, alarmingly spreading themselves through the church, their new modern veils revealing their hair. We also began to be offered a sip of the blood of Christ from a shared cup. The altar boy would wipe the rim of the chalice with a starched white cloth between each person's sip. Dad would never take it. He said he knew all the diseases that the parishioners had, and wasn't going to risk it. I never did, either.

Dad was a gentle, self-effacing man, prone to sadness and very occasional bouts of short temper, usually directed at himself. He had a non-dogmatic and compassionate approach to life, having become wise, not bitter. He had perfected the now-lost skill of saying 'I don't know', but was always interested in finding out if he could and accepting uncertainty if he couldn't. His patients loved him. He was a very good doctor. He had been the doctor for the prime minister, the governor-general, the chief justice and the cardinal. The State, the Realm, the Law and the Church were all covered. He worked so hard. Mum liked to tell the legendary story of when he had been up every night for over a month delivering babies or administering anaesthetics. She found him in the morning asleep on the landing, halfway up the stairs.

One afternoon he took Mark and me to the movies, a very unusual event. Halfway through, text appeared, moving slowly across the bottom of the screen: 'Would Dr Skinner please come to the front desk.' His being called away was our norm.

Catholicism worried him. He saw the distorted, lonely lives that priests and nuns were forced to lead, and the damage done to vulnerable parishioners wracked with fear and guilt, his wife included. He struggled with the laws of the Church in relation to contraception and did eventually prescribe the pill. Abortion saddened him. During that period when Mum was in the middle of having her babies that died, he arranged, as many Catholic doctors did, for unmarried mothers whose babies were up for adoption to come and live with us. They would arrive, quiet and sad, small bags in hand, when their swollen tummies had become obvious. It was such an horrendous cruelty, but at the time it was seen as an act of charity. 'They can always have another one later.' I even heard my mother say this. I don't know what sort of relationship Mum had with these young women — both of them about to lose their babies.

Dad told me once about the time when he went into the waiting area to greet his next patient, a woman with a six-week-old adopted baby come for his first health check. Sitting across from her was the baby's young mother, who had come in for her own six-week postnatal check. She was oblivious that her baby, unseen and unheld, was within arm's reach. He was horrified.

Because of the eight years during which our babies died, our family ended up being in two batches. By the mid-1960s, the big three had all left home. Catherine went nursing, eventually becoming a midwife. Lew went to the seminary, much to Dad's horror, and Chris went to Massey University in Palmerston North. By then our family had become economically secure. Dad had a well-established general medical practice and was a respected and very busy GP obstetrician. What was most important, though, was that he was able to have some time off. His practice had grown enough to take on a partner, and two other doctors, Diana Mason and Heydon Gray, were able to relieve each other for their maternity cases.

Mark and I were the second batch of kids. He was my childhood companion, my best friend. We spent endless hours together exploring Thorndon on our scooters. We used to visit people who were Dad's patients, though only the ones with lollies or cakes. Our favourite was the McCreadys' pub, in the Railway Hotel at the bottom of Pipitea Street. In the huge kitchen, which smelled so different from ours, we could be sure of the twin delights of fresh baking and chats with the cockatoo. Sometimes it would swear. Then there were the ancient and bent-over Ritners next door, who were refugees from Poland. They had a lolly jar. The scariest place, though, was the witch's house on the corner of Hill Street and Tinakori Road. We would dare each other to knock on the door and then run and hide, revelling in that delicious feeling of terror and excitement. She caught us one day. 'You're Dr Skinner's children. I'm going to tell him about you.' More terror than excitement then.

Days would pass at Thorndon pool as we endeavoured to swim more and more lengths and competed to see who could stay underwater for longer. We would head home, red-eyed and hungry, bare feet burnt from the hot pavement. We would go straight to the tins in the pantry to finish off any baking that might have survived. Only then would we tell Mum of our exploits and our latest underwater record. At the peak of her singing ability, when her diaphragm was strong and controlled, she used to be able to do a whole length of the pool underwater. That was our aim.

Mum would be in the kitchen, the mixer on, beating up a batch of some buttery, sugary thing. Goo cake was the best. She fed us and fed us. She was an adventurous cook, using garlic and cream long before anyone else did, except maybe Rosaleen Desmond, another Catholic doctor's wife from up the road in Murphy Street. They shared recipes. Dad had delivered her babies, too.

Mum and I were close. My childhood happened right at her side — in the kitchen helping her cook, in the laundry tentatively feeding the wet clothes through the wringer or helping with the housework. There were plenty of directions: to use a light hand rubbing the butter into the flour for scones, how to dust between the rungs of the Oregon pine banisters, how to make cheese, pineapple and onion on cocktail sticks when we were having people over for a party. She did not send me to kindergarten, she told me, as she didn't want to let me out of her sight.

I was a good girl. My cousins used to call me Saint Joan, and not in a good way. As I moved into adolescence, I became dreamy and quiet, apparently worrying my mother. But I was just biding my time. School didn't faze me, and I easily passed all my exams, except for French. I had lovely friendships. I was secure, loved and free of trauma.

The world into which I was to emerge as a young adult, though, was almost unrecognisable from that in which I had been a child. By 1971, in my last year of college, my quiet adolescence had begun its stretch towards adulthood. I turned 17. From the shelter of St Mary's, the local Catholic girls' secondary school, my friends and I started to look outwards, and watched the world both expand and come closer. By then, Catholicism for us was about social justice. Literal interpretations of doctrine seemed irrelevant and the days of praying to the Virgin Mary to save the Far East from communism were long forgotten. It was our job to 'make the world a better place' and, naive as it might seem now, we were sure we could. We sang 'Bridge Over Troubled Water' with passion. We were horrified at the photos of starving children in Ethiopia and were reprimanded by Sister Phillipa for wearing Youth Against Hunger badges on our school uniforms. We tentatively joined a Vietnam War protest, calling 'One, two, three, four, we don't want your bloody war' all the way down Lambton Quay. It was exhilarating. We had our first glimpses into our privilege and the responsibility that came with it. We protested, we critiqued the way we lived, and we believed in ourselves and in humanity. Well, that's how I remember it feeling.

So much happened in that decade, shaping my perspectives and foreshadowing the future. American soldiers did eventually walk away from the war in Vietnam, leaving the people behind to their own devices. Next door in Laos, a country which was suffering immensely from both civil war and the Vietnam War (now calling it the American War), communism also became established. And in Cambodia, which was also decimated in that same war, civil unrest and the post-colonial gap was filled by the brutal regime of the Khmer Rouge. In North Korea, which was still reeling from the distortions of colonisation and the utter destruction of the war, Kim Il-sung emerged to create *Juche*, an extreme nationalist and isolationist ideology, taking the country into the most repressive regime on the planet. Further west, Bangladesh won its bitter war of liberation from Pakistan, both nations having been colonial constructs. And Russia, in an attempt to maintain a buffer state between it and Western democracies, invaded Afghanistan.

Forty years later I would work in all these countries. War, it would appear, is a toxic companion for birth long into the future.

Still further west, technology developed apace, impacting every bit of life and promising a solution to all our problems. Western faith shifted further from God towards the miracles we created ourselves: the pocket calculator, the Sony Walkman, a computer at home, the orbit of Mars. Ultrasound and CAT scan technologies revealed the inside of the human body. We could see lumps inside a woman's breasts and watch babies, still wrapped in their mothers' bodies, blink at us. The first test-tube baby was born.

It feels to me now that it was in this decade that New Zealand's interest in social justice began to encompass notions of diversity. Ngā Tamatoa (The Young Warriors) emerged, disrupting our assumptions. We watched them on the news and worried. Colonisation and racism became issues of the present moment, not just of history. Whina Cooper led a land march to Parliament and the protestors camped there, peacefully, for six weeks. By the middle of that decade, the Treaty of Waitangi Tribunal had been established.

We began to look at our environment differently, too, protesting nuclear testing in the Pacific and the raising of Lake Manapouri. The first Earth Day was held, and at school Rachel Carson's book *Silent Spring* was in our curriculum. It scared us.

The social and cultural shifts of that decade were enormous. Modern iterations of the gay and feminist movements further altered our understanding of what it was to be human. The second wave of feminism reached New Zealand. At its core was equal opportunity for women. We should be able to do anything that men could do. To be able to do this, reproductive control was essential. By 1972, the year after I left school, New Zealand's population had reached three million and it did not increase for another 10 years. The first abortion clinic opened in 1974, and that same year the Domestic Purposes Benefit was introduced, allowing mothers on their own to keep their babies. The horrific social experiment that had been closed adoption — where mothers never knew where their babies went, and babies never knew who their mothers were — dwindled.

Feminist interest in birth was minimal. Liberation meant freedom from motherhood and from the home. Control over reproduction meant being able to choose not to have babies. Except for husbands being 'allowed' inside the delivery room, little changed for pregnant and birthing women. It was a decade in which almost all small maternity units closed, and birth technologies were introduced, unchallenged. The high-tech centralised hospital became unrivalled as the place where all women should birth. Feminism spurred only a very small increase in the number of women birthing at home.

Midwifery as its own profession became invisible and irrelevant. The Nurses and Midwives Act became the Nurses Act. The word 'midwife' was removed from all professional and regulatory organisations, and finally doctors took over total control of birth. By law, a medical doctor had to oversee every birth, even those at home. There was no fuss. Despite my sister being a midwife and my father a GP obstetrician, I was unaware of this change.

It wouldn't have mattered much to me anyway. At 17 years old it was clear to me that girls could (should) do anything and no girl with any intelligence would consider nursing. Being infantilised in the nurses' home, only to be bullied and disrespected, was not appealing. So, midwifery was out of the question. It was just another type of nursing and never entered my head as a possibility. But the problem was that there was nothing I wanted to do or be. I would be a mother one day, and I certainly would not be working until the kids were all at school. My imagination failed me; although I was unable to articulate it, I could not see how all this career stuff really mattered. Social conditioning had not quite matched the pace of social change, although it took a good 30 years for me to see that.

There was everything and nothing for me to do. But the time for being dreamy was over.

—o—

We lived in a double-brick house in Mulgrave Street, Thorndon. I could sit on the deep windowsill at my leadlight bedroom window and watch everything pass by. Our street had become a motorway off-ramp, so there was no shortage of distractions. I watched the weddings at Old St Paul's next door. Our family used to rate them out of 10 for quality of dresses, cars and guests. We were merciless. I wondered when I might marry and what I might wear; certainly not a white dress and veil. Directly opposite was a small two-storey wooden house that my mother had grown up in. Occasionally I would see groups of young people waiting outside, chatting and laughing. They looked cool. It turned out that they were applying to do a year of VSA (Volunteer Service Abroad) even though they were straight out of school.

I applied, tentatively, along with about 300 other seventh-formers from around New Zealand. There were only 30 places, and a gruelling interview process. I was accepted. I was to go to Ha'apai, a small coral atoll in the central island group of Tonga. I would teach seven-year-olds and live with a local Tongan family. My imagination couldn't reach that far.

During our orientation in Tongatapu, we were warned about culture shock, told not to get pregnant, given a couple of days of Tongan lessons and then pretty much left to our own devices. It turned out that the shock was truly shocking. From my sheltered, privileged, white middle-class Catholic-doctor's-daughter upbringing, I looked out around me and was terrified. I wasn't just looking at photos of what we then thought of as 'poor' villages or passing through on a holiday. It was not theoretical anymore. I was going to be immersed in this world. What had I done? If living here was like this on the *main* island, what would it be like in Ha'apai? They warned me how remote it was and how much tougher life would be there. There was no electricity, no running water, no airstrip, and hardly anyone spoke English. I panicked, my mind flailing around trying to think of ways to escape. There was nobody I could tell. The only outward sign of my distress was that I couldn't eat, at all.

During the slow, rolling boat trip to Ha'apai I wandered the deck of the overcrowded ferry trying not to trip over bodies. Everyone but me was asleep. I remembered, and grieved, for the ferry ride from Picton I had made just weeks before. Late in the afternoon, just as I was giving up hope of getting there, everyone, as if by some cue I hadn't got, started to stir. And there it was, the most beautiful island I had ever seen, so close down to the sea that the tallest part was the top of the coconut palms along the waterfront. It was as if someone had turned my fear switch off and replaced it with a wonder switch. How, I'll never know. That feeling stayed with me all year.

There was no wharf on the island, so we had to offload on to an already packed barge to get to land. A young woman, about my age, waved at me. 'Soana, I have come to get you.' She took me towards an old Tongan man sitting cross-legged in the shade. He waved his stick and called me over. He was Vaha'i, my Tongan father. We walked slowly along the sandy road, through the village, past the old stone church, and past the concrete-block school where I'd be teaching. He chatted to me all the way, smiling and gesticulating. I didn't understand a word, yet I knew what he was saying. On the way back to the boat a year later, I was able to chatter back with him, albeit in that strange colloquial way gained only from immersion in a language and culture.

We arrived at the 'api. Vaha'i, four of his eight children, and their husbands and families all lived there. There were five homes placed around the edge of a large patch of grass, shaded by a breadfruit tree. Some houses were traditional thatched fales, and others single-room wooden buildings. Copra was lying out on mats in the sun to dry, and smoke drifted up through the coconut fronds of the cooking fale. Children, a couple with babies on hips, ran to see us.

'Oku 'eni a Soana.'

The two skinny dogs yapped at us and were yelled off. The pigs and chickens, nosing away in the dirt at the far corner of the 'api, raised their heads briefly to see what the fuss was all about. Gleaming faces emerged from doorways and there were calls of excitement. Vaha'i ordered everyone around authoritatively. Sulunga, the only English-speaker of the family, showed me my room, a small space in the corner of the wooden house. My bed was made, the walls and ceiling were covered in beautiful tapa cloth and a soft woven mat covered the floor. A mosquito net was ready to keep me safe and cosy. It felt like home.

With my Tongan family during my year with Volunteer Service Abroad in 1972.

There was a blue aerogram on the bed. A letter from Mum had arrived on the boat with me. She wrote that after I'd left, she had walked along the beach for hours and had added considerably to the sea level. It was the first and only time I cried that year. Aerograms from her, tightly typed and full of family news, arrived regularly on the weekly boat from Nuku'alofa and there was always one from me on its return journey. Our letters now sit waiting in a box in the attic, ready for me to create something of them. I'm not sure quite what.

My Tongan story is one that's too big to tell here. It needs its own space. And it's not a midwifery story, although two babies were born into the family that year, one named after me. I watched, amazed, as babies were enveloped by the whole family, who shared in their care and, even more importantly, in the responsibility for their care. Even the children, boys or girls, could be found with a baby on their hip. Tonga made a different person of me, impacting on the midwife I was to become. I finished that year with an embodied understanding of culture and its link with language.

The story is also a love story. I can still feel Sione Taumoepeau's delicious body and that sense of being unable to sleep or even to breathe. Everyone should feel like that at least once in their lives. His love letters from America are still tucked away in my top drawer. I made sure not to get pregnant.

I lived a collective life in Tonga, which was revolutionarily different for me. As much as he could, Vaha'i treated me as one of his daughters. I was never left alone. I had new understandings of family expectations, and of human connection. Around me I could see that notions of individual autonomy and freedom could be unreal. One of my most lasting memories is of walking along the sandy road to town, hand in hand with Lelei, the young woman who had met me at the boat when I first arrived.

'Lelei, what do you want to do with your life?' I asked.

She turned to me, mystified.

'I will do what my family decides for me.'

I watched the inevitable onslaught of colonisation and the slipping away of connection. I was part of it and knew it. The seeking of education and more 'opportunity' for families had already become tied up with Western notions of individualism, consumption and of leaving Tonga. Those tensions are still clear half a century later.

I understood the distorted, privileged position I had been given there.

I lost count of the number of proposals of marriage I received at the weekly faiva. There was an obvious injustice in my impending return to New Zealand, free to 'claim the world as my oyster'.

The experience of going on VSA also taught me the value of taking risks, and that fear is not always a bad thing. Unbeknown to me, the seeds of letting go and of embracing uncertainty were planted deeply that year, and I will always be grateful for this.

I have visited my Tongan family in Ha'apai five times, the latest in 2019 for a big family reunion. I have visited with both my husbands (not at the same time), an experience that was mystifying for them, and difficult to explain in English let alone in my very basic Tongan. I have supported family members when they have come out to work, and fundraised when cyclones have hit and volcanoes erupted. My daughter Kena is named after my Tongan mother. I have been the midwife for many Tongan women. Most of my Tongan family now live in New Zealand, and their 'api back in Tonga is cared for by only one couple, left to act as kau tauhi 'o le fonua (guardians of the land). This is an almost universal experience for Tongan families now. All those seven-year-olds I taught back then now live in America, New Zealand or Australia.

At the end of that year, then 18 years old, I took the first ferry off the island once the school year had finished and flew straight home to New Zealand. I was obsessed with having a long hot bath, roast lamb and potatoes, and seeing my family — especially my new nephew who had been born while I was away. But that was all done on the first day home. The next day I went for a walk down Lambton Quay, strolling at the slow amble I had acquired in Tonga, only to be traumatised by people pushing past me so fast, and by the terrible traffic. They hadn't told us about reverse culture shock. Why had I rushed home to this? I wanted to go back. There was nothing for me here.

—◦—

Not long after I got home from Tonga, Dad handed me a small piece of paper he had cut out of *The Dominion*.

'Have a look at this. It might interest you.'

There was a new nursing course starting at the local polytech. It was student-based, not the old hospital-based apprentice model. The students were to get their theoretical learning at tech, and go out for practical experience in the hospital and in the community. They would be supernumerary to the workforce and the theory and practice would be integrated. It was a radical shift for nursing. I was interested, and it seemed better than doing nothing. It was certainly more useful than doing a random degree at university.

So, in I went. The course was both fascinating and terrible. There were only 23 of us and two tutors, Judith Christensen and Jan Rogers. They were clever, and they loved nursing and what it could become. We could see that. But they were only a page ahead of us in the planning, so it was sometimes a little chaotic. It must have been a nightmare for them trying to find clinical experience for us, as we were treated like pariahs by the nurses in the hospital, standing out in our blue zip-up uniforms with, God forbid, no caps. For some reason we were very threatening. I loved learning about the human body and what might go wrong, and the new idea of a holistic, patient-centred focus for care made such good sense. We were encouraged to be critical thinkers and problem-solvers, as opposed to rote learners. And we studied in class the systems that we were working with in the clinical setting. All this was at odds with how nurses had been educated in the past.

We were to get what was called a comprehensive qualification, which included general, maternity, psychiatric and psychopaedic nursing. Our psychiatric clinical placement was at the old Porirua Hospital. The psychiatric nurses there, sometimes hard to distinguish from the patients, absolutely hated us. I remember them locking us in the dayroom of the male admission ward with the newly admitted and very distressed men. The nurses, who then left, were trying to frighten us. In fact, we were outraged. Our tutors came and rescued us. We debriefed with them to try to make sense of the type of care that was being provided. I wish I could remember what they said. How could locking a group of critically mentally ill men in a room with each other, and with two young women, for hours, be seen as therapeutic in any way? Surely it was bordering on criminal.

We went on to experience the complete horror of the 'care' provided at the Kimberley Home, our psychopaedic nursing placement. Psychopaedic nursing, now thankfully a defunct profession, was created to provide care for those with mental disabilities in the days when families were advised to lock away their 'mentally deficient' children. Kimberley was previously known as Levin Farm and Mental Deficiency Colony. Seems to say it all. I was placed in a villa with the 'profoundly mentally retarded' patients. The care was too appalling to describe. They should have burnt that place down when they closed it; horrifically, this was not for another 30 years.

Learning about nursing opened me up to the fragile nature of humanity. I had glimpses of the preciousness of caring and of the intimacy and vulnerability that can be experienced in the nursing moment. My favourite task was to give a very good bed bath: a hot flannel to the face, a massage along the back and across the pressure areas of the buttocks, soaking the hands and feet in the bowl of warm water, then a careful dry between each toe. And fresh, crisp sheets. All the while we would be chatting, and I would be finding out the how and the why of this human.

When I had my hip replacement recently, the rushed nurses handed me a packet of cold wipes. I am showing my age here.

All of us students got together for our tenth anniversary. Judith Christensen laughingly told me that whenever she had been doing the rounds to check up on how our clinical experience was going, I could usually be found hiding in the sluice room, long tongs in hand, taking charge of emptying and filling the steaming bedpan steriliser, avoiding conflict where possible.

It was during the final year of our nursing training that we did our maternity section. We were packed off to Blenheim, as no one in Wellington would give us access to any maternity wards. And it was here that I saw that first birth and was hooked. It is hard to describe the feeling. It was somewhere much deeper than any conscious cognitive process. I should have run a mile given the type of care I had watched. But I didn't seem to have a choice.

Why did I become a midwife? In writing down my family story and the story of my own birth, I thought that maybe I've always been one. I midwifed my mother back to joy and my family back to hope. I have waited for babies to be born my whole life. I grew up surrounded by birth. It was in my DNA. But I had no idea of all that then.

As inexplicable as it might seem now, you had to do a year of nursing before doing midwifery, 'middie' as it used to be called. As a polytech nursing student I had been given a bursary of three dollars a week from the Department of Public Health, and for that they had bonded me for a year. They sent me to Whangārei Hospital, where I proceeded not to

Graduating from the first polytechnic nursing programme in 1976.

nurse but to supervise hospital nursing students (who resented me) to do the nursing. It was bizarre. I wore a crisp white uniform, with bright red lapels to mark my seniority (non-existent), and a nursing cap (ridiculous). It didn't work and was a time best forgotten. The only patients I remember from that time are Mr Pearson, whose pancreatic surgical wound never healed, and the ancient, silent woman in the medical ward, whose faeces I was directed to manually remove, and who died later that day. I've always thought I might have killed her. My experience as a nurse was made manageable only by the frequent visits to and from my boyfriend Paul, who was doing his MA at Waikato University.

As soon as I could, I packed up my Hillman Hunter and headed back to Wellington, getting a speeding ticket in Hunterville. I arrived home to the news that Dad, two weeks before I was to start my midwifery, had decided to give up obstetrics. I had been so looking forward to working with him at St Helens and was disappointed that he hadn't waited even a few months. But he was exhausted, and he looked it. He insisted that he just couldn't last a minute more. In another 40 years I would feel the same.

—o—

The St Helens I arrive at in 1976 is nothing like the old grey building where I had waited for my father as a 10-year-old. Designed in 1960, it is a purpose-built, four-storey hospital, with single rooms for mothers so they can room in with their babies, day and night. There are no nurseries. The utility rooms are in the centre of the wards, so it is the women who have windows with sunlight and fresh air, not the staff. There is light and air everywhere. I can't find out who designed such a birth space for women, but it is a radical departure from what had been before. Each woman has her own labour room, not the curtain-partitioned spaces of the old hospital. There are windows that open in the labour rooms, too, and enough space for husbands and partners to feel comfortable. There is even a waiting room for them. The delivery rooms are also spacious, with floor-to-ceiling frosted glass, and privacy. I think I'm going to like it here. The other student midwives in my class seem great. I'm the only one from the polytech course.

Then we get shown to our rooms. We're all going to 'live in', mainly so we can be on call for births. We are not going to live in a warren of an old nurses' home, but in brand new staff accommodation. There are shared kitchenettes and lounges. I fetch my bags from the car and begin to unpack.

I'm in the right place. I get that feeling again: it's almost home.

2

—

Midwife and mother

The midwife pushed open the swing door from the delivery room, her masked face appearing around the corner.

'Have you got all your delivery observation numbers yet, Joan?'

I am sitting at the midwives' desk in the centre of the delivery unit. We can see and hear everything from there. I am three weeks into midwifery training and yes, I have done the five birth observations required before I am allowed to do an assisted delivery myself.

'Okay, come and do this one. Mrs Kingsly is happy for you to help.'

Mrs Kingsly, Vicky, is on a high delivery bed but her legs are not up in the lithotomy position. I begin to scrub up and dry my hands thoroughly, putting on my gloves using meticulous aseptic technique. I'm apprehensive.

'No time for all that, Joan. Just get those gloves on or you will miss it.'

I quickly swap sides with the midwife, so I am on the woman's right side. She is covered in sterile guards and there is another one under her legs where the baby will be born. I can see its head now when she pushes. She has some pillows under her shoulders and her husband is supporting her to sit up a little.

'Put your hand on the head and support it, Joan. No, not like that. Like *this*. Keep that head flexed. Yes, good. Now, Vicky, when you get your next pain, I want you to push very gently. The baby will be born with the next contraction, and then I'll want you to pant and not push so you don't tear. It's all looking great.'

'Are you okay, Mike?' to the husband.

'Yes, where is the doctor?'

'On her way.'

'Another one's coming.' Vicky, eyes wide open, an edge of panic in her voice.

I put my hand on the baby's head as it stretches the perineum. It's still hard to fathom that a vagina will make so much room for a baby. I feel the reassuring presence of the midwife's hand resting on top of mine, as she helps me understand how much pressure is required.

'A gentle little pant now, Vicky.' She guides the mother.

'That's great, Joan. You will see the head extend now and the face will come through. Not so much pressure, Joan. It does have to get out.'

The baby's face appears bit by bit: eyebrows, eyes, nose, mouth, chin.

'The baby's head is out now, Vicky. Get the suction catheter and suck out its nose. That's enough.'

'Now check for cord around the baby's neck. Oh, no time, here come the shoulders. Did you see that restitution? Some downward pressure for the anterior shoulder. Good. Gently, Vicky. Now up for the posterior shoulder. Careful! Careful of that perineum.'

'Pant, pant.' I pant along with Vicky. 'And . . . here we are, Vicky. It's a wee girl.'

'Give her a good dry, Joan. We don't want her to get cold. She can have the syntocinon now. Give it IV. Great pair of lungs. Look at all that hair. Get that cord cut. Put the plastic clamp about an inch away from the skin. Yep. Now the forceps next to it. No — not so close, we need space to cut. Grab the scissors . . . now cut. Yes, keep going, it's quite tough. Gee, these scissors need sharpening. Could we have the warm towels please. Now wrap her up tight and give her to Mum. Excellent.'

I had not uttered a word.

The doctor eventually arrived, berated us for not getting her there on time, made us put Vicky into lithotomy so she could check the perineum, and generally made herself the centre of attention. I began to see that this (managing doctors' egos) would be an important part of the training.

I was young when I registered as a midwife in 1976, and, as it turned out, naive. The six-month post-nursing training at St Helens had been didactic and task-focused. The women we were meant to be caring for were strangely absent in our learning. We talked of the uterus and the breasts and followed a stuffed doll through a disconcertingly real pelvis, watching and learning by heart the positions of the baby as it made its 'perilous' journey: flexion, rotation, descent, crowning (lovely term), delivery of the head, restitution (the head rotating back slightly to match the angle of the shoulders), delivery of the anterior shoulder, then the posterior shoulder, and then the whole body is born, following the curve of Carus. (Yeah! I can still remember it.) How the women might have been feeling was not mentioned. Pain relief was either a narcotic or nitrous oxide (laughing gas). Epidurals were just beginning and there was only one doctor, a GP, who could do them. He became very popular.

At that stage, the doctors had gained total control of birth, or so they thought. They certainly got all the money for it. A doctor was seen as the primary health professional for pregnancy and birth and it was he (rarely she) who provided all the antenatal check-ups and attended all the births. Mothers looked to him for decision-making. We midwives were discouraged from building relationships with patients in those days, as this was seen as unprofessional. By now we had been completely 'nursified' by registration and by culture, although most of us did not notice this, or particularly worry about it at the time. All midwives had to be registered nurses before doing 'middie'. Midwifery was almost the only post-registration education nurses could get, so it was required if one wanted to make any progression through nursing. There was no talk of research, and none of homebirth, except that it was dangerous and selfish.

—o—

How did maternity care and midwifery in New Zealand get to this? The birth of midwifery in this country, in its professional sense at least, happened at the turn of the twentieth century. Before then, women in New Zealand generally birthed at home, assisted by lay midwives, women who had learned about birth from other women. It was only rich

The midwives at St Helens Hospital, Wellington, just before the hospital closed in 1981. Matron Joy Moffit is in the centre of the front row. I'm in the third row, second from left.

white women who could go to one of the few private maternity homes, which were owned by doctors. Things were to change dramatically. At that time, governments around the world were starting to examine the demographics of their populations, and New Zealand was no exception. They discovered that women (they only looked at Pākehā) were often dying in childbirth and that New Zealand was thought to have the worst rate of maternal death in the world — at least the part they counted. This worried the New Zealand government as they were keen to see faster European population growth. They wanted a lot more white babies. Thus, motivated by colonialist eugenics, although also concerned at the distress caused by the inordinate number of maternal deaths in the European population, they set about trying to improve things. In their midst, as deputy inspector of lunatic asylums, hospitals, licensed houses and charitable institutions, was Grace Neill.

Neill was an ex-nurse, a midwife and a journalist, trained in the UK. She was by all accounts an impressive and thoughtful public servant. Neill proposed that it was trained and skilled midwives who would make the most difference to maternal and infant health. Richard John Seddon was prime minister at the time, and he and his minister of health both enthusiastically supported her. By 1904 The Midwives Act was passed, which created both a registration and an educational pathway for midwives. Neill had to move quickly. The doctors, who were yet to organise themselves into a professional obstetric speciality, were horrified and were at her heels. Within three weeks she had purchased a house which could be used as a small hospital and had begun to develop a three-year professional midwifery curriculum. Just one year later, in 1905, the first St Helens Hospital was opened in Wellington. Neill named it after Seddon's birthplace; she knew how to stroke a big male ego.

The hospital was a radical innovation — the first state-run free maternity hospital anywhere in the world. It provided maternity care for the wives of 'working men'. To have it run by midwives to train midwives, and with doctors excluded, was unheard of at the time. The combination of political support, inspired public servants and speed were all needed to facilitate such developments. It would be another 90 years until change of this sort would be repeated in New Zealand.

For Māori women over this time, the process was entirely different. Their maternal mortality rates were unknown and unexamined. The passing of the Tohunga Suppression Act of 1907, which aimed to replace Māori health practices with Western medicine, was a marking point for the colonisation not only of Māori birthing practices but also of their healthcare in general. Māori women, in the main, continued to birth at home.

By the 1920s, the year my mother and father were both born, the rate of homebirths for Pākehā had dropped to 65 per cent. Four per cent of hospital births took place in the St Helens hospitals, now situated in three urban settings within New Zealand. The remainder of institutional births were in privately owned maternity homes, sometimes owned by midwives. During this decade, doctors created the speciality of obstetrics and formed the Obstetrical Society. They pushed for more hospital births and offered women pain relief — 'twilight sleep' that made women semiconscious in labour, necessitating forceps deliveries for the birth. Babies were born comatose and the maternal mortality rate doubled over this time. The doctors blamed the midwives, but the health department blamed the doctors' 'meddlesome midwifery'. The St Helens hospitals forceps and mortality rate was half that of the public hospital rate.

Sepsis was a prime cause for these deaths. To prevent it, strict aseptic techniques became mandatory in hospitals. New Zealand was the world leader in the use of this intervention, and the maternal mortality rate started to drop. At the same time, though, the Health Act of 1920 had been passed and there were significant gains in public health. Importantly, the birth rate also dropped, a phenomenon which has always been associated with reduced morbidity and mortality. The role of the midwife began to decline. By 1925, midwives and nurses were covered by the same Act of Parliament and midwifery became a post-nursing qualification.

By the 1930s, 78 per cent of Pākehā women birthed in hospital and 17 per cent of Māori did so, too. There was a switch in who had power over maternity care, and by 1935 the doctors had taken over control of obstetrics from the Department of Public Health. The rate of caesarean section tripled. By the end of the 1940s, the hospitalisation of birth in New Zealand was complete. We again were world leaders.

The baby boom that followed the Second World War led to an acute shortage both of maternity beds and of midwives. Incredibly, the 1946 Committee of Inquiry into Maternity Hospital Staffing somehow concluded that the St Helens hospitals were to blame for this and went on to question the need for midwives at all. Blaming midwives would be another theme with which we would all have to live.

By the 1950s, when I was born, birth looked like a sterile procedure in an operating room. Women couldn't move and were delivered flat on their backs, legs in stirrups, covered in sterile drapes. Maternity care was incorporated into the nursing curriculum, and direct-entry midwifery education was phased out. The closure of small maternity hospitals continued, and the control of St Helens moved from the health department, which had zealously guarded it, to the hospital board and into the hands of doctors. By the 1970s, just as I started my training, midwifery as its own profession had become invisible and irrelevant. I had no idea.

—o—

One day, Jennifer Sage, who was the midwife in charge of the delivery suite when I was on duty, suggested that I care for a woman who was having a breech (bottom first) baby. She was in good labour. I had never seen a breech delivery before, but we had studied and practised it in class using that pelvis and doll. It was a thing we were expected to be able to manage.

'You can do this, Joan.'

I sat with the labouring woman, helping her husband to rub her back, and encouraging her to breathe and relax between contractions. I was not relaxed, and did not leave the room. The contractions got longer and stronger, which is usually a good sign for a midwife — it means the birth is getting closer. For me, it was a sign of impending doom. I was in over my head. Once she started pushing, I rushed out of the room to find help.

'Jennifer, she's ready to push.'

'Just go back in and get her pushing, Joan. Let me know when you can see something.'

'But aren't we going to call the doctor?'

'Not yet.'

Her contractions slowed down to about one every five minutes, and I encouraged her to push as we had been taught: hands behind knees, legs pulled up and open, with three long, hard pushes for every contraction. Half an hour later the vagina started to part, and a wee bit of baby's bottom could be seen.

I rushed back to Jennifer, breathless.

'I can see a bit. What now?'

'Plenty of time. Back you go.'

This went on and on. Back and forth to Jennifer. At one stage I had to beg her to come and see, as by now a huge amount of bottom could be seen. It looked to me like it must be very close to coming out.

'No. Keep going, Joan.'

I hated her.

Presumably we eventually moved her to theatre, as we called the delivery room then, the doctor got called and the baby got delivered. I have no memory of it.

—o—

I did my required 30 deliveries, sat the midwifery exam and got my badge. I can still feel the mix of fear and thrill in those early days as a new midwife. I spent this time learning, taking in the realities of the process of birth and of new mothering. But there was a gaping hole. Experience, expertise, wisdom, confidence, all were absent. Building my skills was to be my focus.

I remember the next breech delivery better. Newly registered, I had been allocated to look after a woman who was on her way into hospital in strong labour. We loved these ones. They were usually quick, easy (for the midwife) and joyful. She came in just in time for me to have a feel of her tummy and listen to the baby's heart. No time for a shave or an enema. I could hardly feel the head, it was so far down in the pelvis; or so I thought. The woman gave a huge push with the next contraction — an indication that birth was near.

I rushed her bed along the corridor, her husband helping at the other end. She had to make the climb over on to the delivery bed, up about six inches (shocking how we made women do this at the moment of birth). I did a quick vaginal examination to check that she was fully dilated and ready to push. I ran my fingers around the edge of the baby's head to look for any left-over cervix. None. She was fully dilated and good to go. But then I felt something soft and squishy. Testicles! What was this baby's head doing with testicles on it? A quick, but what felt like slow, brain-freeze occurred. The breech appeared with the next push, following my fingers out, and fast. It looked like I was going to have to do this one.

'Jennifer!'

The unforgettable rule about delivering breech babies was — and still should be, in my opinion — 'hands off the breech'.

I definitely left my hands off this breech. Jennifer came in, held the mother's hand, and softly guided the woman to push and pant her baby out. She gave me no directions. I watched, hands poised, as the baby boy's bottom rose, up and out, following that curve of Carus. There was a little bit of rotation as first one leg flipped out, then the other. The baby's tummy appeared, with the cord pulsing nicely. Then some more rotation and then one shoulder, another shoulder, and arms. The head is often the tricky bit, but this one was clearly coming with no help needed. I supported it and Jennifer panted with the woman as the baby emerged, slowly and gently. We exchanged knowing looks. Hers said 'Well done'; mine said 'I did it'.

This is a tale I liked to tell young midwives I was mentoring into their practice when they missed things. It always gave them a laugh and made them feel better. 'Well, if Joan Skinner can miss a breech, I won't be so hard on myself.'

—◦—

And then I became a mother myself. Matthew Paul Duignan was born at St Helens in 1979. I was so surprised to see him. He looked surprised, too. His wet body slipped into my hands as he was passed to me, his pulsing cord still attached. He blinked and grimaced at no one in particular, then took a breath, almost reluctantly, and cried perfectly.

'It's a baby!' I said. The doctor and midwife were bemused.

'What were you expecting, Joan?' I had been two years a midwife.

I remember the feel of him, the look of him and the smell of him. Each time I have been at a birth since, in whatever time and place, I have recognised that momentary movement of spirit. I feel the space between heartbeats when the first breath is taken. It is simply not possible to miss it.

In preparation for Matthew's birth, my husband Paul and I had practised effleurage, visualisation, breathing and perineal massage, as one did in the 1970s. Psychoprophylaxis was said to prepare one for a natural birth. I was to be in control and have no medication. Many of my friends birthing at the time aspired to this. But I had a long, hard, posterior incoordinate labour which led to pethidine, an epidural, a syntocinon infusion and a Keilland's forceps delivery. 'Typical midwife birth' was a common, consoling refrain. However, I had felt safe. My midwives were my friends, and the doctor had worked closely with Dad. I trusted him. I chose the best. I was at St Helens, my home away from home, my training ground. I knew its smells.

Transferred to the postnatal ward and with the feeling back in my legs, I took myself gingerly to the bathroom, leaving Matthew tucked up beside my bed. On returning, I found him still sound asleep, but with a ten dollar note clutched in his fist. This was Dad's trademark calling card. On my third postnatal day he visited again. I had just got Matthew to sleep after his compulsory, but clearly unsatisfying, three minutes on each side of the breast. Dad leant over into the plastic cot and yelled loudly, waking him and causing him to yell, appropriately, back at his grandfather.

'Dad, what did you do that for?'

He had thought there was a chance Matt might have been deaf, because I had contracted malaria while volunteering for a few weeks at a small rural hospital on the island of Epi, in Vanuatu. When I became pregnant, I was in the middle of taking huge doses of anti-malarial medication. A side effect of these drugs on a developing foetus was deafness. Dad had not wanted to worry me.

I was not the worrying type: some protective psychic force or epigenetic strength from my mother, perhaps. I did not once entertain the possibility that Matthew would not be alive and whole. Notwithstanding that, while pregnant I delivered three babies with unexpected 'abnormalities': Down syndrome, intersex and exomphalos (a stomach wall defect). My midwife friends noticed that I seemed to get all these babies and worried about me. But I was calm and serene through it all (well, maybe not quite all), with an eye-watering weight gain. I floated through those last few months like a galleon in full sail.

In the first few days of new motherhood, I was a competent breastfeeder and handler of the baby. A real professional. Then that all changed, and I can remember the exact moment it did. Back in that postnatal ward, on the fifth day, Matthew, now breastfeeding for five minutes each side, was at last getting a belly full of milk. While I was changing his nappy — efficiently, of course — he did a huge, milky, mucousy vomit, coughed and spluttered, and turned blue. That's pretty normal behaviour, which the midwife in me should have been able to handle. But I panicked and pushed the emergency buzzer. Staff appeared, breathless and with full resuscitation gear, from all over the hospital.

In that moment I moved from midwife to mother. This was the first inkling for me of that instinctual maternal bond, so totally out of my control, almost terrifying in its power. It has served me and my children

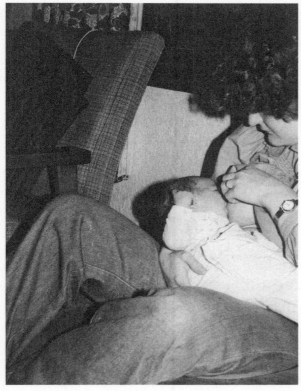

Above: Matthew's christening in 1978. Paul and I were 24, the same age as my mum and dad when they became parents.

Left: The beginning of breastfeeding, a new kind of work.

well. In retrospect, it was a pivotal moment in the development of my midwifery practice. It opened me up to empathy with new mothers that I had not had before. I understood the need for exquisite care when alongside women on their passage into motherhood, especially in the postnatal period. And I have never forgotten this.

This maternal bond is unrelenting. Once I was home, I cried for 24 hours solid for no reason that I could see. Was it the sudden loss of all that lovely oestrogen, a fear of how I was going to mother, or a subconscious freeing from the family story of dying babies? Or was it for my mother? I had no idea.

—o—

When Matthew was five months old, I put on my uniform and went back to St Helens to work, just one night a week. It was so good to be there. I felt like me again, yet I was also a different woman. And things were changing around me. It was 1979, and the second wave of feminism was well underway.

At a staff meeting one Tuesday morning, Lou Costello, the midwife in charge of the delivery suite, said that she had had a letter from a pregnant woman wanting to have her other children with her at the birth. This was a new one for us. It wasn't that long since fathers had been allowed into the birth space. The five of us considered the challenge.

'We need a good plan so that we're ready for her whenever she comes in. Everyone has to be on board.'

'Won't the kids be traumatised? How are we going to make sure they are okay?'

'Well, I think we should have an age limit for kids, and there should be another adult there to look after them. The husband has to be there for his wife, and we can't be babysitters.'

'How are they going to be prepared? Do you think we could bring them in to have a look at the place, so they don't feel too scared?'

'What are we going to do if something goes wrong? I just think it's too much.'

'I think we shouldn't take her into theatre for delivery and definitely shouldn't put her in stirrups. That would really freak the kids out. We should just let her birth on an ordinary bed in the labour room.'

'But those labour rooms are too small.'

There was a pause in the conversation as we contemplated the dilemma.

'Well, let's use our spare theatre, take all the equipment out and put a normal hospital bed and some comfortable chairs in there.'

'Should we get all gowned and masked up and cover her with all the sterile linen?'

'I think so. We can't let our standards slip. The children must stay up the head end, too. Infection could be a problem.'

'Who's her doctor?' Glancing at the chart. 'Oh, he's not going to like this.'

'We can just call him late.'

After all our hours of planning and accounting for all contingencies, the birth was smooth and the family delighted. It was very understated, just like normal. We left the room set up as it was, in case anyone else wanted to have family present. We were also less inclined to transfer women between rooms when they were just about to deliver. It depended on the doctor, of course. But we started to hate the climb up on to the high, flat birth bed for women at the cusp of birthing.

—o—

As I remember it, my sister Catherine did not get saved from that climb. She tells me now that it represented a loss of the normal. Her husband Pete called it a sacrificial table. Catherine was herself a midwife and now a busy mother of three. We had talked about her birth, and she wanted me to be there. I was on duty when she went into labour. It was exciting, and the first time I was a midwife at the birth of someone close to me. It was frowned on at the time, seen as unprofessional. It was thought that the subjectivity of the relationship could cloud judgement, especially if something was to go amiss. So one of the other midwives on duty acted as the responsible one.

Catherine laboured just like I did, hard and long. I can remember her on the high delivery bed, Lizzy's head distending her perineum. It looked like it hurt, a lot, and I could feel a sisterly care, more personal than my usual response. Catherine was stoic and amazing. We had talked about her having a Leboyer birth, which was the latest innovation in the push to rehumanise birth. Leboyer, a French obstetrician, had published his book *Birth Without Violence* in English in 1975 and we were captivated by it. He advocated gentle birthing for a baby, to minimise trauma. The birth room was to be dark, quiet and peaceful. The baby should be handled very gently, placed directly on the mother's abdomen for its first breath and then placed in warm water. We couldn't wait to try it.

Despite the fact that we had traumatised Catherine with the transfer to the delivery room and up onto the birth platform monstrosity, we had planned for her baby to have a peaceful arrival. As Lizzy emerged, we spoke only in whispers. The midwife who caught her placed her very gently straight on to Catherine's bare chest and left her there. This was very unusual back then. I remember the silence as being awesome . . . until the doctor came crashing in through the two swinging doors.

'Oh I see you have already . . .'

'Shhh.'

We hadn't been able to darken the room because of the floor-to-ceiling windows, so Pete shaded Lizzy's eyes with his hands. Catherine had brought a baby bath in, and we filled it with warm water. Pete floated the baby back to weightlessness. There was almost certainly some pressure to let the doctor do his baby check so he could get back to his rooms, but knowing that it was Pat Skinner's two daughters who were featuring would have tempered any impatience.

One of the most magic things for me about having been a midwife is being at the births of women I know and love. I have birthed daughters, sisters-in-law, nieces, midwife colleagues, friends, sisters of friends and old school friends. It would not be uncommon for me to go into a labour room in a hospital birth space to find that Mary Smith was actually Mary Brown who I went to school with (stupid business, that whole name-changing nonsense).

On one of our regular nights out, four of my oldest and dearest friends, the type who have supported each other through all life's stuff, went to the play 'The Vagina Monologues'. At drinks after the play, I commented, 'Do you realise that I have had my fingers in all your vaginas?'

'Oh, Joan, don't! Just don't go there!'

—◦—

We midwives began to feel revolutionary and subversive when we 'let' women have a say in what they wanted, and we started to understand the importance of taking control of our role and letting go of the control of women's birth experiences. We were excited about rehumanising birth, but it was challenging and there was a long way to go. We were in an environment where doctors claimed authority over birth and over us. They were supported by the law. Each doctor had a card of 'standing orders' that we had to obey lest we were to feel their wrath. Each time a woman in labour was admitted, the standing orders would come out and were meant to be followed. Each stage of the birth process had detailed instructions. The doctor provided all the antenatal care, so the women's primary relationship was with them. Midwives were secondary and subservient. When women came in the door of St Helens to share one of their most vulnerable and precious moments with us, we had never met each other.

The same loosening of control happened in the postnatal wards, too. We shifted our care from getting mothers to breastfeed by the clock every four hours to feeding their babies on demand. We stopped timing feeds and did away with routine water or cow's milk top-ups. People had started talking about bonding as an issue and that newborns needed to be kept close to their mothers. So we started to tuck them up with their mothers and pushed the beds against the wall so the babies wouldn't fall out.

We bought front-packs using the ward funds. In the early evening, the crying time, midwives working in the ward could be seen carrying babies on their fronts as they went about their work. And us breastfeeding midwives would express milk before we left for the day so that any babies who needed some extra calories wouldn't have to drink cow's milk. None of that would be allowed now.

On one occasion, the night supervisor came to the ward and said that one of the mothers had to urgently go home for a few hours because there had been a domestic dispute she had to deal with, and could I feed her baby? Later that evening, on her next round, she asked how the baby had fed.

'Really well. He had a good feed on each side and got so much milk he didn't know what hit him.'

'YOU BREASTFED HIM?'

'Isn't that what you meant?' I must admit I had been surprised, but happy to oblige.

Breastfeeding friends' babies was such a normal thing to do in those days. I remember all the babies I have breastfed, and like to tell them now as adults to make them squirm — especially the men. We usually did it to give our friends a break, if they wanted to go out for a meal or a trip to the hairdresser, or just have a few hours of undisturbed rest. But I think I might have gone too far this time.

'No, I *absolutely did not*! What were you thinking? You must never, ever, *ever* tell anyone about this.'

In those early days at St Helens, when women were admitted and while the husband parked the car, we used to 'prep' her for delivery. The doctor's written protocols, which we had accepted unquestioningly, required the woman to have a perineal shave, an enema and a bath. This was all in the name of infection control, a harking back to those 1920s puerperal sepsis outbreaks. We would check these standing orders routinely, to see what the doctor's orders were. Some required that every woman should have 10 milligrams of Valium so that they would not get agitated.

In quiet times, sitting around the staff area, smoking, we started to question all this. Jill, one of the midwives who had been to a conference (extraordinary in itself), talked about a presentation which said that there was no evidence for shaving or enemas. And, in fact, there was some evidence that indicated they might increase infection rates. And she had a copy of the journal article which we put on the notice board. This was radical. We had never seen a piece of research like this, let alone pinned one to the wall.

We all gradually stopped shaving women, as well as stopping compulsory enemas and baths on admission. There was no edict or formal policy change. There was no in-depth discussion that I remember. One by one, we just stopped. We didn't consult the women. For those who sometimes asked for an enema so that they didn't move their bowels as the baby was born, we usually obliged, even though we knew that nature usually emptied the bowels during early labour.

We didn't ask the doctors about any of these changes, and they usually didn't notice. It was the first time we had even considered that there might be evidence to guide our practice; but even more than that, it was the first time most of us had experienced the power of autonomous action. We saw we could be on the woman's side. Although there was limited change initially, and it might have seemed trivial, this time marked a shift in our beings. We had turned our hearts and our brains towards women for the first time. It felt different. It felt exciting.

We also stopped putting pink covers on the girls' cribs and blue on the boys'. I remember that decision. We hated the assumptions that those two colours made about who and what this little person was to become. And it was not just about the girls. By that stage, many of us were raising boys and wanted freedom for them, too; freedom to become who they might be.

—o—

There were also changes of a different kind coming. One morning in the delivery suite, there was a shiny new machine sitting on a trolley. It had an impressive number of buttons, dials and wires, and paper that could provide a printout not unlike the ECG machine. Very similar, as it turned out. It was to listen to the baby's heartbeat and measure the mother's contractions. This machine was a cardiotocograph, a CTG — a machine that went 'bing'. There was no research evidence to support its use. But it seemed, to the doctors at least, like a good idea to be able to pick up changes in a baby's heart rate. If the rate dropped, we could then summon doctors urgently and would have an emergency caesarean section, presuming that this would save the baby's life. A 'crash Caesar', as we called it, was quite exciting, as we believed we were rescuing a baby from brain damage or death.

It was used as much as it could be. We only had one, so it was in demand.

'I think you can have a go at the CTG on Mrs Acton today, Joan.'

I wheeled the shiny new machine into Carla's room. She was lying on her side, moaning through the contractions, her husband keeping a cool cloth on her face.

'We are just going to put this machine on you for a while, Carla. It will tell us how well your baby is coping with the contractions.'

How could she refuse?

'Can you roll over onto your back, please, so I can feel where to put the transducer.'

I then cut a piece of stretchy tubigrip, large enough to cover her whole abdomen and tight enough that the transducers wouldn't move. It was always too tight for the woman. Then the transducer that picked up the contractions was placed at the top of the abdomen, and the heart transducer was covered in gel and moved around the lower part of the belly until I got a clear signal from the baby's heart.

Meanwhile, Carla's contractions continued, and I paused when she moved to breathe. Finally, I got it going: paper running, lights flicking, heart bleeping. Theoretically it meant that we really didn't need to be there anymore, an efficiency improvement. The hours that we would have spent with labouring women, hands on their abdomens to sense the strength and progression of their contractions and listening regularly to the baby's heart with a little plastic funnel were now superfluous, supposedly. What did it matter that during this time beside the woman we also connected, encouraged, stroked, smiled, chatted and breathed with her, reassuring her husband that all was as it should be?

Carla hated the monitor. And so did I.

She couldn't lie on her side, because every time she moved I had to reposition the transducers. Her husband's eyes moved from his wife to the printout, and his attention moved from her breathing to the *blip-blip* of the baby's heart rate. Every time it lost contact and they couldn't hear the blipping, they worried. Labour care became monitor care. It seemed hopeless. Unless, of course, the woman had an epidural. With an IV drip in and paralysed from the waist down, the mother could sleep and lie still. Forceps deliveries, and the now ubiquitous caesarean sections, were waiting in the wings. More technology on top of more technology.

I don't remember us midwives ever questioning the value of the CTG. Maybe we thought it was inevitable. Current research has shown that use of this machine on women with normal pregnancies increases the rate of intervention with no improvement in babies' outcomes. Despite the fact that all current national and international guidelines now state that this machine should not be used when a pregnancy is normal and healthy, it continues to be used for just this purpose.

This time marked a milestone in birth practices. Women themselves (and, of course, we were women too) were finding their voices and seeking autonomy, especially over their bodies. As midwives, we were beginning to respond. We took steps, albeit small ones, to prioritise the wishes of the women over those of the institution, which was soundly under the control of medicine. But despite this change, we did not foresee the tsunami of technology and centralised biomedicine that was approaching. We were oblivious to where birth practice was headed. No wonder the doctors couldn't care less about our stopping shaves and enemas and offering birthing options for women other than being in lithotomy on the high birth bed. They had much more impressive things in mind. The CTG machine was just the start.

—◦—

The first palpable threat to St Helens in Wellington had become obvious in the mid-1970s when the Wellington Hospital Board, the governing body for the region's public hospitals and under the power of doctors, decided that it needed a new, modern, fit-for-purpose (for doctors, not women, as it turned out) maternity unit. They also needed more 'clinical material' to establish a viable medical training programme. The birth rate had continued to decrease markedly, and by the 1970s most women in Wellington, if they chose their own doctor, went to St Helens, which by now had its own new, purpose-built building (for women, not doctors) with single postnatal rooms and a spacious labour and delivery space. Although GPs and specialists could now 'take' their privately booked patients there, the medical staff from the main hospital maternity unit could not use it, and they resented their exclusion, especially since now most Wellington births happened there. The board proposed closing St Helens.

But they had not considered the popularity of St Helens with both mothers and GPs. After a huge rallying of support and just before the local-body elections of 1977, the board decided to postpone the closure of St Helens indefinitely. Although I was a brand new midwife at that stage, I have no memory of all this. Apparently, the midwives at St Helens were silent over the proposed closure and played no part in any fight to keep it open. We were compliant and silent. I was stunned when I discovered this later. I am forced to look closely at the 22-year-old me and reflect on the processes of politicisation which were gestational not only for me, but also for many of my midwifery colleagues. We were unaware or uncritical of the fact that 'unmarried' mothers whose babies were for adoption and Māori and Pacific mothers were less likely to birth at St Helens. Inequity of healthcare had yet to be brought to light as the critical health issue it was and still is.

In June 1978, after the elections for hospital board members, and less than a year after they had indefinitely delayed the closure of St Helens, the board, now safely re-elected, reneged on its decision and announced that it was to close after all. They stated that it was too late to halt the

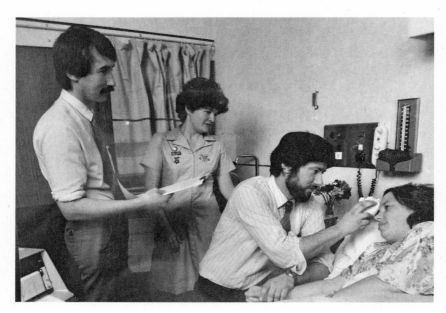

Above: A photo taken for a Wellington Women's Hospital antenatal brochure produced in 1984 to show parents what they could expect: an obstetrician, a midwife, and a labour in bed attached to a CTG machine.

Below: The concrete monstrosity that was Wellington Women's Hospital in 1983. The birth space was in the basement.

construction of the new maternity unit. This time, no amount of protest changed their minds.

The news of St Helens' impending closure was shocking for us midwives. We did know that there had been strong pressure for the two maternity services to amalgamate. But now it was real. More worrying was the fact that midwifery education at St Helens was to end, and would become just a small part of a postgraduate nursing diploma.

—o—

I had become pregnant with Matthew in 1978, the same year that the decision to close St Helens was announced. By 1981, the year it actually closed, I was pregnant again. I was still working my one night a week. As a group, we midwives had started to feel anxious and despondent about the impending closure. What was it going to mean? Trying to be a bit positive, I suggested, 'Why don't we go down and have a look at it? We're going to have to make the most of it. It's brand new so it should be right up to date with the new advances.' A more sceptical co-worker commented, 'You think so? How many of us have had any input into it? None. I don't like your chances, Joan.' The boss had been down to see it, but she was very reserved and uncommunicative about it.

'Let's arrange a visit tomorrow after work. I think we need to know what we are going to.'

The next day, seven of us piled into a couple of cars and headed down the hill. Although we had seen it from the street, up close the building looked like a multi-storey hunk of grey concrete. We were let through the locked front door where women in labour would enter. We stayed together, wandering around, unable to believe what we were seeing.

'What is this room for?'

'Looks like some kind of interview room. Why do we need an interview room?'

'I don't know. Maybe on admission? Crazy. We won't be doing that.'

'Come and look at this. It's a bloody prep room for shaves and enemas and a bath. What century was this place designed in?'

We were now becoming worried. Then a distressed call came from around the corner. 'Oh no, come and see this!'

It was Pam. We joined her in what was one of the labour rooms. It was tiny; just room for a bed, a locker and one small chair. And it was dark. There was a shared toilet area and no window.

'Are all eight rooms like this?'

'Looks like it.'

'Oh, what have they done?'

It was worse than we could ever have imagined. Shock, horror, disbelief and grief came in waves as we walked deeper into what we could only describe as a dungeon. They had put the delivery unit in the basement, as if it were some sort of torture chamber from which women's screams couldn't be heard. There was lino the colour of baby's poo on the floor and halfway up all the walls.

'Where are they meant to deliver?'

We walked further into the dungeon, past the large reception desk, presumably where the staff would congregate. There was a massive whiteboard with columns already laid out for the patients' names, the doctors' names (of course), the stage of labour and anything else of interest displayed for all to see. It seemed we would have to push the bed of a woman about to birth past all this. Pam began to cry. The whole thing looked like it had been designed in the 1950s.

We tentatively pushed open the door of one of the four delivery rooms. It was huge. Really huge. Bright lights and more poo-coloured lino. No bathroom. A high and horrid birth bed with its poles, the sort we were trying not to use at St Helens, was in the middle of the room.

'Who is still making these things?'

Then we noticed the whiteboards and lost it.

'That is for teaching the fucking medical students. While women are birthing? Please, God, no.'

There was silence except for muffled groans, sobs and the occasional 'fuck' as we explored the other three delivery rooms, appropriately called 'delivery theatres' on the plans. We then discovered the nursery where the newborns, separated from their mothers, would be checked over, weighed and dressed, before they were returned — who knew when? Their mothers, newly birthed, were all put together in a 'recovery area'.

We were done for. We held each other. Shed tears. Any remaining skerricks of innocence had fled. An inner fury caught fire.

All this signalled the next step for midwifery. We intrinsically knew that we had to try to work two birth paradigms. The new modernism of science and medicalisation called us to embrace new technologies and interventions to control birth — in order, supposedly, to make it safer; meanwhile, the emerging voice of women, fuelled by the second wave of feminism, called for women's reproductive rights and freedom to birth as they chose. There was a palpable tension as we began to try to figure out how to do both at the same time. At that stage, though, we were mainly just plain angry.

I was deemed to be too pregnant to help with the big move, and by the time I did my first shift in the new hospital, it had been open for six days. We had been very apprehensive about merging staff and having doctors around all the time. I remember those first few months as being chaotic, but in the best possible way. No rules had been written; no guidelines developed. And we were pissed off. We refused to use the spaces as intended. There was no 'prepping' at all. We would use 'early labour' spaces for the whole labour and for the birth. At least those had windows. There would be no moving to the ghastly delivery room if we could avoid it. We took beds out of the rooms and put the mattresses on the floor. We got a birth stool and used it as much as we could. Some of us would not wear our uniforms. It felt marvellous. But it was too little too late.

The doctors didn't know what had hit them when we made them get down on their hands and knees to deliver babies, when we stopped opening their gloves and tying up the back of their sterile gowns. But they quietly and cleverly bided their time.

Meanwhile, it was time for me to leave and prepare for the birth of another baby.

3
—
Claiming
space

We chanted as we marched from Parliament and up Molesworth Street. Thousands of us. It was July 1981, and there was no way we were letting a whites-only Springbok team play rugby in Aotearoa. Never. We had spent weeks plotting and planning our protest. The whole country seemed to have dropped their lives to focus on the tour. No one talked about anything else. For the first time, it seemed to us, New Zealand was polarised across and between us all.

Paul and I and our friends had regular meetings at our place to plot action. Six of us planned to stop the TV transmission of the Wellington test match by covering the transmitter on Tinakori Hill with a piece of material lined with aluminium foil. It would have to be big. We would put strings on the edges and attach rocks for tossing it over the dish. The guys would be in charge of the throwing. Us women would be the getaway car drivers. My job was to sew the huge cover. We got a disconcertingly large pile of op-shop curtains and I sewed them together . . . for hours. We then had to get the foil attached somehow. Someone got dispatched to buy aluminium foil from supermarkets — not too much in each one, lest we attract attention. We did several dummy runs up Tinakori Hill, and discovered, just in time, that the intended satellite dish was for telephone, not television, transmission. So, it was back to just marching. The curtains made great painting covers, but I think I am still using up the foil.

As the march passed the Murphy Street on-ramp, the organisers split our end of the crowd off and headed us on to the motorway. Paul and I somehow ended up at the front. We crossed both lanes, turned and sat, blocking the motorway. Irate drivers tooted and shook their fists.

'Amandla! Amandla! Amandla awethu,' we called back.

I felt my mood shift from determination and excitement to anxiety and entrapment. I would have liked to go back home to Mum, who was looking after Matt, now two years old, and watch Princess Di's wedding with her. But I didn't. Kena chose that moment to roll over inside my belly. Knowing her now, she would have been saying, 'Don't you dare move, Mum. I'm fine and I want to be here.' It is one of her claims to fame that she started being an activist while still in utero.

She was born in January 1982 at the new Women's Hospital, two weeks late and from a posterior position, just as Matthew had been. It was another shocker of a labour. The anaesthetist's needle was hovering over my spine, ready to put in an epidural, when my body suddenly decided to evict the tardy child. I pushed her out. I hadn't felt Matt's birth because of the epidural I'd had that time; this birth felt like the closest visit I would ever have with death, until the real thing. As Kena's head appeared, my midwife friend encouraged me to put my hand down and feel her, anticipating delight and joyous maternal connection. It does happen sometimes.

'No! That will never come out!' I cried, heading back to suck on the nitrous oxide as hard as I could. But she did come out, and with no stitches required. For just a moment, I couldn't have cared less what I'd had. It could have been a goat for all I cared. *I was still alive.* Once I realised that I'd survived and had taken a couple of breaths, I was okay. It was such a good lesson for me as a midwife. Sometimes women need a moment before they turn their attention to their baby. Sometimes, it takes a lot longer.

Just by the by, that baby was a sleeper, a feeder and a smiler. I have been known to tell people, 'If you haven't had a baby like that, keep trying.'

For me, the early part of the eighties was dominated by mothering. I was in full physiological mothering mode. It felt instinctual and comfortable. Paul was working as a researcher for the Federation of Labour, the old CTU, so we could just afford a house in Mount Cook, right by the park and alongside some native bush. We demolished walls, paint-stripped, sanded, painted and wallpapered. Our pride and joy was our new rimu kitchen. Our friends were all around, but most importantly, our extended family was in Wellington, too. The children had siblings, aunts, uncles, cousins aplenty, and two sets of doting grandparents.

We built long-lasting friendships. It was not the norm for mothers (the white, middle-class ones I knew, anyway) to return to full-time work, and we were lucky enough not to have to. Four of us set up a weekly sewing group. One would have the children for the morning while the others met up with our sewing machines and sewed. Most of our children's clothes were homemade or hand-me-down, except for the occasional treat when someone's parent returned from an overseas holiday with some Mothercare clothes. My speciality was corduroy dungarees. All our furniture was from the op shop and everything in the kitchen was too, except for what our mothers gave us, or the pottery casserole dishes and crystal bowls we got as wedding presents. A wedding register would have horrified us. We had a commitment to working and living as much as we could in community, and social justice was our imperative. We women all kept our surnames, we would not put pink anywhere near our daughters, and our boys were never allowed arms of any sort (although they were inclined to make guns out of their toast crusts). Paul and I decided to have no television. We never went out for coffee, and very rarely for a meal. We had friends home for meals and picnics in parks.

Many of those friends were social activists and disillusioned Catholics. Three were ex-priests, since 'defrocked' and married. It was not just youth who fled Catholicism in the 1980s. On our way out of it, though, we did feel a lack of an active spiritual community, so we decided to create one. Twelve of us, and all our children, spent a couple of years taking turns at each other's houses, creating spiritual rituals and sharing reflections. We broke bread (from the Newtown hot bread shop) together and had a shared meal. But it was chaotic and was well-nigh impossible to sustain, with up to 18 two- to ten-year-olds running riot in our homes. It took us a week to recover and put everything back into a semblance of order. We dreaded our turn, and understood then why people made churches and created priests. Very sensible. Once a few of the marriages started to end, the group found its own quiet conclusion and we breathed a sigh of relief.

When Kena was a few months old, I returned to doing my one shift a week on night duty at Wellington Women's, again in the delivery suite. Inevitably the place was much more organised than when I'd left it and there was little sign of the anarchy we had created five months ago. There were guidelines and protocols and it had developed its own culture. There seemed to be effective relationships between the midwives and the doctors, but I noticed that no one was putting mattresses on the floor anymore and everyone was in uniform. It felt good to be on night duty. The nights always seemed to be more peaceful than the days; the house surgeons, the registrars and the obstetricians were less keen to come and intervene. When it was packed full and humming, the night would fly by. When it was quiet, we would restock, chat, knit and drink a lot of coffee, or be summoned up to the postnatal ward to help mothers feed and settle their babies. But it remained a difficult physical environment in which to make birth humane.

There was still a lot of momentum in the community left over from the battle against the closure of St Helens. The second wave of feminism was still in full flight, and it seemed preposterous that all women should be expected to birth in a tertiary hospital. Pamela Messervy, a Wellington midwife and a close friend from my student midwife days, and Ros Capper, a staunch local feminist and St Helens advocate, had started planning for an out-of-hospital birth centre in Wellington pretty much as soon as St Helens had closed. The plan was for birth-centre midwives to work from the same continuity of care model that the homebirth midwives did. They set up an incorporated society called Birth and Beyond and proceeded to gain the necessary approvals and persuade the authorities of its viability and acceptability. They had a small group of committed midwives and women in the community who were all keen to help. I joined them at about the same time as I went back to work. I still have a vivid memory of chairing Birth and Beyond's first AGM in the Mount Victoria Community Centre in 1982, with three-month-old Kena sound asleep in her red Mothercare cocoon on the floor under the table.

I was just 28 and it was my first step into feminist activism. It felt daunting but exciting. We wrote proposals and submissions, went to meetings and fundraised to equip the new centre. One celebrated meeting we had was with the Wellington City Council to get approval to open the centre which, we were told, would have to be covered under the Private Hospital Regulations if we ever had more than one woman in the place at the same time. Ros and Pamela went to present our submission. Michael Fowler, the mayor at the time, commented, 'Oh, I see the ladies have not brought their lawyers.' Their main concern, so Pamela recollects, was screaming women disturbing the neighbourhood. 'They want us to stay in the dungeon,' I thought. In the end they approved. I suspected they thought we would never be able to find enough funding.

The next task was to persuade the Wellington Hospital Board to give us a house. This was a big agenda item. It took another year, and a lot of lobbying, but we got it — an older-style house in Newtown that had been used by the hospital to house its medical staff. We were so close now. The city council just needed to approve it as suitable for a birth centre. But not only did they *not* approve it — they condemned it as unfit for human habitation. We wondered what the backstory was. A cynic might think that the provision of an unsuitable house was deliberate.

In the meantime, four of the women in the group had had babies, and all had opted to birth at home. It seemed that as a group, we had all gradually shifted our allegiance to supporting homebirth. We realised, as we planned the birth centre, that it would offer no more safety or care than midwives already provided at a homebirth. As Bronwen Pelvin, one of our earliest and most radical homebirth midwives, said, 'There are plenty of birthing centres in New Zealand. They are called home.' We decided to wind up Birth and Beyond and refocus our efforts on supporting the homebirth movement.

Thirty years later there is still no birth centre space in Wellington and the Hutt Valley where women might leave their homes to birth.

—o—

In 1984 Matthew started school in the bilingual Māori class at Newtown School, and Kena turned three. Paul was keen to become a clinical psychologist and he was accepted into the course, so we decided it would be a good time for a switch of roles. I went back to work full-time as a midwife in the delivery suite of Wellington Women's Hospital. We could see it from our bedroom window, and it felt reassuringly close to the children. I would also be doing shift work, which meant I could work around Paul's lectures and Kena would not be in childcare for too long — something that we valued.

They were pleased to have me back, and I joined the staff happily but with some apprehension. I would miss my children, but I knew that more time with their dad would be good for them. It was also time for me to make the turn back into the 'real world'. I put on my green zip-up uniform, attached my name badge and my midwifery medal, and headed out the change-room door to join the staff for my first day shift in six years. It was familiar territory and an easy transition. My friends were all pleased to see me; the doctors quizzed me: 'What are you doing here at this time of the day, Joan?'

However, working full-time reconnected me with the realities of this terrible birth space and the futility of attempting to provide a positive birth environment here. Someone had donated a spa bath while I was on maternity leave and it was installed in a back room, despite the outrage of the infection-control managers. The 'prep room' we made into a labour/birth room, so women didn't have to move to birth. There was more space for family members to be present, something that was happening increasingly often. But that was about it.

Our attempt to start a birth centre had been unsuccessful but the homebirth rate didn't seem to be going up, partly because the midwives were paid a quarter of what we were paid in hospital, and partly because it was becoming increasingly difficult to find a doctor to 'supervise' a midwife at the birth. There was a lull in midwifery action in Wellington. It seemed that over that past three years, midwives had accepted that this was now how birth was to happen. The fire we felt about protecting women from this dreadful environment had faded. I can't put my finger on why. Maybe it was the sheer volume of work, or the domination of medicine, or the increasing, unquestioned use of technology. Or maybe we just didn't care enough.

So how was birth happening then?

In a typical 'patient journey', as management-speak coined it, once a woman's contractions had started she would ring the hospital and talk to any of the midwives on duty. She would have been instructed by her doctor not to ring him (seldom her). The ward clerk would fetch the notes which described her medical and obstetric history. That is all we would know. We didn't know *her*. We knew nothing of how the pregnancy had been, or what her wishes for the birth were, or what she might have been worried about. Nothing. Her notes would be put in the 'pending' pile. The charge midwife on duty would allocate her to one of the four midwives on duty. Her name, the name of her doctor and the name of the allocated midwife and anything of interest would be on the board, there for all to see. When she arrived, she would be shown into her small, dark room. She would change, often into a hospital gown, would pass urine for us to test, then immediately get on to the bed for the midwife to do the basic assessments. She would have a routine vaginal examination.

By then the husband would have arrived, having parked the car. Unless she was close to delivery, the woman would have the fetal heart rate monitor applied. This meant that she had to lie on the bed very still and have two transducers placed on her pregnant tummy. The machine would bing and flash with the baby's heartbeat. It printed out long strips of paper that could be examined in detail, even though at that stage, and probably still even now, we couldn't really tell whether we needed to be concerned. The machine was on a trolley and took up a whole side of the tiny room, blocking access to the woman from that side. It captured the total attention of the husband and staff and made being an actual midwife almost impossible.

For pain relief, women could have an injection of pethidine or could have nitrous oxide gas if they were thought to be close to delivery. They frequently became distressed and there was little we could do to help. We hardly knew them; we were drowned in protocols and guidelines and the clock dominated our decisions. Few of us midwives fully appreciated yet the importance of being out of the bed to labour. Even if we had, the room was so small that active birthing would have been impossible. Out in the corridor there was more space but no privacy. No one took the bed out of the room anymore. There was no room for additional support people. Not surprisingly, the rate at which women had epidural anaesthesia increased. Eventually there was a full-time anaesthetist in the delivery suite, ready to put a needle in anyone who so much as moaned. It was marketed as 'women's choice'. It still is.

We midwives might have another labouring woman to care for, maybe even two, and some postnatal women waiting to feed their babies, have a shower and get to the ward. And there might also be someone in early labour just about to arrive.

'Can you have her, Joan? Your postnatals should be gone soon. Are there any beds left in the ward?'

We could be absent from a labouring woman's side for some time. Occasionally we would be called to help with an emergency caesarean section, so the midwives who were left 'on the floor' would have to reallocate the care of all the women for the hour or more it took to complete the operation. By now the typical picture was one of a woman trapped on a bed, plugged into a machine, a plastic catheter in her back, a drip in her arm and contraction-stimulating drugs being administered through another bleeping, flickering device.

As the birth approached, we would detach the machines, push the woman in the bed through the corridor, past the staff area where there was usually a group of midwives, doctors and sundry others to stare at her, and then into the massive, fully lit delivery room. The doctor would be called. In the delivery room she would have to climb on to the hard, high, flat delivery bed and would be covered in sterile drapes. The machines would be reconnected. When the doctor arrived, usually hale and hearty, the midwife would stand aside. If the woman managed to push the baby out herself, well and good. We would dry and wrap the baby and then give it to the mother to hold. We had just begun to hear that bonding might be important. If the mother took too long to push the baby out, we would put her legs up in stirrups and the doctor would place forceps on the baby's head and pull it out. If the women had not booked with a GP or an obstetrician for her care, or if she was deemed to be at very high risk of serious complications, the house surgeon and registrar on call — both unknown to her — would attend. The midwives changed shift every eight hours, the doctors every 12 hours. We tried to be kind and encouraging.

That was hospital birth in the 1980s and it was not going well. It didn't seem much different from that first birth I had seen 10 years before. There were some women, of course, who managed to proceed through the birthing process fast enough to avoid all this intervention, but their births, I have to say with some dismay, were less memorable. I worry that for midwives working in delivery suites in the 2020s, this picture of birth is still the same. Only now there are fewer of them.

—⚬—

Eventually I was promoted to being a Charge Midwife, which meant that every shift I was on, I had to manage that place. I became an expert in caring for the most complex of cases, and in teaching and supporting other midwives to do the same. I really had birth nailed, or so I thought.

One Sunday, I walked down the hill for my afternoon shift, leaving Paul with the children. They were all going off for a picnic afternoon tea and a swim. I put my uniform on — a blue one now, because I was 'in charge'. I dropped my bag in my locker and put my dinner in the fridge. I would not get to eat it.

The place was quiet. There was no one in the corridor, the changing room was tidy with no sign of clothes thrown about or used surgical gowns in the laundry bag. There was no pile of dirty cups in the kitchen and no family members getting themselves a cuppa. The kettle was cold. 'Great. We might have a nice quiet afternoon,' I hoped.

I turned the corner of the corridor and did a quick check of the whiteboard. Only four women here, and two had already delivered. One had had a caesarean section. The midwives on the morning shift were all sitting around the desk, having coffee and waiting for us so they could head home. By the time the four of us on afternoon duty had arrived and had done handover, there had been two phone calls from women in early labour who would probably be in soon.

'There's another three out there niggling, too,' the morning midwife coordinator commented. 'You might get busy.'

The hospital supervisor came by to do her early check and looked at the board.

'It looks pretty quiet,' she said. 'Could one of your staff go up and help in the ward, Joan? They are pretty full up there.'

'I don't think so, Jan. We have five women out in the community, all niggling.'

The four of us on duty all stood by the whiteboard. I held the pen and asked if there were any preferences for who they wanted to look after. My job was to allocate the midwives to the women.

'It looks like we might be getting busy, so I think we should try and get the postnatals up to the ward ASAP,' I suggested.

Aolani was our nurse aide on duty for the afternoon. She had been a midwife in Sāmoa but couldn't get registered in New Zealand. It was her job to do the stocking and the cleaning. It was shameful really. She could often be spotted, mop in hand, leaning on the door of a labour room chatting animatedly but surreptitiously with the Samoan family inside. The difference it would have made for that family to have had her care for them is immeasurable. She had worked with us since our St Helens days and knew the place better than we did.

'Aolani, I think we may be about to get busy. Could you please start by checking that the stocks in the rooms and on the trolleys are complete?'

Then the phone started to go crazy.

'Hi Joan, it's Tim here [the neonatal paediatrician]. Just to let you know there is a 27-weeker in prem labour being choppered in from Blenheim. Her ETA is about 15 minutes away. I've called the obstetric registrar and there is a bed in the neonatal unit for the baby if we can't stop the labour in time.'

I had no time to tell anyone before the phone went again.

'Hi, it's Mary O'Hara here. I rang about half an hour ago because I was having some contractions. But I have started bleeding so I thought I should ring you.'

'Hi Mary. It's Joan here, one of the midwives. Yes, that was a good idea to ring us. Can you tell me how much blood is coming out? Is it just a little bit on your pants or is it flowing out?'

'It's like a heavy period sort of amount.'

Oh, that's not good, I thought. 'Okay, Mary. I think you should come in so we can assess the bleeding and check on the baby. It can all be normal, but it's worth being safe. Do you live far away, and have you got anyone to bring you in and to look after the other children?'

'I'm just here in Newtown at Mum's and she is going to look after the kids. My husband can bring me in right away.'

'Fantastic. Well, see you soon. Do you know how to get here?'

I added the two new names to the board, allocated midwives to them and went to let them know that we were shifting up a gear. 'We have an APH [antepartum haemorrhage] and a 27-weeker on their way in. They should be here in 15.'

I got back on the phone, found beds we could move the two postnatals to and rang the registrar on call to warn her we would be needing her very soon.

Meanwhile, one of the women we had in early labour moved swiftly into strong labour, hefty noises emerging from her room. 'Oh good, that will be one out of the way soon,' I thought. Anne, the midwife looking after her, would be fully tied up now. She had also been allocated to care for the woman who'd had the caesarean section, so I took over that, did her recordings and helped her attach her baby to the breast. It would be an hour or so before she would be ready to go to the ward. She might have to wait a bit longer. Her epidural was still working well, so she was pain-free and happy to just be with her baby rather than be rushed upstairs.

Shirley, in her usual efficient form, had her postnatal woman ready to go up, so I rang an orderly to come and help. Aolani turned the room around in double-quick time and Shirley arrived back just as the doorbell buzzed and the ambulance arrived with the woman in premature labour. Shirley took over looking after her, and I knew that meant she would be out of action to help anyone else for a while. But she was very experienced, and I could rely on her to know exactly what to do.

The front doorbell went again, and I went to let Mary and her husband in. She had a towel soaked in blood between her legs and was looking pale and frightened.

I grabbed a wheelchair, and we went quickly to the room closest to the caesarean theatre.

'Hey, Mary and Sam,' I said. 'This doesn't look so good. I'm going to listen to the baby to make sure it is okay, then I'm going to get the doctor here. Sometimes this much bleeding means that the placenta is starting to separate, which it shouldn't do before the baby is born. But you're in the right place now. Just to warn you that you might need an emergency caesarean so that we can stop the bleeding.'

While the doctor was on his way, I put an IV in and turned the monitor on. Mary and Sam were relieved to hear the baby's heart rate, but I was less impressed. It was much too fast and lacked the variability that a healthy baby's heart should have. This baby needed to come out, and fast.

Just then Anne rang the buzzer for help, as her woman was pushing. Sarah, the fourth of our team, who was in the next room looking after a first-time mother in labour with an epidural and a syntocinon drip, had to leave her to answer the bell.

'Can you get me the delivery trolley, please, Sarah. No time to take her to theatre.'

There was then the noise of running past the room I was in. I put my head out the door. 'Any problem, Sarah?'

'No, she's just delivering fast,' Sarah commented as she pushed the trolley into the room. A lusty baby's cry could already be heard.

All that was in the first hour of the shift. Before long, we had called an extra midwife in from home. The whiteboard was full, the place was full of doctors of all descriptions, and family members were coming and going. The maternity unit supervisor came to help. She made a trolley of tea and coffee as there was no way we could stop to make it ourselves.

Both Mary and the woman with the premature baby had emergency caesareans. We had four more admissions, three normal deliveries, a ventouse suction cap delivery, and a woman with pre-eclampsia who was transferred down from the antenatal ward with very high blood pressure who needed intensive care. And I was in charge!

Despite all this, I stayed calm — on the outside anyway. I sure was pleased to have three experienced midwives and Aolani on with me. We didn't get off till one in the morning, two hours late. I grabbed my uneaten meal from the fridge, and my bag from the locker room, which was now strewn with clothes and used theatre scrubs. I was buzzing, full of adrenaline, still on alert. That was my day-to-day work, and I was good at it. I could 'do' a normal labour and birth with my eyes closed, and I had also acquired the skill of managing complex pregnancies and emergencies.

Strangely, although we were striving to care for mothers and babies and to control the outcome of the births, the women themselves could seem lost on a shift like this. I can see that now in the language we used. A deeply human experience becomes inhumane, and the possibility of midwives being connected with women as they birth impossible, as the focus moves from the woman to the demands of the organisation.

—○—

There were two things that really bugged me. The first was that healthy, well women with uncomplicated pregnancies absolutely did not belong in that environment and it was impossible for us to provide appropriate care for them. But the sense of the time was that this was the safest place to be. All the doctors and all the equipment were close to hand. Nowadays, we know that it was too close. But in the 1980s it felt like pissing into the wind to try to persuade anyone that birthing out of hospital was not only safe, but was actually safer. We had to wait 30 years to get the evidence that would bring validity to our deeply experienced intuition. And even then — despite the evidence and despite national and international recommendations to keep women out of hospital unless they need it — hospital birth is still considered by most of the population as the safest place to give birth.

Wellington Women's was the hospital where any mother who had a very complicated pregnancy or who birthed prematurely had to come for care. They came from a large area in the central part of New Zealand. And they needed to. Every possible piece of equipment was at hand, and the staff were experienced and confident. But having said that, I was alarmed at the poor quality of care that was actually provided to these women. They stayed in the antenatal ward of the hospital, sometimes for weeks, and then were transferred to the delivery suite, mostly for inductions of labour. They were sometimes with us for days and would then often have a longer time than usual in the postnatal ward. Anxiety, fear and loneliness were their constant companions. We would try to support them by sending a social worker or an occupational therapist. It was a pathetic attempt, I thought, that reflected the centrality of the needs of the institution and of the doctors, not of the women.

I drew up a proposal for a continuity of midwifery care model for these women. My thinking was that a woman could have a midwife who could be hers right from when she was admitted into the hospital. She would get to know this midwife, who would coordinate care, be an in-between person with the obstetric team and ensure that as far as possible, any normal aspects of becoming a new mother could be enhanced. The midwife would be part of a small team and would be on call for the labour and birth, and then could follow up in the postnatal period. These midwives would be experts in complex care, but would also bring a midwifery focus, that of being a skilled companion and advocate. When the women birthed, they would always have a midwife with them who they *knew*. The proposal had lots of buy-in and the midwives were excited. My last task was to get the proposal past the Nurses' Union, as there needed to be a variation to the employment contract to allow flexible working hours. They refused outright to even consider it.

No one's interests except the doctors' were met at Wellington Women's Hospital. Women anticipating a normal birth had an unnecessarily isolated and disturbed experience. Women with complex and challenging pregnancies were rotated through the hospital as if they were commodities for medical education and research. Midwives were de-skilled and relegated to be doctors' handmaidens, despite all our futile and fledgling attempts to claim back our essential nature — that of being with women.

Apart from not having to move beds down corridors during labour and usually having a familiar midwife in labour, not much has changed in the culture of the delivery units in our major hospitals. A midwifery PhD, completed in 2020 by Suzanne Miller, which I examined, stated:

> Ironically, the very attributes that make the tertiary hospital the ideal place to be when birth is complex or the unexpected happens ('poised-ness' for action, being a 'well-oiled machine' for emergency care, surveillance and control) are the same attributes that create a dis-abling environment for physiological . . . birth to unfold at its own pace. Once 'nested' within the tertiary hospital setting the impact of social, professional, and industrial discourses overwhelms the salutogenic factors that should protect normal birth.

In other words, in 30 years little in the tertiary hospital has changed. Her PhD thesis made for a distressing read.

—o—

But even worse things were happening to midwifery in the 1980s, this time at the hands of nurses, not doctors. With the closure of St Helens, the education of midwives was moved to sit within the Advanced Diploma of Nursing. It was a one-year course undertaken in technical institutes. The course was woefully inadequate in several ways. First, the nurses who emerged from the course as midwives had very limited clinical experience, and were not ready to function over the full scope of midwifery practice. Between 1981 and 1987 only 23 midwives a year graduated, as compared with the St Helens programmes which had prepared on average 157 midwives a year. This huge gap in the midwifery workforce numbers was still being felt 30 years later, especially when my cohort all started to retire.

The change to the Nurses Act of 1983 meant that all midwives who provided homebirth services had to be nurses. Our professional body was the New Zealand Nurses' Association (NZNA) and within that there was a Midwives' Special Interest Section where midwives could discuss midwifery issues. Our regulatory body was the Nursing Council. Midwives were powerless to act within these two organisations. We were outnumbered; but not, as it turned out, outwitted.

Back in 1972, a Canadian nurse had been contracted by the Nurses' Association to look into reforming nursing education. She recommended that nurses should be educated in tertiary institutions instead of the apprentice-style preparation that was based in hospitals. A new polytechnic nursing course started in 1973, and I was in that first class. The Canadian consultant also recommended that midwifery registration be abandoned, as it was an outdated and irrelevant profession, and that midwifery be restructured as a post-basic diploma in Maternal and Child Health Nursing. This was, not surprisingly, the Canadian model at the time. The recommendation was not followed through by the Nurses' Association till the mid-1980s. Despite a strong and united position taken by the Midwives Special Interest Section that recommended retaining midwifery registration and separating midwifery education from the nursing diploma and extending it, the NZNA went ahead and produced a policy statement that notionally supported midwifery, but only as a post-basic nursing qualification on a par with any other nursing speciality. The effect of this would be the end of midwifery in New Zealand.

When we realised what nurses were planning, we became active in the defence of our profession. Although the Special Interest Section had no formal power, it proved vital as an arena for midwives to develop a nationally coordinated response. Throughout the country we lobbied nurses, and outnumbered them at their meetings, so that we could get remits supporting midwifery to the national nurses' conference. Then we nominated and seconded midwives to be the delegates at the conference. It was surprisingly easy.

I volunteered to be nominated as a Wellington delegate. I was to propose the Wellington remit that the NZNA accept the World Health Organization definition of a midwife, which did not require a midwife to be a nurse first. We had done our homework. Enough regional branches supported it for it to be passed. Then there was another remit, I think from Auckland, which proposed that midwifery education be removed from the Advanced Diploma of Nursing and become a full-year course at a polytechnic. We got that through too, and could hardly believe we had done it. It was a powerful lesson for us. Many nurses were angry with us; others were delighted.

There was also another force in action, probably the most pivotal one. Women who wanted to birth at home needed to have a doctor who would agree to, in effect, oversee the midwife. And there were fewer and fewer of those. Some parts of New Zealand had none. Joan Donley, a staunch homebirth midwife in Auckland, along with the Homebirth Midwives Society, joined forces with the Home Birth Association to fight for a change in the Nurses Act so that midwives could work autonomously, and women could birth at home. 'Save the Midwives' was born, led by a wonderful clear-headed woman called Judi Strid. Judy and Joan were both canny operators. Their relationship was where the notion of the midwifery/woman partnership originated. We needed to look after each other. Our mantra became: 'Midwives need women need midwives need women need midwives . . .'

Most of the political activity supporting midwifery happened in Auckland. This was where most homebirths occurred and where the core of consumer action was based. Alongside the homebirth association and the local midwives, the mothers were a powerful force of action.

Finally, after 15 years of being under threat, midwives became politicised, activated and motivated. And furious. Well, most of us. In Wellington we lobbied every organisation we could think of and all our members of parliament. I volunteered to present our case to the Women's Electoral Lobby and the National Council of Women. I was unused to public speaking then, and was a nervous speaker. I had to remember my mother's words. Summon my mad McGrath.

I remember endless discussions about why midwifery was different from nursing. We agonised over it. The arguments included:

'Nursing is about illness, and midwifery is about health and life.'

'Florence Nightingale was the origin of nursing. Midwifery has nothing to do with Florence.'

'Our history comes from a different source.'

'Midwifery is the oldest profession. The first ever women to birth would have had a companion to help them.'

'Nurses are subservient to doctors. We should have nothing to do with them.'

'Nurses are overwhelming us and overpowering us. We need to escape them.'

'But there are so few of us.'

For the first time, many of us had to think about what midwifery was and could be about, why it was valuable and what we were trying to achieve. And we had to think much more clearly about the women. In retrospect, nurses probably did us a favour. We would never have been able to activate and politicise so many midwives had the nurses agreed, without coercion, to provide a separate midwifery course.

We all began to understand that a change in the Nurses Act would be required for midwives to regain autonomy. Joan Donley's local MP was Helen Clark, who would eventually become the minister of health and the prime minister. Helen has related how Joan started to lobby her from 1983 onward and was a persistent and persuasive operator.

There was one last piece of the midwifery reform process which would prove to be the underbelly of midwifery reform and autonomy. It was a strange bedfellow. It was neoliberalism, the free-market reform which began in earnest in the mid-1980s, and enabled a sociocultural shift that touted deregulation and reduced state control. It was the backbone of the new politics. Almost ironically, it facilitated midwifery's autonomy. But that is a story for later.

—◦—

By 1987, I knew somewhere inside me that I wasn't finished having babies. I still can't work out quite why. Maybe it was that deep hormonal mammalian need to reproduce, or maybe it was fear of the future without babies, a future in which I would have to craft a life for myself. In the end, it turned out that I just could not have had a life without Timothy in it.

It was February 1987. I conceived easily and I was pregnant the first cycle we tried. Later that year, Paul finished his master's degree and got a job as a researcher in what was then known as the Alcohol and Drug Research Centre of the University of Auckland. I agreed to relocate, but it felt wrong. I was leaving my mother and father, my extended family, my friends, my work, my home, my passions, my support, all my connections. It felt like I was leaving my life behind.

Dad took us to the airport. I was in the last trimester of my pregnancy, blooming, grieving and nesting, all at the same time. I was tearful and scared and felt strangely alone. He held me tight.

'You go well now, girl. We'll see you soon.'

I whispered in his ear, 'I don't think I'm going to be very good at this.'

4

—

Being
with
women

I sat on the balcony of our renovated but rented house in Devonport, Auckland. The yachts flew by, leaving Rangitoto on its own, connected to the earth, spread out like one of Mum's passionfruit biscuits. Matthew and Kena were settled into their new school. Devonport was a fairy-tale place, a peaceful corner of Auckland, where I hoped to feel settled in these last few months of pregnancy. There were the comforting vistas of sea on both sides of the peninsula. I planted a wisteria which headed off at great speed around our veranda, bathed in Auckland's warmth and humidity, far away from Wellington's gusts. Paul went to work each morning on the ferry. I continued to feel alone and bereft.

The midwife was coming soon to talk with me about my having this baby at home.

'Well you know, Joan, you have to make the decision yourself,' she said eventually.

I remember her as being nice and clearly very experienced. She listened carefully to my obstetric history and heard my hesitation, but I have no memory of her name or face. As I closed the door behind her I knew deeply that I needed to go home to birth. I called my friend in Wellington, Chris Hannah, and asked her to be my midwife. I told Paul that I was going, and Mum that I was coming, and waited till I was a week past my due date to get on the plane. The children were excited to be going back to Roro's and to be having a new baby. Paul took time off work.

I had an induced labour a week later at Wellington Women's Hospital, a syntocinon infusion, an epidural and a Keilland's forceps delivery. I felt weirdly at home. Timothy was beautiful. I had that perfect feeling of silk against my cheek again and that almost orgasmic tug at my nipples. I was satisfied and nurtured. That was it. No more babies needed.

It's not uncommon for people to say to me, 'I suppose you must have had all your babies naturally at home?' 'Well, not exactly,' I would say. 'It depends on what you call home.' I realised that at the time of my births, the physical space was less important for me than knowing and trusting who was with me. I could not imagine having someone I didn't know being with me and was horrified that women would ever have to do this. For hundreds and hundreds of women, that unknown midwife had been me. I still feel worried that I might not have always been as attentive a midwife as I could have been. If you are one of those women, I am deeply sorry.

This knowing of the need for a relational experience with the midwife was not intellectual, but visceral. Even though I had not birthed at home and had never even seen a homebirth, I knew then that I would become a homebirth midwife — because at that stage it was the only way to provide continuity of midwifery care, the only way to build that relationship of trust that I now knew women needed for birth. It became a commitment: to fight for all women, everywhere, to have a midwife they knew alongside them as they entered what possibly would be the most vulnerable state they would ever be in.

I still have a residual doubt about whether I would have succeeded in a homebirth. Deep-seated issues related to too many dead babies in my family, medicalisation burnt into my genes, previous shitty labours, and the fact that I hadn't even seen a homebirth, would have got in my way. It would have taken a very stroppy midwife to tell me, 'There is no reason you can't do it. Just get on with it, Joan.' I like to think I would've.

Pregnant with my third baby, and having retreated home to prepare and to wait, my mother and I talked of birth and of her dead babies. She seemed, at one level, so matter-of-fact. My sister and I, both midwives and now in our later years, remain mystified at how she managed all this. We both regretted that we'd never persisted to get through our mother's stoic exterior to share and to comfort. Although it might well have been for the best that we didn't.

Of the actual births of all her 10 babies, alive or dead, she had no memory at all.

'You know, Joan, I have never seen a baby being born.'

'Oh Mum, that's awful! Why don't you come and be with me when I have this one? A lot of mothers come to births now.'

Eyes light up. 'Are you sure?'

I was so hoping that this baby would be speedy and easy, but I stuck to my usual childbirth routine. A very overdue start followed by hours of unproductive contractions. Damn posterior babies. My mother was with me in the hospital, and as the day progressed to evening she looked anxious and exhausted. Every time the midwife came into the room, she asked, 'Can't she have some pain relief yet?' I heard the edge of fear in her voice. Her face was grey with worry. By midnight, I too was exhausted and in real need of some more upbeat energy around me.

'Mum, this is taking an awful long time and you look terrible. Why don't you go home, and we'll ring you when the baby arrives?'

I've never seen anyone put their coat on and get out of there so fast.

She never did see a baby being born.

—o—

We returned to Devonport, and I tucked up in the house with Timothy. I remember so much about being with him then, consciously laying down memories in the bit of my brain where I would forever be able to recall them at will. I wasn't going to be doing this a fourth time. But, eventually, it was time to think about midwifery again.

With Tim as a six-week-old, I attended my first midwifery meeting in Auckland. As the minutes of the previous meeting were read, Timothy, feeding hungrily and noisily at the breast, exploded loudly into his nappy, sending runny yellow poo up his back, down his legs and over my lap. I couldn't have been with better people, people who erupted in laughter, with many offers of help to clean up. New connections were made. It seemed through those decades that many of us midwives were also coming in and out of new motherhood. We understood the need for nesting and withdrawal and would relish the arrival back into the scene of a midwife and her latest baby. Some came back earlier than others.

Leaning over the cot one night to pick up a chubby two-month-old Timothy, I felt something rip in my back, and I collapsed to the ground. I had ruptured a disc in my spine, and badly. I was eventually transferred to hospital by ambulance, with lots of nitrous oxide, had a week of pelvic traction to relieve some of the pressure on the disc, and then spent three months flat on my back; it was a year before I could walk properly again. My parents and Paul's parents took it in turns to come from Wellington to help, and ACC funded a full-time helper to do the housework and help with Tim. Life with a three-month-old baby and two young children when unable to move was pretty shocking, and I still remember going into a sort of emotional shutdown which allowed me to not complain or fret too much. My prolapsed disc could be interpreted, and was by some, as my subconscious working out some way to keep my family around me. It was all horrible, except for Tim, and I still find it difficult to talk about. That was pretty much 1988 written off.

Later that year I did make it to the national conference of the Midwives Section of NZNA. It was in Auckland, and it was my first outing on my own since my back injury. I was keen to go, as I knew it would be an interesting conference and it was time to reconnect with midwives. For so long we midwives had been talking about splitting from nurses, and of claiming autonomy from doctors. I thought things might happen at this conference. Caroline Flint, a midwife from the UK, was a keynote speaker. She had set up a successful continuity of midwifery care scheme and written a book about it. I was also apprehensive and tentative. Would anyone even remember me? Did I have any life as a midwife left?

It was soul-soothing to be back with some of my Wellington midwife friends at the conference and to realise that I still had a career. Caroline Flint was a perfect speaker for us at the time. There was strong support in the audience for her approach. Then Joan Donley got up and talked to us. Her now-famous phrase, 'Are we midwives or moas?' got a standing ovation. We yelled back, 'We are midwives!' Not an extinct species. It was time to act. As we sat down again, it was clear that we were ready.

But how would we get from the middle of a conference based in a nurses' organisation, with all its constitutional rules and regulations, to our own midwives' conference? What was the protocol? (Can you believe that we were still being such good girls?) I stood and put my hand up.

'I propose that we close this conference now and open the first national conference of the New Zealand Midwives' Organisation.' Someone seconded it; nobody discussed it, they were all so excited. It was passed, almost unanimously.

Settled in Devonport and with the family complete, I turned my mind to
a new stage of life as a midwife.

It was momentous, thrilling, and happening. I was back in midwifery, and my bad back was relegated from life-defining to a minor irritation. There was a lot of work to do. A small group of us volunteered to write the constitution. I have fond memories of being at Joan Donley's home, dreaming up what midwives could be and what we wanted to achieve. She was so focused. She had a huge bed that was covered in piles of paper except for the bit she slept in. She had ditched her husband long ago (her words), and her children were all grown. We gathered there or in her tiny kitchen. Joan had the first mobile phone I had ever seen. It was just an ordinary landline, but with a cord so long I think she could have taken it to most of her births. We would pause for lunch or tea, and she would send us into her chaotic but productive garden to fetch random leaves for one of her famous 'weed salads' or a herbal tea. She had been a homebirth midwife forever, it seemed, and was the authority on all things birth. She could be cantankerous and demanding, but we all loved her.

We came up with a draft constitution that we were happy with, but it was radical for the time. We wanted to call the new organisation the Aotearoa College of Midwives, and we created a structure where consumers were represented at every level, with voting rights. We also wanted to create a structure that could facilitate working alongside and in partnership with Māori midwives. (This did not happen till 1996, though, when the first representatives of Ngā Maia o Aotearoa me Te Waipounamu joined a College national meeting and worked towards an understanding of how co-governance might function.) We sent our draft around the country for consultation.

At that time, it would be misleading to describe all midwives as being activists. Not everybody was on board with the changes, and many didn't care. There remained some resistance to our splitting with nurses, and an unsurprisingly conservative streak had a habit of finding its way into the discussion. We needed as many members as we could get, so in the end we compromised. The name 'Aotearoa' got changed to 'New Zealand', but we did manage to lock in the centrality of our relationships with women. We were the first professional organisation in New Zealand and the only midwifery organisation in the world to build this partnership with women at every level of our organisation.

I loved being with Joan. One day, in a small pause in our writing and thinking and over a comfrey tea, I broached the subject of me wanting to start doing some homebirths but never having seen one.

'Do you think I could maybe come out with you?'

She looked at me dismissively. 'There's no way you need to see a homebirth. Just go and get started.'

'But I don't even know what equipment I need.'

'Come with me next week and we'll go shopping at the medical warehouse,' she said, with her still-strong Canadian twang.

It turned out that one didn't need so much, according to Joan. We wandered around the warehouse. Actually, Joan almost ran. She let me buy a sphygmomanometer for measuring blood pressure; two pairs of forceps for clamping the cord; some scissors and a needle-holder for suturing the perineum; some oxygen; a Pinard stethoscope (a plastic funnel for listening to the baby). And that was it. When I suggested I might like a Sonicaid (a type of electronic foetal monitor), she looked at me scathingly.

'What would you need that for?'

I had wanted to get back to work, so I was doing two afternoon shifts a week in the postnatal ward of North Shore Hospital. Our next-door neighbour in Devonport was happy to look after Tim, Matt and Kena after school. Paul would come home from work early most days I went to the hospital, so it worked well. Still, homebirth was calling. There were no domiciliary midwives living on the North Shore, but there were women birthing at home, and midwives had to travel over the Harbour Bridge to get there.

I eventually made an appointment to meet the two doctors who did homebirths on the North Shore. We still had to work with doctors. They were keen, and Paul was supportive, so, just like that, I made sure I had all the equipment I needed (a lot more than Joan had recommended) and all the paperwork done. Within days, I got a call from a woman who lived just around the corner and who wanted to have a homebirth.

'Of course,' I replied, in a cheerful and confident voice, much more positive than I was feeling. 'Why don't I come around and say hello and we can have a chat about it?'

I took Tim with me in the pram and walked the five minutes to her home. I paused in front of the unrenovated bungalow with its overgrown garden. What was in store for me? I was stepping way out of my comfort zone and had no midwifery support nearby. For the first time, I wondered what a homebirth was like. It was no longer theoretical.

I knocked on the door to be greeted by Maria and her partner Ross. Although dishevelled, the house had a warm, homely feel. There were comfortable old couches, mismatching kitchen chairs around the Formica table, and a delightfully unrenovated kitchen. An old-style Italian coffee-maker was simmering on the gas stove and the air was filled with the delicious aroma of fresh coffee. Maria and Ross had just returned from Europe to have their baby in New Zealand. The house was rented and they were hoping to be able to stay there at least for the next year or so. Maria was due to give birth in a month; her pregnancy had been normal thus far. Tim settled down on the floor beside me with some toys I had brought. We chatted about their travels and their hopes for the birth.

'You probably want to know a bit about me,' I said.

'Roger [one of the doctors] said we would be your first homebirth but that you were very experienced. He said you were highly recommended and he would be at the birth too.'

'I'm pleased you are okay with that. The other thing to let you know is that I have Tim here and he will be coming to most of the visits with me. My partner will almost certainly be able to look after him when you are in labour. But he might have to be with me for some of your early labour too. You have to feel comfortable with that, so have a chat once I have gone, and let me know.'

The coffee was good and strong, which was to prove very useful during the labour. It was long. Eight hours into it, Maria's strong contractions petered out. It was midnight. I had come early and set up all my equipment on a table ready to go. I was hypervigilant and drank a lot of coffee. Maria was doing amazingly well, and Ross was calm and present. The baby was ticking along and giving us the odd wriggle to tell us he was all right. I did worry when the contractions dwindled in intensity and then stopped altogether. Nothing I could encourage got them going again. It looked like I might fail at my first homebirth. I called the doctor, assuming that he would recommend a hospital transfer, but he was reassuring and got out of bed to come and see us. Roger brought his air of calm confidence into the room. He did a vaginal examination and Maria was four centimetres dilated, nearly halfway there.

'I think you're just tired and probably a bit dehydrated. How about I put a drip in to give you some fluid, you have a bit of sleep Maria, and we'll see if the contractions pick up again? How do you feel about that, Joan?'

I had never, ever heard the like in all my time as a midwife. My experience at that time told me she needed significant intervention, definitely a hospital transfer (I wouldn't think that now).

'That's a great idea,' I said.

Roger went home; Maria and Ross tucked up in their bed together. There was no way I was going to sleep. I sat bolt upright at the kitchen table for the next two hours, worrying and drinking coffee.

Sure enough, Roger was right. The contractions started again at about 3 a.m. and in full force. Maria knelt up against the couch and pushed and pushed until this beautiful baby emerged into my hands and into his home. I had that delicious feeling of overwhelming relief and sheer thrill that midwifery can give. This time, though, I felt a twinge of something more: humility and privilege. How lucky was I to have come to this place in my world, a place where I could share and support a woman to birth? I had not felt this so powerfully in hospital.

It was grand. We were all elated. Ross cracked open a bottle of bubbly. He had put some strawberries to soak in brandy as the labour started, and now put one into each champagne flute. It had been a long labour and I had not eaten anything. I wandered home a little crookedly and climbed into bed beside Paul.

'How did it go?' he asked.

'Good. Guess what?'

'What?'

'I'm a homebirth midwife.'

'Have you been drinking?'

I was already asleep.

—◦—

My next two births went well. They were such new experiences for me. The most profound thing was watching women birth. That may sound crazy — I had seen hundreds of births, maybe even thousands. But watching women labour and birth in their own environment was revelatory. It seemed like a different process altogether and I felt like I was learning birth all over again. The continuity of the relationship with the women and their families that I hankered after was as precious as I had anticipated. It was in this environment that I came to understand and internalise the exquisite care needed when supporting women to birth and to mother.

The postnatal visits were always a delight. Tim, aged two, with a head of long, soft golden curls and quiet tentativeness, was my steady companion. He became expert at retrieving things from my kit and was especially keen on getting the scales out. It meant that soon I would be holding a baby aloft, wrapped in a nappy that was attached to the scales with a safety pin. It never failed to amaze him. (He would've made a wonderful midwife. Instead, he became a theoretical physicist.)

I only had three homebirth bookings at a time, one for each month, yet I had to be on call all the time, day and night. We didn't have cellphones, just pagers that went 'beep', and there was no message and no number to ring. Whenever I went anywhere, I had to be close to a phone. It was not a lifestyle made for a busy mother of three children who liked to be out and about. It was also incredibly poorly paid. Even though domiciliary midwives had just had a pay rise, I still made more money doing one shift at the hospital than I would make for all the homebirth care for one woman, including the antenatal visits and four weeks of postnatal care. The doctors who supported us to do the homebirths were exceptional (and paid properly). They were very supportive and totally collegial. It felt weird to be treated with such respect by doctors. It doesn't happen that often. It would be a whole new world if we ever did get our autonomy back, I reflected. For me, at least.

That time came much sooner than expected.

On the evening of 22 August 1990, Parliament passed amendments to the Nurses Act which reintroduced autonomous midwifery practice in New Zealand. It went so much further than we could have dreamed, providing the statutory recognition of midwives as 'safe and competent practitioners in their own right'. Helen Clark had made a good job of it. The amended Act separated nursing from midwifery, recreating midwifery as a separate and distinct profession with its own specific expertise and training. It also gave us the statutory right to prescribe medications, order and interpret diagnostic tests and scans, and study midwifery without prior nursing qualifications. I remember sitting by the radio in my lounge in Devonport, listening live. I could hear women in the public gallery cheering. It was a monumental change, with implications much bigger than any of us imagined.

Helen Clark then went on to describe the payment schedule that she proposed. She had decided to put us on the same pay scale as doctors. 'Oh my God!' I yelled out. I rang Judy, my sister-in-law and midwife buddy in Wellington. 'What colour BMW are you going to buy?' we laughed. 'She really did it. The whole bloody thing!'

Chatting with Heather Simpson, Helen Clark's PA, at a Labour Party fundraising dinner many years later, I heard the tale of how she and Helen had sat down one night and worked out what needed to be done. The first thing she commented on, as I remember, was that although they knew they were giving autonomy to all midwives, they thought it would really only be the homebirth midwives who would pick it up. The changes they made were very much in response to Joan Donley and Judi Strid's constant pressure about the growing lack of doctors who were prepared to support homebirth. They had also consulted the Nursing Council, who they found unhelpful and negative about midwifery autonomy, as Joan had warned. They could see that we needed to be set free from nursing.

'And what are we going to pay these women?' Helen had asked Heather.

'Well, equal pay for equal work,' Heather reported saying.

As minister of health, Helen Clark had had several losing battles with doctors, mostly in relation to trying to control the cost of GP care. Putting midwives on the same rate of pay as doctors would be a real coup. And it was. Doctors were caught unprepared. Susan Lennox, one of Wellington's homebirth midwives at the time, was married to a GP. When she told him what had happened, he said, 'Surely not. That can't have happened.'

At last we had become midwives. We were definitely not moas.

—◦—

Writing my PhD thesis 15 years later, I reflected on the key elements that had come together then to make autonomy happen. Although it really began the day a woman sat with another woman to help her birth, I identified that the modern-day genesis of midwifery autonomy lay in the coming together of six strands, most of which were generated during the 1980s. The first was doctors' withdrawal from homebirth, which activated homebirth midwives and women to push for midwifery-only care. This, along with the centralisation of maternity services into main hospitals, which further reduced women's birth options, worried both women and midwives a lot.

Another strand was the magic combination of visionary people in key places at the time, such as Joan Donley, Helen Clark and Judi Strid, plus wonderful women, mainly consumers, who were strong, united and active. Judi Strid, in particular, with her 'Save the Midwives' organisation, managed to motivate and unify midwives and consumers right across the country. Then there was the Cartwright Report on the experimental treatment of cervical cancer without consent at the country's largest women's health service. It was released in 1988 and caused a huge cultural shift in the way consumer rights, especially those of women, were prioritised. The consumer voice became important.

Then there were the nurses who, by minimising midwifery education and then threatening to end it as a profession altogether, motivated us to form a separate professional organisation and to join forces with Save the Midwives. Finally, there was the neoliberal, free-market political environment in which less government, less regulation, professional freedom and competition were to the fore of policy development.

They made for a strange tapestry, these strands. But we headed into the last decade of the millennium as free to be with women as we liked. It was up to us now — or so we thought.

—o—

Jane's was the first homebirth I did without a doctor. She lived in Takapuna, and Tim and I headed up one afternoon to do the first visit. Now I was to do all the antenatal care, including the blood tests. Laboratory technicians and chemists had to get used to midwives' test requests and prescriptions. Some struggled, which is to say they revolted. Up until then, only doctors had been allowed access to such hallowed tools. Resistance to our autonomy was to be from then on, and to some extent forever, our constant companion.

It was Jane's second homebirth, and she was very happy to have me as her midwife and not to have a doctor as well. I must admit to being quite nervous, especially when she added 'Pete's a doctor, Joan. But don't worry about him. He knows nothing about childbirth and is really happy to have another homebirth.'

I needed to find another midwife to be at the birth with me: a second pair of hands was crucial. My good friend Heff, who had done midwifery with me, volunteered to help. She was the perfect person to be with me. She was experienced and had a lovely calm, cheerful persona. This homebirth, though, would be a first for both of us.

Jane did not have a single problem to worry me. She had a textbook pregnancy and labour, and birthed her daughter serenely on her hands and knees. She had a normal blood loss, and not a stitch was required. The baby breastfed like a dream and everyone was happy. Heff and I both acted like we had done all this a million times. We were supportive, confident and encouraging. I didn't *feel* confident, though.

I did all the postnatal checks and blood tests myself, filled in the birth certificate and referred Jane on to the Plunket nurse and back to her GP.

23 October 1990

Dear Dr Reynolds
Re: Jane Calcutta. DOB 13/3/60
Baby: female, DOB 15/9/90

I am referring Jane back to you as her primary medical practitioner. Jane had a normal pregnancy throughout, a normal four-hour labour and delivery at term. I have copied all her laboratory tests to you so you should have these on file. She had a normal blood loss and required no sutures. Baby Kirsty had Apgars of 9/10, weighed 3450 gms and has been breast feeding well since. Her hip check was normal, and she had her heel prick completed on day 4. Her discharge weight was 3830 gms. I have given Jane a prescription for condoms as this is her choice of contraception at this time.

Jane has a copy of all her maternity notes which I have suggested she bring to her six-week visit with you when she plans for Kirsty

to begin her immunisations. Feel free to contact me if you have
any concerns.

Yours sincerely,
Joan Skinner RM

I'm not sure about other midwives, but for me the shift to autonomous practice was momentous. Others talked about the experience as being 'just normal', 'long awaited', or 'feeling right'. For me it was 'Wow I've just done a whole pregnancy and birth without a doctor and no one died.'

It got a lot better quite quickly, especially when Chris, a young midwife who had recently settled on the North Shore, offered to be my back-up. I was in my element, and thrived. Midwives needed to upskill fast, some more than others, so we organised workshops where we could build and develop our skills in suturing, putting in IVs, antenatal assessments, neonatal checks and resuscitation, interpreting tests, hip checks . . . all those skills that had been taken from us. We developed an accountability framework where we would have our entire practice regularly reviewed by both peers and consumers. No other health professional in New Zealand did that. We could be very tough on ourselves.

It wasn't just homebirth midwives that needed to upskill. The change to the Nurses Act meant that women could have a midwife and also birth in the hospital. And the money was good. At last, all midwives could make a living from it. I could stop working in the postnatal ward. Midwives exited hospital employment in droves and set up as what they called 'independent' midwives. Some would offer homebirth as well, but most initially offered continuity of midwifery care alongside doctors and in the hospital. It was called 'shared care' and was very popular with women for a while. It seemed to women that they could have everything. Philosophically there were challenges, as midwives were sometimes slow to embrace the role of advocate for undisturbed, normal birth (and some never did).

It was a busy time. Over those years we also had to continue developing the frameworks for our work. We worked on a code of practice; standards for practice, service and education; and referral guidelines. We produced a statement on safe options for low-risk pregnancy. We relished the autonomous professionalisation of midwifery.

But we also lost something. It might seem a little sentimental, but something about the reciprocal relational nature of the work had shifted; ever so slightly at first, but increasingly over time. Maybe it was because we were so badly paid back then. Women, somehow, valued our company and our actual being. There was a give and take, a genuine human connection. I also felt that there was a level of appreciation and a lack of entitlement. The change, I think, was a shift from trust to accountability, from friendship to respect, and from gratitude to expectation. It puzzled me why it had changed, and I couldn't work out why being paid properly and being valued as providing an excellent service would impact so negatively on a relationship. We had pride in ourselves that we were doing a new type of professionalism based in relationship. But I remained unconvinced.

A sign of the change was that it was increasingly seen as inappropriate and less than professional for me to bring Tim along to the visits. Women became surprised that Tim was with me, and I could tell they were becoming disapproving. I felt sad about that.

PART TWO

LOVE AND FEAR

5

—

The life–death–life cycle

The same year that midwives claimed back autonomy in New Zealand, my father died. He was only 70. He had just retired and was settling into writing his memoirs, playing golf (which he was very bad at), and being a grandfather (which he was very good at). He delighted in us, and we in him. At last he was getting some rest after a lifetime of dedication to his patients. And now he and Mum could have some time together, uninterrupted.

But a tendrilled, fast-growing brain tumour got him. My brother Lew phoned me to tell me what the scan had found. I walked along Cheltenham Beach to pick the kids up from school, in a state of numb dissociation. I looked out at the sea and felt what it might be like to never see it again. I found midwives to take over the care of my women, packed up the kids and flew home to Wellington, something I should have done much earlier.

His dying took only six months.

It was six long months and six short months. It was both horrifying to watch him fade away from us, and boring. I would spend hours with him, watching the same game of cricket on the TV again and again. Waiting and waiting for death. His short-term memory had gone. Eventually we had to stop everybody except close family from coming, as the tumour eventually wound itself around his pre-frontal cortex and he lost his inhibitions. That was when we saw the first signs of agitation and aggression appear.

He had a few days in the hospice to get his sedation sorted. He came home to us semiconscious but peaceful, occasionally smiling in recognition, and still able, for a while, to enjoy a spoonful of Mum's chocolate mousse or watch his four-year-old grandson using his dying body as a racetrack for his cars and trucks. There had been only a tiny window in the early days when he was himself. Steroids and the tumour took his brain away early. Day after day, it was our job to make sure he was free from pain, danger and distress. He died at home with all but one of his children around him.

Being alongside Dad at this time had been both meaningful and meaningless. It was my first experience of loss. Up until then I'd had everything I'd wanted, was accepted for everything I applied for, and succeeded at everything I attempted. I had been loved deeply. I was privileged beyond measure. But as it turned out, I had been only half alive — the easy half.

I was also struck by how similar death was to birth. The waiting, the wondering, the pain, the taking-over of caring. Letting living do its thing, gathering around, connecting, helping, cooking, the seeking of the wise woman to help. Tears and joy, gratitude. My sister Catherine had become a palliative care nurse — not an uncommon career move for a midwife — and her experience was so reassuring.

The death of my father left a horrible dark hole which I never wanted filled. There was no way I was going back to Auckland and leaving Mum. I found a school for the kids and a place to live, and I settled back into Wellington. Paul joined us. He needed to finish off his PhD, so I got a job as perinatal unit manager, the new name for the Charge Midwife, at the Hutt Hospital. It was miserable. This was when we had Crown Health Enterprises instead of hospitals. We were meant to compete with each other. It's hard now to understand what they were thinking. But in the 1990s, neoliberalism and managerialism were both unleashed. The new CEO and his management team had their offices redecorated in pink and grey; meanwhile the showers in the postnatal ward rotted, and women had to bring in their own sanitary pads and were required to go home as soon as possible after the birth.

It was my first and last experience of middle management, stuck between men (now businessmen instead of doctors) who reduced my budget every time I met with them, and staff who became more and more irate at the poor care women were getting. We did have several (futile) attempts at introducing some new ideas, one of which involved the community of mothers being involved in planning how we looked after them. After all, we were told that neoliberalism was intended to open up unimagined opportunities for innovation.

The whole thing was a mess. Nothing worked, and I felt like a failure and a fraud. And Dad was gone. I would hide in the hospital gardens with a coffee and a cigarette whenever I could, and hold myself together to keep functioning, trying to work out how long it would be before I could run, and what excuses I could give. After a year of this, they closed the postnatal ward and I was another budget cut. I was liberated, wiping most of the year out of my memory and never going anywhere near management again. It was time to get back to homebirth. Midwifery was thriving in New Zealand, and I was missing being part of it.

—o—

In the two years since midwives had regained their autonomy, there had been huge changes to the way maternity care was provided. Midwives had exited hospital employment in unexpectedly high numbers, to work in the community. The women loved knowing their midwives, and they were at last seemingly in control. Grandmothers delighted in the birth experiences of their daughters. For many, being present when their daughters birthed opened up memories of their own. I have had many cups of tea while debriefing new grandmothers about their own births. Seeing their daughters birth so powerfully helped to heal the damage caused by the terror, cruelty and helplessness they experienced as they birthed these daughters 20 or 30 years ago.

It had been a remarkable transition. In just two years, midwifery had changed from being seen as an outdated, nearly extinct profession to being a core provider of maternity care. By 1993 the first question a pregnant woman would often be asked was, 'Who is your midwife?' It was a world-leading change. The new College of Midwives thrived. We started direct-entry midwifery degree programmes around the country. There would be no more nursing for us. We developed our own standards for practice and ways to monitor them. We asked the government to provide a separate regulatory body. Consumers were represented at every level of our organisation. Māori midwives developed their own organisation and

The Wellington Home Birth Midwives Collective in 1993. Back, from left:
Adrienne Cathie, me (and my big hair) and Helen Cussins.
Front: Bridie Foster and Judy Skinner (now Stehr).

worked alongside the College. Midwives right around the world envied our freedoms, and many came to work and study with us. We loved it too. Across the country, midwives carried pagers, stayed on call 24/7, and formed relationships with women and their families that we had never been able to before.

By the time I had dusted off my equipment and headed back to work, Wellington was buzzing with midwives. Before the law change there had been only one midwife in Wellington providing homebirth services. Now there were plenty. Four of us decided to formalise our working relationship and we set up the Wellington Homebirth Midwives' Collective, the first of its kind in the city. It was a way to share our experiences, help with the problem-solving and decision-making, and, of course, to cover each other when we needed time off or needed to be relieved for sleep. A second pair of hands could be vital in an emergency or as a relief when everyone was getting tired. We formed strong links with the women who ran the Homebirth Association.

We made a great team. We met weekly and shared information about who was due to give birth and any concerns we had. We had a monthly coffee morning where all the women were welcome to come, either before or after their birth. They could meet each other and meet all four of us, in case their main midwife was off call. This was important. Women needed to know very early on that they might not get their 'own' midwife at the birth. These discussions were sometimes hard. In fact, we rarely missed one of our births and stayed on call almost all the time. It made midwives' lives complicated.

Our weekly meetings were usually at my home in Glenmore Street, as it was the most central. Our pagers had the same number, and technology had now progressed to being able to leave a message. We all saw all the messages, which were sent out to us by an operator somewhere. She got to know our lives quite well.

Message from Bridie: Sorry will be a few minutes late.
Just finishing off a postnatal. Will bring custard squares.
Message from Joan: No prob. Bring milk.
Message from Kirsten Guy for Joan: Contractions have started.
Still mild. Will ring when stronger.
Message from Judy: Want me to see Kirsten on my way?

Will be passing.

Message from Jenny for Judy: Mum, where is my hockey stick?

Message from Bridie: I don't think Helen will be coming.
She was up most of the night at Chris's birth. It was a bit tough.
Tell you when I get there.

Message from Paul to Joan: The House is sitting late tonight. I won't
be home till midnight.

Message from Joan to Judy: No thanks. She'll be fine. She is super
confident. I'll ring her later.

Message from Jenny to Judy: Do we come straight home after school
or go to Dad's?

A cellphone would have come in handy.

—◦—

Eventually we were all gathered for that weekly meeting. Helen made
it too, but she was sleep-deprived and distressed. We debriefed with
her about the birth. She had rushed Anna, one of her women having
her fifth baby, to hospital because the baby's heart rate kept slowing
down. She birthed just as they arrived, and the baby was pale, floppy
and unresponsive. The neonatal unit staff got her breathing at about
three minutes but they had been rude and critical of Helen in front of
the parents, who were already distressed. Then she got tied up with the
endless documentation, admission forms and incident forms, talking to
doctors and then transferring Anna to the postnatal ward. She had felt
criticised by everyone.

'Is there anything I missed? What if the baby is brain-damaged?'

We went over her decision-making with her, to check how that went.
It felt to us all as if this was a safe environment not only to truly reflect
on what had happened, but also to take a good look at what mistakes
might have been made. Many midwives go straight to self-blame when
something unexpected happens, and we need lots of support to get
through it. We do make mistakes sometimes, and it's so important for
us all to learn. We thought that Helen's decision to move to hospital was
spot-on, and that she should have been congratulated, not condemned.
But backlash was inevitable. There was a part of New Zealand that was

horrified at midwifery-led maternity care. This attitude was sometimes overt but most often semi-hidden, ready to be revealed whenever a birth outcome was difficult. Then, we would hear or feel some variation of:

> Midwives kill babies. Doesn't everyone know that? How come we leave these girls with only three years of training at a polytech and no medical supervision to manage one of the most complex, dangerous parts of life? How did we let that happen?

'Next time we get an unexpected outcome, I think we should always call one of us in straight away. It's too hard on your own,' I suggested.

'Well, I thought of it, but I didn't want to wake you.' Helen blew her nose.

'Oh, you should have. Then we can do some of that paperwork or the postnatal care, or just be there,' Bridie said.

'Let's make it a thing for us all,' Judy suggested. 'Time you went home to sleep, Helen. We'll do your visits today. We probably need to talk about this some more. Page us when you wake up.'

An extra-strong pot of coffee and all the custard squares were gone. We settled down to do our usual business, keeping each other up to date on the women we were looking after, getting advice about issues we were having, checking on who was going to stay on call over the weekend and, of course, just generally how everyone was. We also needed to plan who was going to work over Christmas. Even though it was only May, we were starting to get Christmas bookings. There was the inevitable diversion to holiday planning, who was having whose children for Christmas, and Bridie's hilarious story about her husband being Father Christmas last year.

'I need to talk about Jan.' I brought us back from holiday planning to the job at hand. 'She's 10 days overdue. She had some acupuncture today and I'll give her a stretch and sweep tomorrow if there is still no sign of labour. Just in case she delivers on the weekend, 'cause I'm off, everything is ready at her place. The syntocinon is in the fridge and she has all the linen organised. They are on the third floor of an Oriental Bay apartment and there is pristine white shag-pile carpet everywhere. Just saying. Good luck with that. It looks like Kirsten might deliver tonight. Are you still okay to do second for that, Judy?'

—o—

My pager went off at 9 p.m.

'Joan, I think the labour has started.' It was Jan, not Kirsten.

This was good news. An induction of labour and a hospital birth had been on the cards if she hadn't birthed by Monday. The contractions were still only 10 minutes apart. We agreed that she'd ring me back when the pains were closer and stronger or if she was worried about anything. But that was the end of sleep for me. There is nothing quite like having someone ring to say labour is starting just as you are thinking about bed. I knew she would be fast once she got going because she had her first baby in just over six hours. I put out the clothes I would need, loaded all my equipment into the car, and warned Paul that I would probably be gone in the morning so he would have to get the kids off to school. Just as my head hit the pillow, the phone rang.

'Joan, I think you need to come now. Jan's started to have really strong contractions and she thinks she wants to push.'

I leapt out of bed, grabbed my clothes and flew out of the house. I arrived a little short of breath, with my two bags of equipment over my shoulders. The apartment was toasty warm and dimly lit, some quiet jazz in the background.

'No baby yet. Good.'

Jan was clearly in strong labour, though. She was leaning over the end of her bed moaning and rocking through nice, long, strong contractions. She glanced up as I quietly entered the bedroom. A look of relief to see me, but no smile.

'Oh God, I'd forgotten how terrible this is. I don't think I can do this. How long have I got to go?'

Funny thing about midwives. We describe long, strong contractions as 'nice'. We get excited when they get even worse and are usually very pleased when the woman gets shaky, vomits and is adamant that she cannot do it anymore. It means the baby is close.

'Wow. You are doing beautifully. You seem very close now. This is all normal, Jan. Let's just do one contraction at a time and you will have your baby here soon.'

An hour later, and there was no change. She should really have had this baby out by now. Something was holding it up.

'How about I have a feel to see what this baby's up to?'

Sure enough, she only had a little bit of cervix left to go. But it was swollen and refused to budge even when I tried to help stretch it over the baby's head. Midwives know it as an 'anterior lip' and it can be a real bugger.

So, we had to change tack. Time to move, time to change position, time to walk. Patience and lots of encouragement were needed.

'You're doing so well, and it won't be long.'

Another hour passed, and I tried all the tricks of the trade to get that last bit of cervix to go. Jan paced up and down her apartment. I was aware of the white shag-pile carpet. Jan couldn't have cared less. Thankfully, the baby's heart rate was good. I phoned Judy and asked her to come, as I thought we could all do with some new energy. She needed to be there for the birth anyway. Surely we must be close now.

Judy took Jan into the shower, hoping that the flowing water might help, and I curled up on the couch to catch my breath and have something to eat and drink. It's this sort of uncomfortable time when you realise how uncertain and unpredictable birth is. I felt the intense level of alertness and anticipation flow out of my body as I sipped the hot tea. I let it go and rested, trusting Judy to pick it up for me. There are times when midwives hate cervixes and hate their jobs. *What are you doing this for, Joan?*

Within minutes, it seemed, bellowing and grunting emanated from the bathroom. It was music to my ears. It was sounding fast.

Judy called, calmly and gently, 'Joan, the baby's coming so I . . .'

I was already there.

'Greg, bring the towels and the birth kit . . . quite quickly, please.'

Jan was standing in the shower, holding on to the taps as if her life depended on it. Judy was in the shower too, bending down with her hand on the baby's head as it emerged. She was wet.

'This is all perfect, Jan. I have the baby's head here.'

I caught Jan's eyes. 'Jan, I need to turn the shower off now. Greg is here to hold you so you can let go of the taps. Here's the baby now. No big pushes. Just gently. Reach down now and you can feel his head.'

The baby arrived just as I turned the shower off and with an enthusiastic cry, not dissimilar to his mother's. Judy ended up holding a slippery, wet baby, mid-air, still attached to his mother. This is a midwifery skill that takes a lot of practice. I grabbed the towel off the heated towel rail and Judy popped him into it. We were all joyful, except Jan, who was catching her breath for a second, her mind coming back into the room.

Then she was very joyful. Another midwifery skill is getting a mother and her still-attached baby from the bathroom to the bed over pristine white shag-pile carpet.

—◦—

Being back with birth was a sort of homecoming for me. But things at home were actually not going so well. Mum became ill. She was in pain all over her body and was too nauseated to eat. She tried valiantly to carry on, to summon back that stoicism that had saved her before. But her 'mad McGrath' deserted her this time. I went to lots of her specialist appointments as they scoped and scanned and blood-tested. They didn't find anything. It was cruel that the medical system, which had sucked up so much of Dad's time from her, failed her when he was not there to keep watch.

Eventually my sister Catherine in Melbourne came up with the diagnosis. Mum had a not uncommon immune disorder called polymyalgia rheumatica. A small dose of steroids each day removed all her horrid symptoms. Dad would have picked it. But it was too late for Mum, as during that year from hell the only thing that helped her feel a little better was a brandy. And that got her. To this day, I regret not bundling her up and bringing her home. But things at my own home were not going well either.

Paul had found a job at Parliament, running the Labour Party's research unit. But I think it stretched him too far, and to somewhere he didn't want to go. Mike Moore was Leader of the Opposition at that time. He was chaotic to work for and Parliament had a toxic working environment. I could tell that Paul was struggling and I knew we were not in tune with each other. I was emerging from a decade of full-on motherhood with just a day a week of midwifery. Tim had started school, and I was trying to work out what was next for me and feeling very unsettled about it.

One night we were sitting together in the lounge and Paul said he wanted to tell me something. He said that our marriage was over and 'that it would be good for us to separate while we still have time to create new lives'. Just like that. There was no warning. He needed to repeat it several times until I heard him properly and before I understood that he really did mean it. He had never discussed it with me before. He had decided it all by himself. I curled up into a ball, unable to breathe or speak. Paul had to ring for my sister-in-law, the helpful one, to come and be with me. I just felt like my whole world, my dreams, my hopes for the future, had all gone, and at the hands of a man who I thought was my soulmate. It was beyond believable.

We had another year together and I can't remember how I managed to last. We both turned 40 and put on huge parties for each other. Paul organised a surprise helicopter trip over all my old Wellington haunts, at which he had arranged people from my past to be there waving. We flew over schools, homes, hospitals, the polytech, and the final triumph was a HAPPY BIRTHDAY JOAN sign made from wallpaper on the side of Mount Victoria.

I spent the year in denial, so much so that I didn't even talk about it with my closest friends. It was my horrible secret. I tried to make myself the strong, independent, interesting woman I thought Paul might want to stay with. There was no way that my kids could be from a 'broken home'; I was sure it would ruin them. The mother lion in me emerged. I did self-development courses, I did fire walks and bungy jumps, I went to university to start a master's degree. I had a make-over. I tried to never complain or demand. I read *Women Who Run with the Wolves*. I tried never to think that Paul would really leave us. There was no way he could.

Meanwhile, the delight of my work provided a balance to support me. I managed in true 'daughter of Ro' style to function as wife, mother and midwife with as much contentment, confidence and determination as I could. Looking back now at this time in my life, I certainly benefited from my mother's gift of stoicism and denial. Nobody, not even me, knew the torment that I was living in. It allowed me not only to function, but indeed to thrive in my work.

Judy and I worked closely together. We had homebirths all over Wellington, from Ōwhiro Bay to Pukerua Bay; we had long first-time labours and ultra-quick experienced mothers; we had a woman with a postpartum haemorrhage in Plimmerton and an unresponsive baby in Seatoun. The last two were both just fine but did require a precautionary transfer to hospital once we had them stabilised. These were my only two transfers while I worked in Wellington. It's funny how we can remember the bad stuff so clearly and so much later.

We had to do some hospital births, too, as there were not enough women wanting homebirths to enable us to earn a living. One memorable day, I had a hospital birth in Wellington followed straight afterwards by a homebirth in Thorndon. Then, just as I was sitting on the edge of my bed taking my shoes off, my pager rang and it was another woman heading to Kenepuru Hospital in labour. All three births went well. After all that I slept the sleep of the just. In those days, it would only take one good sleep to get me back on track. Nowadays I couldn't even do one all-nighter. Midwifery is not a job for the faint-hearted, or the old and weary.

—o—

Midwifery is not just about the actual birth. Most of our time is spent with the women before and after the birth, and it is in these times that relationships are built and women are supported into motherhood. One of the important moments of care is the six-week check, a rather understated phrase that signals the end of the midwife–woman relationship. Of course it involves a range of tasks, and reams of paperwork and computer work to do. We weigh the baby, check it over from top to toe again. And then we check the mother from top to toe, too: breasts, lactation, involution of the uterus, lochia, perineum. We make sure she has a GP to go to, a referral to a Plunket nurse, and that we have talked about contraception and sexuality. And all the other stuff we do.

But then we have to say goodbye.

—o—

Six weeks after Ahuwera was born, it was time for me to say goodbye to her, and to her mother and grandmother. Ahuwera had been breastfeeding well, about every three or four hours, and was a settled, happy baby, apart from in the early evening when she liked to stay awake for a while.

'Stan is enjoying her company. He misses her a lot since he went back to work,' Irihapeti commented. Ahuwera gave me a big smile as I wrapped her in a nappy to hang her from my scales. She was well over her birth weight.

'That's a very good weight gain, Iri. You've clearly got a wonderful milk supply,' I said. Marama, Iri's mother, had gone to make us one last cup of tea.

Ahuwera had been born at home after a long, overnight labour. During her pregnancy, Iri had explained to me that she had been a tamariki

110

whāngai and that both her mothers would be with her during her birth. For one of her mothers, Iri was the last of seven babies. For the other, she was her first and only. Iri was 40 at the time of this birth so her mothers, who were cousins, were older, probably in their late seventies. I didn't ask.

Marama poured the tea while Iri dressed Ahuwera and put her on the breast. Over the previous six weeks we had talked a lot about the birth, but it was time to check in again, one last time, to see how Iri had been processing it, and whether there were any questions either of them wanted to ask me. A birth can sometimes feel very different six weeks later.

'Well, Joan, that birth was amazing. I was very unhappy about Irihapeti having a homebirth, but it went well in the end. I really trusted you, you know, and I'm pleased I did.'

I had felt blessed to be at Iri's birth. She had laboured so well. But it wasn't fast, so the three of us, Marama, Tui and I, made a good team. I could tell when I arrived that they were worried, as they were hovering over her, with frequent queries to me about how she was and whether they could do anything to help. It was part of my job, I saw, to shift the scene away from anxiety towards calm, patience and positivity.

I could see the relief in their eyes as they saw that I was confident. I balanced the need to keep them too busy to worry with making sure they had rest spells and enough to eat and drink. Pacing their energy was important; I did not want to exhaust them. It didn't take long before they were confidently encouraging Iri during her contractions. We tag-teamed the night away. I can't seem to remember where Stan was most of the night, but I remember that it nearly killed him when he had to hold Iri up during the two hours she spent pushing.

I remember every second of the birthing. There was such relief that the long night was nearly over. We all watched as the dark curly hair on the head of the baby came closer and closer. Ahuwera was born with such calm and joy. Marama was right by me, watching her granddaughter emerge with awe. Tui was wiping Iri's face with whispers of encouragement, and Stan, his face contorted with the effort, was using every last bit of his strength to hold Iri as she bore down. Tui and Marama together chanted a karanga as the baby emerged. I handed her straight to Marama, who held her, spellbound for a few seconds, and then handed her back to me, tears flowing down her face. 'You take her, Joan.' Later that morning Tui left for home in the Waikato, to take the placenta for burial.

As we drank our last cup of tea together, Marama commented: 'When we had our babies, they tried to stop us having them at home. We used to birth easily at home and someone who had birthed a lot of babies would come and help. And the father was always there. We knelt to give birth and baby was always caught from behind. It was very private. When they first tried to tell us to go to hospital we just stayed at home, especially if it wasn't our first. There was a local doctor in Putāruru who used to come to the births, but we always waited till the baby was born before we called him. He used to come out and have a cup of tea with us. We'd get our best cup and saucer ready. I think he knew what we were doing but he never got the authorities on to us.'

'Where did you have your babies?' I asked.

'I had my first three at home, but then went into the hospital for the next lot. It was bad. They wouldn't let anyone in, put me on a hard bed, and then put my legs up so everybody could see. It was so shameful. But now I see there are births in homes again. Honestly, you Pākehā! First you say we can't have our babies at home, now you tell us we can.'

I don't remember replying. Maybe it was just with a rueful smile.

As I gathered my things and packed up my birth bag, Marama said 'You have been a wonderful help for us all and I have enjoyed our chats.

'You, Joan, are to stay being a midwife till you are a very old woman,' she instructed. 'Here, I have something for you. Sit there just a minute.'

She rummaged in her purse and brought out a piece of pounamu, carved in a heart shape and engraved with the word 'whaea'.

6

—

Being different and the same

On Labour Day 1994, Paul finally left. The loss of my dream was extreme. I was stoic on the outside, but inside I was paralysed with terror, and it was only my children that kept me breathing. Somehow I found the energy to focus on 'the three left at home', as my mother had. Paul may have been looking around to see what was next in his life, but it seemed that *my* life was over and my children's lives were ruined. I couldn't eat. I took a week off work, as I was in no state to make decisions. And then I went back because I needed help to keep moving.

My first day back on the job, I was walking through what the locals called 'the Bronx' in Petone, my kit in hand, on my way to do a postnatal visit. I could put one foot in front of the other, but I was numb. From the third floor of the council flats, a familiar face with her usual big grin leant out and waved.

'Hey Joan, how're you going girl?'

'I'm doing okay, Rona. How's that baby?'

'Sleeping, I hope. Who are you off to see?'

She had opened me up a little, just by that call-out. My feelings came back, but softer, warmer, with a little less terror. I felt a bit more me than I had before. My life had collapsed, yet my life — my real life — might just be getting going again. I had underestimated what being a midwife meant to me. It had kept me connected; it was good for me. Rona would have been very surprised by what she'd done. Twenty-five years later, I can still hear her voice. She had been one of the first women I had looked after in my new job as a midwife working for the Hutt Union and Community Health Service, HUCHS as we called it. I had been working there for about six months. It was the perfect place for me to be.

Six weeks after Paul left, it was Christmas and I dreaded it. How would I manage? I offered to be on call for the morning, as Paul was taking the kids to his family. They had been my family too. I had no idea how I would cope with that. So I prayed that someone needed me for a long, hard labour. I would need complete distraction. But it turned out not to be so. Paul called and the children headed off down the steps with him. We were all sorts of smiles. The children looked back at me.

'Bye, Mum.'

I could see the worry for me and for them in their eyes. Matt was pale, and Kena bewildered. Tim was too young, I think — I hope — to be distressed. That we should not have all been heading off together was unimaginable for me, but there it was. The family was broken. I had mustered all my strength to make what morning I had with them as Christmassy as possible. Christmas tree, presents, ham and cheese croissants, fruit juice and fizz. I'd eaten almost nothing for two months and had finally got skinny again. People said I looked fantastic.

As my husband and my children all walked away, I closed the door and fell against the wall, sliding slowly to the floor. It was agony to breathe. A strange groaning was coming from somewhere and I thought I might die. I was cracked open again. How often would I have to do this? I had an unexpected out-of-body experience, sitting on the stairs looking down at myself. I could not stay together.

'Oh, you look like they do in the movies when they do the whole "slide down the door weeping" routine. It does feel terrible, eh? That pain really hurts.'

I knew I couldn't die because I was on call. I managed to start breathing again and got up off the floor. Thank God I *was* on call, or I would have headed straight for a glass of wine. I would also get the kids back (What a disgusting concept. How could that be me?) after lunch, so I needed to hold it all together.

My pager stayed ominously quiet and it looked like no one wanted me, confirmation that I was intrinsically unlovable. It was ironic that the one Christmas when I needed to be too busy to think, nothing happened. Then I remembered Lizzie. She needed a postnatal visit.

Lizzie was 35 and this was her first baby, which was a total shock for her as she had been told she had a hormone imbalance and could never have children. No contraception, no permanent partner — but then a pregnancy. We didn't see her until she was seven months pregnant, as she thought she was just getting fat.

I loved looking after Lizzie. Despite having what seemed to me to be the toughest life, she was funny and kind. Her baby had been born six days ago and it was one of those labours that midwives love. A 'surprise us, won't you?' kind of birth. At six o'clock in the morning, Vanessa, another midwife in our group who had done the night cover, rang to say that she'd been up all night with Lizzie at the hospital and Lizzie had no one else with her.

'I think she is finally getting going, Joan. She's still only three centimetres, so she's got a way to go. But I've been with her since ten o'clock last night, so I need to get a bit of sleep. Do you think you could come and relieve me? No hurry.'

I took my time, as it looked like it was going to take a while. I had a shower, washed my hair, and even had some breakfast. By the time I got to the hospital, Lizzie was yelling obscenities and heaving down on the baby with everything she had. There was no time for us to have a handover. Vanessa, still there and now wide awake, was putting on her gloves as the baby appeared.

'Gentle pushing now Lizzie.'

'Fuck ooooooooooff.'

Six days later, on that Christmas morning, I arrived at Lizzie's front door. I had no idea what to expect, as I hadn't been to this place before. Lizzie had been a bit transient and it was hard to find her sometimes. The crates of empties at the door and the rubbish in the stairwell worried me. Christmas can be a tough time for lots of people. I am not alone, I thought.

'Hey, Joan, mate, happy Christmas.'

'Happy Christmas, Lizzie. Thought I'd come and see how you're doing.'

'C'mon in. What are you doing here? It's bloody Christmas.'

'You haven't had a visit for a few days. Time to weigh that baby.'

Would this excuse do? I'd have loved to have told her about my morning so far, but I hesitated. I'd cry, which was not very professional; although it was probably more about me not wanting to expose my vulnerability. I had resisted doing this with almost everyone over those months. The thought of being pitied was almost as bad as being abandoned. I hate pity. I knew that Lizzie would definitely not pity me. I thought I could have found a kindred spirit at covering the hard stuff up.

'Where is everybody?' I asked, looking around the sparse living room. It had two worn old couches, a Formica table with non-matching chairs, and a huge flat-screen TV perched on a coffee table.

'They've all gone up the coast for Christmas.'

'How come you stayed here?'

'Well, they all just get pissed and fight on Christmas Day. I don't want my baby's first Christmas to be like that. I thought I'd just stay here on my own.'

'Cool. How's that baby? Shall I have a look at him? Then I'll check you over.'

Lizzie fetched the baby from her room. He was tucked up warm and cosily asleep.

'Do you mind if I wake him?'

'Yeah, nah. He's due to wake up for a feed, so no sweat.'

'What have you decided to call him?'

'Jesus. Hah . . . nah. Rongo.'

Rongo was tubby and content. He was already over his birth weight and was feeding about every two hours.

'He's so hungry, Joan. I think he needs a bottle.'

'No way. He's just thriving on your breast milk. Babies normally feed very often in the first few weeks. It keeps your milk supply up and means he gets lots of cuddles. How much help are you getting?'

'Fuck all.'

'Anything I can do?'

'Move in?'

We both smiled.

'Want a coffee?' she added.

'Yes, please.'

We settled down together in one of the sinking couches. I watched as Lizzie put Rongo on the breast and he sucked at her nipple like he was half-starved. There was plenty of milk. We chatted, and somehow the misery that had threatened to take me out seeped away. We shared a bar of chocolate.

'What are you having for a Christmas feed, Liz?'

'I got a cooked chicken from Pak'nSave. What are you having?'

116

'Not a clue.' It was the end of fairy-tale-perfect Christmases for me. 'I'm off to my brother and sister-in-law's later. Picking up my kids from their father on the way.'

—○—

The joy of building relationships with women and being able to be alongside them right through their childbirth experience was precious. At last, midwives in Aotearoa were supported to do this. We were paid well, and we could work without doctors dominating our practice. We made decisions and helped mothers make theirs. Mothers had the choice of birth places and birth attendants.

But while the 1990s may have been wonderful for us, for women on low incomes things became worse. The neoliberalism which had overtaken the world in the 1980s had made its way to New Zealand. In 1990, the National Party won the general election, and the new government let loose an avalanche of neoliberal policies that increased support to the rich and privileged, who, it was believed, would grow the economy. Wealth would, they proposed, 'trickle down' to the poor. Ruth Richardson's 'Mother of all Budgets' in 1991 slashed all social benefits and abolished the universal family benefit altogether. Of course, wealth did not trickle down and an enormous disparity developed, still present today. Many families, either on a benefit or on low wages, could hardly afford to house and feed themselves, let alone seek healthcare. Their health outcomes plummeted.

From 1987 the union movement, whose low-paid members were suffering terribly, together with concerned leaders in the community, saw the growing gap and established five low-cost primary health services in Wellington and Auckland. They were community-owned and community-led, very different from the model of GP-owned, privately run health services. The cost of a visit to a Union and Community Health service was $10, as compared with the $50 that a GP visit cost. Despite maternity services remaining free, families on low incomes often did not access maternity services till very late, sometimes not until the birth. And their health needs were often greater.

In 1993, the Union and Community Health service in the Hutt Valley (HUCHS) decided to investigate the possibility of employing midwives to provide the same degree of continuity and commitment that other women had but that HUCHS mothers were not accessing. I got a call one afternoon from a man called Peter Glensor. He had started the primary health service in the Hutt Valley. They were offering midwifery care but only had one midwife. She was working 24/7, was exhausted and needed help. 'Would you be interested in joining us?' he asked. At that stage I was still working in the homebirth collective but we didn't have quite enough homebirths to keep us all busy. HUCHS was an appealing proposition. My friend Chris Hannah was the midwife for the Newtown service, and I liked how she talked about it. What made it especially attractive was that it had a strong social justice approach. It was community-owned and -run and all the staff, including the doctors, were on a salary. And it cared for families with minimal income and complex lives.

'We are having a social event on Saturday, Joan. Why don't you come along and meet the team?' Peter suggested.

I was welcomed by a slight, bearded man in a cream felt top hat (slightly grubby), and a heavily embroidered waistcoat that fell to his knees. 'I got them from the tip,' he announced proudly. He had a huge smile and piercing blue eyes. Chris Hannah had said, 'That man is a saint, Joan.' He was nothing like what I expected, but he emitted the type of energy and positivity that was appealing. The team was clearly relaxed with one another. I liked them all. I had worked with Siloma, the nurse from the Petone clinic, when we were both at Hutt Hospital. There was a mixture of staunchness and self-deprecation in the group and I could tell they were close. I was in.

It wasn't long before there were four midwives in the service. It turned out that almost all the pregnant women were happy to have us, and word got around the community that we were okay. I worked part-time, as I had started a master's degree in midwifery. I also wanted to continue doing some homebirths. Four was the minimum number of bodies we needed because we had to have a midwife available 24/7, and needed to cover sleep, weekends off, sickness and annual leave. In HUCHS, though, our working model was different from that of other midwives. The 'independent' midwifery model that most midwives in the community adopted, and that we followed in the homebirth collective, was to function as if self-employed although we were funded by the State. We had control of when, where and how we worked. The HUCHS model was structured specifically so that the community was in control and all the staff were accountable

The Hutt Union and Community Health Service (HUCHS) mothers' group learning how to perform CPR on babies at the Pomare Community Centre. I'm second from right.

to them. We were all employed by the service and worked as a team. The board ran the service, not the doctors.

In focusing on low-income families, we cared for a population with higher rates of ill-health, both physical and mental. The underlying poverty also included housing problems, meaning that many families were transient and vulnerable. Accessing maternity care was frequently the least of their concerns. At the time I joined the service, only 30 per cent of households had a telephone. The service had nurses, doctors, midwives, community workers, social workers and receptionists. A shared kaupapa was essential. Equity and social justice were at the core of our work. We were not only health providers, we were also social activists.

Most of the patients were Māori, Pacific or former refugees. This was reflected in the management board and in the staff, and there was a strong culture incorporating tikanga Māori. Facing up to the issues of colonisation and racism was integral. Other community and iwi-owned services were being set up in other parts of the country, and we joined together eventually to form a national organisation called Health Care Aotearoa. In the late 1990s the Labour government of Helen Clark drew on this model for what became the New Zealand Primary Health Strategy and the emergence of PHOs. It was a thrilling place to work.

While I was there, the Petone centre outgrew the corner space of the community hall where it had begun in 1993. With the explosion of new patients, new staff and new services, there was simply no room. Peter used to sit on the floor with his laptop on top of his lap, alongside a supermarket bag of his papers. This was his office. He would move between the two sites in Petone and Pomare, keeping us all positive and working hard despite the service having little money. Community work was in Peter's bones. He was very good at getting people excited, involved and, very importantly, keen to donate. Lever Brothers, the soap factory opposite the Petone centre, made a huge donation to enable an old school prefab to be trucked in and attached to the community centre. Peter also persuaded various DHB staff to give us their old examination beds, desks and chairs, and even their computers.

I loved the work. It felt useful and meaningful. To this day, it remains the best job I have ever had. I loved working in the team, and seldom felt overwhelmed by the challenges of the job. I thrived in the diversity and in the difficulties that inevitably came our way. I learnt a lot.

HUCHS staff catching up at a local Petone café. From left: Sally Nicoll (midwife), Muriel Tunoho (community worker) and me.

Much as with the homebirth midwives' collective, the four of us HUCHS midwives met weekly. The nurse, the doctor and the community worker were all included, and at each meeting we worked our way through the notes of every woman under our care, checking that we weren't missing anything and that we were meeting their needs. Someone usually brought muffins. Food is important for midwives. Most of us are a little round. We started each meeting by discussing the new bookings.

Sally began.

'This next one is a new patient to the service. Her name is Loma Luatafi and she's just moved down from Auckland with her four children. I saw her yesterday to book her in. She has moved in with the Faleotalas in Taitā. I couldn't work out whether her husband is coming down or not.'

'Oh, that's going to be a squash,' Siloma, the nurse, commented. 'That house already has too many people in it.'

'Yes. She's started looking for somewhere to live but it's not going well. Do you think you could pop around and see them, Muriel? They could do with some community worker input and they said they'd be happy to meet you. I also didn't ask about any benefits she might be on. Depending on her husband, I guess. She had all normal births before, but we need to watch her blood sugars.'

'Sure. What is their address? Are they still up in Lockwood Crescent?' Muriel asked.

'Do you know if she is a resident?' David, one of the doctors in the service, asked. 'The hospital is starting to get very tough on billing non-residents for maternity care now.'

'No, she's not,' Sally answered. 'I'm not sure how we can help her with that. How much are they charging for a birth now?'

'I think it's around $2500,' David replied.

'There's no way they can pay that. Maybe she could have a homebirth and we could bypass the DHB,' I suggested.

'That's not a bad idea, Joan. Do you think she will want to, Sally?' asked Chris.

'I'm not sure. I'm all for it, but you're the only one of us that has ever done a homebirth, Joan. Let's have a talk about it when Vanessa's back. We'll all have to be on board.'

Siloma remembered to ask, 'When you go back to the Faleotalas' house, Sally, could you please take the grandmother's blood pressure? And see if you can get the family to bring her in to the clinic because she is overdue for her diabetes check. They usually bring her in every couple of months, but we haven't seen her for ages.'

'Sure, no problem.'

'This next one is Kath,' continued Sally, getting back to the process at hand. These meetings could easily go on for hours and we all had work to get to. 'She delivered two days ago. A nice short birth and it was all normal. She had the whole whānau with her apparently. Vanessa looked after her and said it was a great event.'

'Yes, I've been visiting her the last couple of days at home,' added Chris. Vanessa was having some days off. 'Kath went straight home to her mum and they are doing fine. I reckon everyone should have their babies at 17. They do it so well. Actually, she'd be a great one to talk to our antenatal group about giving birth, and she might be up for it next week. I'll ask her when I see her later.'

Along the way we also talked about Ana. Ana was Tongan and I had been a midwife for her two sisters and her cousin, so she was keen to have me for her midwife too. I seemed to have become the local midwife for the Tongan community. It felt special. I could still speak a bit of Tongan but it had a colloquial edge, which was often a source of great amusement.

We had discovered that Ana was having twins, so she needed to consult with an obstetrician at the local hospital. I couldn't go to the appointment with her as I had hoped to, but I shared the result of the consult with the others.

'It didn't go well at the obstetric appointment. Ana told me that Howard [the obstetrician] said that because she had twins, she was too high-risk for us and all her care should be transferred to the hospital team. He didn't mention sharing her care.'

'How was Ana with that?' asked Sally.

'She seemed okay. But I don't think it will go well. She'll have no continuity of care and no midwifery input. I think I'll just keep an eye on her. I wish I had gone to the appointment.'

'That hospital has gone over the top with taking women off you midwives,' added David. 'I think they might be doing it to claim the funding. Most of our women have risk factors, so I think we need to have a meeting with the hospital. Let's talk to Peter about it.'

We worked our way through the rest of the notes, and the muffins, then headed back out to work. I had an antenatal visit booked in Taitā, and while I was there I planned to pop into two homes of women I hadn't been able to find for a while, and who were overdue for visits. Chris was heading to the hospital to visit one of 'our' women who had had an elective caesarean the day before. Sally had a pile of paperwork to do and a meeting with the manager of Kōkiri Marae about offering to do some antenatal classes there. Hopefully, Vanessa was curled up relaxing somewhere. She had just had a very busy week and needed to catch up on sleep. I suspected, though, that she would be with her daughter, helping with her new moko. She was thriving in her new grandmother role.

—o—

A couple of months later, we at HUCHS started offering homebirths. Siloma took our decision to start doing homebirths to heart. Most pregnant women using the service saw her first, to get a pregnancy test. She seemed to have suggested homebirths to them all. 'We've got midwives in the service now. Why don't you have a homebirth?' There were some interesting moments for us when we had to reassure some women that while they were probably not candidates for a homebirth, we would still be there for them right through, just the same.

During that following year, our homebirth rate was the same as that of the general population. I was very proud of that. The only hard thing was that a significant proportion of those numbers involved Pacific women without residence visas, who had birthed at home to avoid the hospital bill. Initially we thought that we were being kind and clever, saving them so much money. But later we found that they were ashamed to have had their babies at home, and so were their husbands. Hospital was seen as a more prestigious place to give birth. Their homebirths in New Zealand were often joyless despite all our attempts to praise their achievements.

The first homebirth we had was Tania's. It was her second baby, and her partner's first. She liked the idea of a homebirth when Siloma suggested it. Her obstetric history was fine, and she had no health problems. So we agreed to care for her at home. Tania lived in a small one-bedroom flat and her partner, who did not live with her and whom we did not meet till the birth, was a member of Black Power. This was to be my first homebirth so far outside my comfort zone. I couldn't explain my reluctance any other way than some expression of my white, middle-class privilege. But it was time to put my commitment to equity into action. Tania and I had the usual homebirth conversation about the importance of being as prepared and as healthy as possible for birthing at home. And then we waited.

She rang in the middle of a busy day of appointments to say that the contractions had started and were getting strong. I arrived to find her on her hands and knees on the floor of the small living room, moaning and rocking with each contraction. Her partner was sitting on the couch, with his patched jacket on, watching her. He seemed out of his depth, or shy, or hating being there — I couldn't tell which. But he was there, which I had not been expecting.

'Hi Willie. I'm Joan. Good to meet you.' I couldn't get eye contact with him.

'This is too hard. No way am I doing this. I need to get to hospital,' said Tania, panicking.

'You are in such nice strong labour. It doesn't look like you are far off. How about I check to see how the baby is and how far you have progressed? Then we can have a chat about what to do.'

Women giving birth at home often demand to go to hospital during the transition to pushing. We rarely take them. Deferring, distracting and delaying usually work. I helped Tania to slowly roll over onto her back, then I got down on the floor and had a feel of her tummy to check on the baby's position and feel how far down its head was. I listened to her baby's heart, which was pounding away happily. Then I put my gloves on and did a vaginal examination. She was eight centimetres dilated but the baby's head was just a bit off-centre.

'Tania, you are so close to being there. Your baby is doing fine. There will be no time to get to the hospital.

'Let's stand up and lean up against the mantlepiece. You can rock your pelvis to help the baby come down. Willie, come on over and rub Tania's back while she has contractions.

'Yes, that's great. Nice and firm, just like this.'

Oh, a shotgun on the mantlepiece. I ignored it.

'Yes. That's perfect.'

Soon there was a little bit of grunting happening, so I called Sally, who was the second midwife for this birth. I got my gloves and my instruments out, turning the oxygen cylinder on, making sure that anything else I might need was on hand.

'Willie, can you hold Tania while she squats during her contractions? It will really help that baby around the corner. You might like to take that jacket off as it's going to be hot work. But before you do that, can you please put that heater back on and get me some more towels. Everything needs to be nice and warm for the baby. This is all very normal, Willie. This baby will be here soon, and Sally is on her way.'

Willie stripped his jacket off and threw me the towels. Still not a word from him.

With the contractions getting very strong, Tania moved into that overwhelming, uncontrollable pushing phase. It terrifies some women, but Tania was right into it. There was no more time for her panic — this baby was on its way. The head started to distend the vulva just as Sally slipped into the room. We nodded at each other. I put my gloves on and gently supported the birth of the head. Sally went to get another towel.

'Easy now, easy now. Just gently bring the baby's head through, Tania. No big pushes. Look down here, Willie. You can see your baby's head.'

Once the head was out, Tania reached down and stroked the thick black hair, an amazed, relieved smile on her face. With the next contraction the baby was born, and I handed her straight to Tania. The baby coughed, spluttered, and looked straight up at her mother and father.

'It's a girl,' Willie smiled, wide-eyed.

Once the baby had settled and Tania had had time to catch her breath, Willie carried them both to the bedroom. They were all still attached. We covered the baby with another warm towel and popped the duvet over them all. Sally and I went back to the lounge to give them some time together.

Later, when the placenta was delivered, the baby was on the breast and Tania was tucked up with a cup of tea and some toast, Willie and I sat on the back steps of the flat and had a cigarette and a cup of instant coffee.

'Fucking hell. That was full-on.'

HUCHS provided a health service for Black Power at Petone, and for the Mongrel Mob at the Pomare centre. It was important not to get them mixed up, and when we got new curtains we had to be careful what colours we used. We birthed all their babies. They were staunch allies of the service and kept us and our buildings safe. One weekend, someone broke into the Petone clinic and stole all our computers, which was devastating. During our staff meeting a couple of days later, five Black Power members knocked and then came in carrying five computers.

'Here, we thought you might need these.'

—◦—

I had started to recover slowly from Paul's leaving. I got a brand new mattress and turned the bed around to face the other way. I kept the self-help book industry in business and found an excellent therapist who was reassuring, especially about the children. Apparently, studies had shown that children who have some trauma in their lives but who are loved and supported through it learn that bad things happen, but that they can get better again. It builds resilience in them. Who knew?

I was determined not to become bitter. I had seen this happen to too many divorced women. I didn't want that to happen to my soul, or to my children. I played the perfect ex-wife (mostly). People admired Paul and me for how well we had separated. I worked hard at letting him go. It hurt. I rewired my neural connections with the mantra 'He doesn't love me, he doesn't want me'.

One Saturday morning I was making the bed and listening to the radio in the background. The words 'the meaning of suffering' caught my attention. Kim Hill was interviewing Hugh Tennent, a Buddhist meditation teacher. I listened closely and knew that this might be a path for me. Having found out when the next retreat was, I headed off to Tauhara for a long weekend of silence. It was perfect — hard, but perfect. The teachings were enlightening. From then on, I immersed myself in the practice, attended local meetings when I could, and meditated as much as possible. Every year for the next 10 years or so I went on a long retreat. They were silent, sometimes joyful, sometimes terrible as I watched my mind get into all sorts of tangles. But it was always helpful. The Four Noble Truths, the basis of the Buddhist dharma, have consistently supported me. Suffering (Dukkha) is a part of existence. Its origins (Samudaya) lie in craving and attachment. The end of suffering (Nirodha) comes from seeing and letting go. And following the eightfold path (Magga) will support one's walk to enlightenment and freedom.

I remain an irregular but committed meditator. My two favourite Pali words, as my family will attest to, are 'anicca', which means that everything is impermanent and uncontrollable (this comes in handy when something precious gets broken), and 'papancha', the habit of overthinking and over-reacting, which perseverates and prolongs suffering. What has been seared into my being, though, is the deep reality of connection and interdependence, not only between all humans but with everything on Earth and in the universe. Funny that I would begin to feel that most profoundly when my own world had split apart.

I continued to work with my therapist as I started to look to my future. My biggest fear was ending up renting an 'ex-state house in the back of Johnsonville' (that was my mother speaking!). I know it was very non-Buddhist of me, but I had seen the loneliness and poverty of too many ex-wives, and I dreaded it. 'Well, we will have to find you a CEO,' the therapist laughed. The next visit I announced that I had found myself a CEO already, and that I had stayed the night with him.

'Oh, good on you,' she said. 'Who is it?'

I knew she wasn't going to like the answer. 'My boss. Peter Glensor.'

Peter and I slipped easily into loving each other. Early in our relationship we borrowed a Waikanae beach house and had our first weekend away. Paul had my kids; Peter's ex-wife had his. We talked and talked about our lives, our families and our friends. We made love until we just couldn't anymore. It was surprising. Peter made me a big feed of bacon and eggs. I needed it. No man had ever done that for me before. I managed to get him into the sea for an icy swim despite it being May. He was hooked and happy.

Everyone, including my kids, thought it was too soon after Paul. It had been only five months. But Peter was there, he wanted me, and I didn't want to miss the chance. If I had waited the statutory year or so alone, post-divorce, he could've been long gone. All my friends and family wondered if this was my rebound relationship and they worried. It was, and it wasn't.

We moved into our big house on the hill in Korokoro, overlooking the harbour, on the day Princess Diana died, 31 August 1997. I cried most of the day. It was nothing to do with Di — it was just such a momentous move, and it was so final. We had six children between us so needed plenty of space. It turned out to be the perfect spot, with magical views over the harbour and hills, and tons of room for as many family and friend gatherings as we could fit in. The children were stars, and our 'two sets of three', four boys and two girls, formed sound relationships with each other.

—o—

Proposing to me became a habit of Peter's. Every so often he would say, 'Let's get married.' I would always reply, 'No. Why?' This went on for several years, until one day he proposed to me over the frozen chickens at Pak'nSave, his favourite shop after The Warehouse. 'Oh, all right,' I replied. Anything to stop the nagging. At the checkout he said, puzzled, 'Did you just say yes back there?'

Our friend Joanne told him off. 'It's a very funny story, Peter, but it is not good enough.' So, true to style, he proposed to me again, this time on one knee and with a dozen long-stemmed red roses, on the balcony of Caffé e Cucina, Chapel Street, Melbourne. He had wisely consulted my sister in the planning. It was completely over the top, but a delicious treat and made for a great story. I still had no diamond, though. (I dislike diamonds.) We found a black silky waistcoat in a posh men's store in Chapel Street for him to wear at our wedding, just in case he thought of wearing his rubbish-tip one. Then we went off to Daylesford for dinner and a night at the Lake House. Peter had told the staff everywhere we went that he was planning to propose, and they waited apprehensively in the background until he gleefully announced to them that yes, we were engaged. At least we got a few free drinks out of it — not something likely to happen in Pak'nSave.

As we arrived in our exquisite room, with its huge and inviting bed overlooking the lake, Peter began to feel and look very sick. His temperature soared so high that I thought he must have septicaemia (blood poisoning). I worried all night as he turned redder and redder and moaned like a dying man. It turned out to be an infected ingrown toenail. That man is expert at creating good stories. Or maybe he is just expert at living them.

We married at home in our backyard with friends and family. It was not a quiet affair. We had 150 guests, who all brought food to share. There were aunts, uncles, cousins, brothers and sisters, nieces, nephews, kids, friends, workmates. Everyone except my mother, alas, who was too sick

Peter, me and our children at our wedding on Waitangi Day 1999.
From left: Tim being cuddled by his sister Kena; the two big boys,
Matt and Ben, in the back; Kim, Sarah and her fiancé Richard.

to come. It was one of those special Wellington days, not a breath of wind, not a cloud in the sky, and toasty hot. We were bagpiped in by Peter's uncle, with all our six children, one with her fiancé, our first in-law (maybe a grandchild one day). I wore red. My sister Catherine officiated. We blessed rings, blew bubbles, sang love songs, read from the Bible and from the Buddhist Dhamma. Peter and I were gifted white scarves of welcome from each other's families. We shared stories and blessings. We laughed and laughed. The kids played trumpet and saxophone, accompanied by a keyboard, and we had a string quartet over drinks and dinner, then a jazz band so we could dance late into the night under the stars. And we did.

That was the year a millennium ended and a new one began. I had graduated with my master's degree in 1999 and had been awarded a PhD scholarship at Victoria University, so had reluctantly stopped work at HUCHS. There was a growing demand from midwives for postgraduate study, so there would be some teaching for me at the university. I decided to carry on doing some homebirths as I thought it was important to stay connected to the world of birth. By now, Peter was heading up Health Care Aotearoa, the national organisation to support New Zealand's community-based health services. He had also just been elected to the Hutt City Council and then to the District Health Board. There were big changes coming for us.

On New Year's Eve, we stayed up all night to celebrate the new age with our friends and our children. We went down to Petone Beach to watch the midnight fireworks and to wait and welcome the fleet of waka being paddled through the mist over a millpond harbour. We could hear the chanting of the kaihoe long before we could see them. Then we went home to our house on the hill to share breakfast on the deck and watch the first sunrise. We had come prepared to share reflections, blessings and hopes. The new light seeped in through the thick mist without us noticing.

7

—

It's risky

As I drove past the house, looking for a park, I could see that the front door was wide open. It was three in the morning. I parked the car, grabbed my birth kit and headed inside. For some reason, Mike's electric bicycle was lying abandoned across the footpath, like a signal to panic or some portend of disaster. I stepped carefully over it.

When I arrive at a homebirth in the middle of the night and find the front door open, I am reasonably sure that if the baby hasn't already arrived, it's not far off. I picture it. A soon-to-be father rushing backwards and forwards to the door, as if it might somehow help to bring the midwife faster. Meanwhile, the woman is disappearing into her mountainous contractions, her body tense, every muscle joining in to bear down and birth the baby. As she emerges between contractions, in the few seconds she has to catch her breath, she demands of her husband, 'Is Joan here? Why isn't she here? Where is she?'

As I approached the door, I could hear a baby crying. *That sounds good. All done,* I thought. I took in a breath, then let it out slowly. It had always been an automatic response, me staying calm in the face of pretty much anything. My being rushed and anxious wouldn't help anyone. I strode into the lounge, where the baby's crying was coming from, wondering what to expect.

Sure enough, there was Kate and the already-birthed baby; but Kate was standing up in the birth pool, not lying in it. Women usually stay in the water to birth, especially when the baby comes quickly. She and her mother were both holding the slippery, crying baby against Kate's belly. The cord was still attached. Shock, amazement and a touch of terror had filled the room. 'Oh, thank God you're here.' And then there was the early flicker of relief and joy at the corner of Kate's mouth, and then wide-eyed wonder. 'It's a boy!' Her two-year-old daughter was sleeping soundly upstairs. I did a quick midwife scan. All seemed well. The baby was pink and crying, the blood loss looked normal, the placenta wasn't delivered. The grandmother looked a bit traumatised. But there was no sign of Mike.

'Well done, Kate,' I smiled as I grabbed a towel off the heater and wrapped it around the baby. 'He looks perfect. If you let me have him for a tick, you can use my shoulder for support to step out of the pool.' It's a tricky manoeuvre. 'Did you birth underwater, or did you stand up?'

'Joan, I had to get up. I was too scared to stay under.'

'That's all good, Kate. Did you catch the baby, Sally?' I asked Kate's mother. She was still looking pale and shaky, but she was tending to the couch, covering it with the plastic pad and some towels, ready for Kate to lie down. Deeply mothering.

'I did.'

'Good job. That must have been frightening.'

'Well, someone had to do it. We couldn't have him dropping into the water,' Sally commented, the colour coming back into her cheeks. Was that an edge of rebuke in her voice, I wondered? Well, fair enough, I thought. The fight-or-flight mechanism was probably still lingering. And flight is not an option for a mother.

'Where's Mike?' I asked.

———o———

The phone had woken me at 3 a.m. At that hour I always assume it must be a labour starting. 'She's pushing, she's pushing!' someone yelled at me. Why do they always have to tell me things twice? And who is this? I switched into full awareness.

'Ah, Mike. That's great. Remember what we planned if Kate births fast again. Get her to puff and pant the baby out as slowly as she can. If she is in the pool, she can stay there. Remember, we talked about babies being safe underwater as long as they haven't had their face in the air. Wrap the baby in a towel and keep it warm. If the baby doesn't start breathing straight away, give it a good dry with a towel. It will be fine. Fast is okay.'

There was silence from Mike and then a roar in the background.

'I'll be there in 10.' I hung up.

I leapt out of bed. There was no time for a shower or to clean my teeth. I grabbed random clothes from the end of the bed in the dark, and a jacket from the hall cupboard. The coat-hanger crashed to the floor, waking the dog who barked me to the car. Speeding down the road, I went over all the things I needed to remember. Kate was Rhesus negative, had a previous bad tear and breastfeeding difficulties. 'Concentrate, Joan,' I told myself. 'If you miss the turnoff you'll be screwed.' The billboard ahead yelled SPEED KILLS. 'Not in birthing,' I thought, despite taking my foot off the accelerator a little.

Lately I had started to recognise an element of fear in me as I approached a birth, a feeling that I had not experienced before. I always used to be alert and attentive because it is part of our work. But recently fear had been creeping in with a level of tension and anxiety that was disconcerting. It was spoiling birth for me. I wondered if other midwives felt this, or if it was just me. Taking a deep breath, I refocused on the job at hand.

Back in the birth room, Mike appeared — ashen-faced and sheepish from the bathroom where he had just been throwing up. His mother-in-law's freshly baked fruit cake had been a bit much for his terrified tummy.

'I'm sorry, Kate, but I just couldn't vomit in the birth pool.'

'Worse things have ended up in a birth pool, Mike,' I laughed.

Joy and calm began their journey back into the space. We had left the baby naked on Kate's tummy for over an hour. She had pushed the placenta out as the baby sucked hungrily and competently at the breast, and Mike, now fully recovered, cut the cord. Then he went to wake up his daughter. She smiled and poked at her little brother before falling back to sleep in her grandmother's arms. I left them to it, grabbed a large piece of cake from the kitchen bench (breakfast) and closed the door quietly behind me.

—◦—

The new millennium was now well underway, and midwifery in New Zealand was thriving. Women had embraced the new way in which maternity care was being delivered. By 2001, around 75 per cent of women had a midwife as their main maternity caregiver.

But there were still things amiss. The promise offered by midwifery autonomy was that women would choose a normal, natural birth and would increasingly choose to birth at home. But somehow almost all women still wanted to birth in hospital. Something strange was going on. Then the backlash against midwifery intensified. We frequently made the front pages of the newspapers when a baby had died or was born very ill. Doctors had never been on the front page over problematic births, yet we were increasingly vilified and made accountable for any unexpected outcome. There were so many places we had to be accountable to: the hospital hierarchy, the Health and Disability Commission, the Accident Compensation Corporation, the Midwifery Council and the Health Disciplinary Tribunal, the police and the coroner. And the press, of course. It was a brave midwife who survived all that unharmed. Most didn't. All this also got in the way of being openly accountable to the women.

We knew that what was happening was about gender and power, but the underlying assumptions were buried so deep that they were hard to fathom and hard to fight. I wanted to find out more.

Midwives were seen as 'baby-killers' — despite there being no shift in the numbers of babies that died in New Zealand each year. In 1995, the College of Midwives had asked Professor Murray Enkin, an obstetrician researcher from Canada with a commitment to natural birth, to come and speak at our College of Midwives' Conference. He said that if he could, he would put up a billboard that said 'BABIES DIE'. It was quite confronting, even for us.

In New Zealand around 600 babies die every year, either before or soon after birth. There was no increase in these numbers when midwives regained autonomy. However, the worry is the lack of *decrease* in this rate. Despite all the technology and all the research that has been thrown at the problem, it will not seem to budge. The Perinatal and Maternal Mortality Committee in New Zealand has recently commented that of the deaths that are preventable, most are strongly associated with poverty, institutional racism, women with major health issues becoming pregnant, and an ageing population of birthing mothers. Midwives are not baby-killers. But the backlash went on and on. It frightened many of us.

The other issue that worried midwives during the 1990s was that our role seemed to be changing. We had always claimed to be the specialists in normal birth, yet normal birth was dwindling in front of our very eyes and continued to do so. By 2017, only 23 per cent of women giving birth for the first time had no medical intervention — it became abnormal to birth normally. For us, birth was a natural, physical, social and spiritual event, which sometimes needed intervention. This 'birth is normal' perspective was in marked contrast to the dominant medical approach, which had developed within the patriarchal, techno-rational and misogynistic social framework that saw women's bodies as flawed and birth as normal only in retrospect.

Despite midwifery autonomy, we began to see that authority over birth still lay with medicine, and in the assessment, management and supposed control of risk, and that many women still seemed to believe this. To make things even harder, the medicolegal environment became overactive at this time. If there was a poor birth outcome, the first thing asked was 'Who is to blame?' — and it was easiest to go for the midwife. And they did. We worked with a continual double-edged sword of anxiety: risk for the mother and baby, and risk for us. Despite autonomy, we were at risk of becoming irrelevant.

And so that edge of fear crept into my practice. I was increasingly becoming hypervigilant about backchecking my work, and it seemed that I was losing my nerve. Since the late 1990s I had been providing ACC with what they called expert advice when a claim had been made for injuries that a midwife had been accused of causing. When there was an 'unexpected outcome', as they called it, it was crucial that there be a midwifery voice to balance the obstetric voice. It wasn't long before I was also providing advice to the Health and Disability Commissioner and to the coroner and being pushed out of my comfort zone again. I would have huge case files couriered to me nearly every month, and it was my job to decide whether the midwifery practice was 'reasonable given the circumstances at the time'. Appearances in the Coroners Court as an expert witness was not a skill-set I had been expecting to add to my midwifery practice.

There was little room for midwives to admit their error (if they had indeed made a mistake) without terrible consequences, and at that stage there was no accountability by health institutions or managers when system failure had contributed. Doctors were very quick to deflect responsibility on to the midwife, even when they themselves had failed in their willingness to assist her. It felt as if the doctors, the health system and the media were all joining forces to lay the blame on the midwife, the least powerful person in the whole birth process. The parents usually joined them. It was such a horrible time for all of us, a genuine modern-day witch hunt. There seemed to be no way of being heard. The only way to escape was to flee.

—◦—

Recently I had a rummage in the attic to find my old birth notes. The box was heavy, and I sat on the floor and emptied it, birth by birth, recalling all the women I had been with. There was a pile of photographs of babies, of all sorts. Some were with parents, some were just being born, and some were with me. Some photos were taken by me, as I had a spare camera in my birth kit for times when families didn't have one. There was also a folder of cards and letters from parents. I lost all track of place and time as I revisited the families and their births. It got dark and cold. Peter eventually came looking for me.

'Peter, I found all my notes. I had forgotten so much. Look at these photos. Shame I can't use them. They tell such an amazing story.'

He sat down beside me and flipped through some of the photos. 'You look very young in some of these.'

'Yes, and thinner.'

'Do you remember them all?'

'Most of them, but not all. There are so many Pacific faces, too. I'd forgotten how many Pacific families I cared for.'

'I'll bring them all down, Joan, and you can carry on in front of the fire. It's freezing up here.'

Back in the house and warming up, I spread out the photos and matched them up with the notes. Two birth registers were at the bottom of the box. These were legal documents that we had to keep as a record of our work. I flipped through them. As well as the usual data I gathered, such as type of birth and how many visits I had made, there was a column for my comments. I seemed to have commented only when things were not straightforward. But it did happen quite often. Over five months in 2002, when I was the primary midwife for 20 women, there were 10 women with significant complications. This was when I was working at HUCHS, and a 50-50 split of straightforward births and complicated births was typical.

My comments about the more complex births included these:

RN — Active hepatitis C. Babe's father active IV drug user. 18 antenatal visit attempts. Home only twice.

FR — Planned homebirth but had twins in hospital
[Oh, I remember that these were the only set of twins I've delivered. It was thrilling.]

MD — Disappeared for a large part of the pregnancy up north. Husband in prison. Hard to find.

LT — Came from Tonga at 38 weeks. No English, eighth baby. Seven normal births in Tonga. Large baby and unstable lie. Drs decided for elective caesarean section!! Babe never fixed at breast. *[I remember how frustrated we were by our medical system, in which Pacific women with a history of normal births at home ended up with interventions and caesareans once they got to New Zealand. It was not uncommon.]*

DR — Heavy drinker, smoker and drug user. Itinerant and aggressive. Babe adopted by aunt.

OM — Antepartum haemorrhage, emergency caesarean section. Premature. Babe very slow to gain weight. Comps started at 6 weeks, including Weet-Bix!!

SM — Pregnancy a result of rape by ex-husband. Some time in Women's Refuge. To Auckland with babe straight after birth.

EK — Stillbirth. *[This was incredibly traumatic, with several full case reviews. The parents were initially very angry, but when the wider whānau became involved we had an extraordinary meeting of regret and forgiveness.]*

CQ — Concealed pregnancy. Sisters took over care of baby.

AT — Big baby, shoulders stuck. Episiotomy and obs called, but got the babe out myself with a bit of a pull! *[This was one of my homebirth mothers. Two previous births at home, but this time she said she felt like she needed to be in hospital. Did she know something I didn't?]*

PR — Female genital mutilation. Called obs to repair perineum. Husband very anxious and suspicious. Wanted her stitched up tight again.

BO — Homebirth after previous caesarean section and gestational diabetes. *[Whew!]*

The idea of what was normal and what was risky became more and more challenging in all midwives' lives, not just in mine. The possibilities of what might happen to women and babies were infinite. The challenges of the last birth in the list above exemplified our dilemma. Bronwen had had a caesarean section for her first baby; she had then developed gestational diabetes during the second and third pregnancies. Most midwives — and all doctors — would insist that these two conditions together are risky enough to require a hospital birth. But Bronwen wanted to birth at home again. She had birthed at home twice since her caesarean section, and was very aware of how to manage her blood sugars. This reduced her risk, but it was impossible to quantify it.

In the end, risk decisions are often value-based and are more cultural than scientific. We compromised. Bronwen agreed to see the obstetrician and the diabetic specialist during her pregnancy, reducing my risk should something go wrong. I agreed to be her midwife and to support her at home. She birthed her baby, Hana, normally at home two weeks before her due date. Complexity and normality it appears are not mutually exclusive.

Hana turned 21 recently and Peter and I went to her party. Dad had sometimes gone to twenty-first birthday parties of children he had delivered. He was known for his engaging and funny public speaking. During his speech he would retrieve, from the inside pocket of his jacket, the maternity card containing the details of the child's birth and would proceed to read out such details as the mother's weight gain and the number of stitches. It caused much hilarity. He delivered all eight babies

Hana's birth at home just seconds after she arrived; she is in the arms of her mother, Bronwen, and surrounded by her family.

of one woman over his 40 years in practice and he was the local doctor for three generations of her family. He would faithfully bring out each child's birth card at each twenty-first. They would have felt deflated if he hadn't. I did not read Bronwen and Hana's birth notes out at their party.

Times have changed, especially around birth. Fifty years on from those 'old days', the relationships with, and expectations of, birthing women are radically different. Generally, women in New Zealand now have control of their fertility, have their babies later, often have work to return to, and expect risk to be managed. I have heard midwives complain, blaming the anxiety about risk on women:

'Women just aren't the same anymore. They want everything to be perfect and they want us to be responsible for it.'

'They've become control freaks and are really scared that something might go wrong. They want all the risk removed from life.'

By 2000, risk and fear had become fascinating for me. I wanted to make sense of it somehow. I knew it was much more complex than just women's behaviour. Why were we becoming more scared when we had never been safer? What was happening in society that people had become so risk-averse? Is all birth risky? Does that mean that nothing is normal? If I'm getting fearful, are most other midwives feeling this too? How do other midwives make sense of risk? What might help us to keep working alongside this fear, and to support women in their fear too?

It might seem a bit excessive, but I did a PhD to answer exactly these questions.

—o—

For months I buried myself in all the disciplines I could, to see how others viewed risk: psychology, sociology, epidemiology, anthropology, philosophy, ethics. It was riveting. But in reading the midwifery literature, I noticed that there was little deep analysis of risk, and that midwifery itself had been poorly theorised. We seemed to feel somewhat insecure about our own knowledge base.

I set out to fix this. I wanted to ask midwives how risk was affecting their lives and how they managed to keep themselves connected and responsive to the women they cared for, while at the same time keeping themselves safe in their practice. I travelled from Northland to Invercargill and gathered midwives together in small groups to share experiences. We would sit about, often after one of their weekly team meetings, and eat the food I provided (it had to be good — I was feeding midwives, after all). We often started with discussing how it felt when we discovered an unexpected risk factor. The conversation in my PhD research transcript looked like this:

Me: How does it feel when you find something is not going well?

Midwife 1: It's a horrible feeling really. It's almost a physical sensation of disappointment and anxiety. [You can feel the] loss in your tummy. You know we are going to go to a different place. Yeah, that gut feeling that's almost a tachycardia as well.

Midwife 2: Something has changed.

Midwife 1: You say to the woman, 'Now we're going to have to go down a different path.' And there is a loss of that possible ideal birth that you were looking forward to.

Midwife 3: Yeah! That's the word to me — loss. On one level you're dealing with a grief situation.

Midwife 2: Because you've lost the normal process that you were hoping for and that was expected. And it is certainly for me a common scenario when suddenly GPH [also called pre-eclampsia] rears its ugly head.

Midwife 4: Or the breech.

Midwife 5: Yeah, and they were somebody who was really down to earth, trying to have a normal birth at the local unit or at home. And it's taken out of your hands with the complication and things just start to escalate. And you're not only dealing with the clinical side, you're dealing with the woman's emotional expectations and processes, and the family's. Because you're their anchor, you're the one they have known all the time. But I mean, in the hospital situation it would be different again because you're acting a lot quicker than in an antenatal situation and if we've got something happening here, we've got to go there.

They were also, as I had been, increasingly anxious about the medicolegal implications of their work:

Midwife 6: I think about it all the time. A classic thing that I think of often is, like on Friday night, you might be on call for the weekend, but you just think, 'Oh I've got through the week and no work planned for the weekend.' And someone rings up and says, 'I didn't feel my baby move today or for two days' or something like that. 'Why didn't you ring me earlier?', I think.

Midwife 7: Yes, when I was out and about. And there's an absolute obligation that you must attend to this straight away, that you have to go and do a CTG or give them a printout or whatever, to protect yourself.

Midwife 6: Whereas before you may have said, 'Oh well, just lie down for 20 minutes and see how many times the baby moves, and give me a call back and we'll discuss it then.' And you know that ninety-nine times out of a hundred all will be well, but . . . yeah. It's a killer.

Midwife 8: I find that really interesting because I thought the older hands would have said, 'Just chill out.' Whereas as a new practitioner I feel obliged that I must do the CTG. I must check. I must do the bloods. I must go and find out or do whatever is indicated at the time. And I've felt that I've been medicalised by checking everything so thoroughly. But it was an old-hand who said recently, 'Cover your arse', you know. You've just got to do it. That was interesting.

Midwife 6: I'd like to talk about that because for me, constantly in my practice, I'm aware of the eagle hovering, like ready to come and have a go if you make a bit of a slip or a misjudgement or you miss anything. And I think that that constant reassessment of what's going on continues even 30 years down the track. You're constantly thinking, 'Are we okay here?' But I think it takes quite a toll. Because I think for me, and I would consider myself an experienced practitioner, I'm very conscious of that. And it's not only for the woman's protection. It's the medicolegal protection for myself that I'm considering. Because I'm pretty happy with what's going on.

My favourite quote of all the discussions came from an experienced midwife who spoke about the unknowability or uncertainty of birth and therefore of midwifery:

Midwife 6: And I think there's a huge area of grey. And the more I've practised, the more grey there is, which makes it harder. Because you're always on edge, making the decisions without clear boundaries of when to bail out. I've got all this space in here [pointing to her heart]. I'm swimming around really, thinking, 'Now, am I okay, can we keep going, what if she does this, what if she does that?' And I find the grey area is the hard bit. I mean the black and white are easy, but it's that big grey area, and the more I practise the more grey there is.

The young midwife in the group was dismayed, as she had hoped that the more experienced she became, the less grey there would be and the more certainty she would have. But the older midwife commented that the more experienced she got, the more comfortable she was with the expanding grey. Anything could happen and she needed to be prepared and alert, not scared. 'Fear in birth,' she said, 'was a real downer.'

The midwives also unpacked the problem of 'normal birth'. One young midwife in her first year of practice commented thus:

Midwife 9: I found I had to redefine normal when I started practice. Because I had a concept that when you're physically well, that you're emotionally stable and you're financially or economically stable, too. And that was normal. Now what I found in reality was that there's always one leg missing on the stool. And I had healthy strong

144

women with absolutely no money and no partner, or he's a criminal. It just was awful. But that was normal for her. And then I had people with really stable relationships and financially they are okay, and everything is hunky dory and then physically, bang, we've got something wrong. So, it just seems to me every single client has one leg missing on the stool and that to me is now normal. And that's life. There are problems and that's normal. So, my picture now is that you're bloody lucky if you get all three at once.

Her mention of the three-legged stool stayed with me as I analysed the transcripts of the focus groups. Eventually, when my computer screen became inadequate I wrote out the dozens of sub-themes on separate pieces of coloured paper and spread them over the floor of my study. I spent hours and hours wandering around them, regrouping and rearranging them to try to make some sense of it all. How would I be able to describe all this?

The centrality of the birthing women became clear. The 'with women-ness' of midwifery was paramount and all the midwives' talk referred back to this. There were also three interlinking strands that stood out.

'Ah,' I thought, 'it looks like a birth stool.'

Birth stools have a long history as a midwife's ancient tool. Traditionally, the midwife used it to help support the woman as she birthed her baby. But this time, my birth stool was to support the midwife.

There are a number of characteristics of three-legged stools that make them relevant to midwifery practice. Having three legs makes them sturdy and stable. Provided that they are reasonably in proportion, the legs do not have to be exactly the same length or shape. They are resistant to wobbling, and as long as they are well connected, they are secure and long-lasting. They can be different sizes and made from different materials but they are still recognisable and functional. All of this makes the birth stool such a useful analogy for midwifery — with all its variations of experience, knowledge, perspectives and work settings surrounding the woman at its centre.

Using a birth stool as a theoretical model for current practice works well, I thought. 'Being with women' was the seat, the centre of things. Each of the three interlinking strands, or themes, became a leg. The first related to the midwives' understanding that they needed to be

Peter had this three-legged stool made for me when I graduated with my PhD. It is a conceptual model of what supports a midwife to provide sustainable, accountable, quality and woman-centred care. Birth stools have been used by midwives for centuries.

knowledgeable, skilled and up to date. And they needed to be accountable to the woman for their practice. I called this leg 'being a professional'. The second leg was 'working the system' — midwives work in, and often have to manipulate, the system and the power relationships in order to help women get what they want and need. The third leg was managing the complexity and unpredictability of their work.

Initially I had struggled to work out what to do with all the midwives' stories from their practice. I had expected them to talk about risk and how it made them feel; I wanted their opinions, I thought, not their stories. But whenever they could, they started off on yet another tale: 'I had a woman who . . .' or 'At one birth last year, I tried to . . .' or 'We went to a meeting at the hospital last week and . . .' As interesting as the stories were, I couldn't help feeling like precious time was being wasted. However, once I began to construct the stool, I saw how the stories fit — they were the struts holding the stool together, making connection possible.

Each story revealed the complex and contradictory nature of midwifery, connecting midwives' practice to the real stories of the women for whom they cared. The midwives used stories to illustrate their role as professionals and to show how the system they worked in functioned. They used stories to explain and justify their opinions and their actions. And they used them as a tool for reflection and learning. Stories held the whole complex thing together.

Peter had a three-legged stool carved for me as a graduation gift. The grandchildren use it now to reach the basin to clean their teeth when they have a sleepover with Papa and Narnie (that's us).

Risk as a concept is now ever-present in my mind's eye. I watch how the anxiety of the times overpowers us. I watch how our children are expected to parent, and mourn the loss of free exploration for the grandchildren. Our children have to, and do, consciously construct risky situations for their own children. We used to call these times normal, like playing cops and robbers on Tinakori Hill, or spending the whole day on a scooter around Thorndon. We wouldn't have dreamed of being taken to or picked up from school. Yet kids are much more likely to die in a road crash on their way to school than get abducted by a child-molester. People know this, but the new norm is that leaving kids exposed to any risk at all is reckless. Yet we drive them around in carbon-emitting tin cans, at speed.

It is apparent to me now that whether a particular action is denoted as risky is not a factor of any objective measurement of danger. Instead, it is more a measure of the power of one group to assert control over others by defining what is meant by risk, and which risks are prioritised over others. Post-structural theorists posit that risk is an act of surveillance and control, not one of individual choice. The decision about where to give birth is an example of this. Despite sound scientific evidence that healthy women with well babies should not give birth in a major hospital, the controllers and authoritative knowledge-holders (doctors and health managers) will not encourage or provide support for out-of-hospital birth. Those most vulnerable — pregnant women and their families — are immersed in this risk-averse environment and are understandably less likely to challenge those who claim to have authoritative knowledge.

What midwives in New Zealand have learnt since we became autonomous is that the way we organise midwifery care will not, of itself, make enough of a difference to how women birth. It is the social and political context in which we practise that has more of an impact. So, we just have to change society! Or at least take part in the change.

I now understand deeply that midwifery is a counter-cultural movement. In analysing the midwives' talk in my research, I surmised that the essence of our work as we moved into the new millennium was not simply to be 'with women' (although there is not much that is simple about that!). We are the 'in-betweeners', negotiating the diverse perspectives and decisions of women, their families, doctors and institutions. We also need to negotiate gender diversity in those giving birth, and we need to be aware of our own biases as we seek to enable the woman to truly be in control of her childbirth experience. I coined the term 'paradigm broker' to describe this incredibly challenging yet undervalued work. The birth stool is a model that could be of help here. I also saw midwives as the knowledge-seekers, the surprise experts, the holders of the possible and the mistresses of the uncertain.

I have come to understand the important place that midwives have in the world. We are in a position to answer the global call for a new way of being and of working: one that embraces diversity, that can use technology when it is needed, but one that has a profoundly different take on life. And doesn't that make perfect sense, given that we work with birth? We are at every birth. We literally hold the next generation in our hands. How we help them into life and onto this precious planet is crucial.

Midwives support mothering. We should not be passive servants of society's expectations, but should take a lead in moving the world forward. And I think we need to claim that space and support the move for an improved humanity. We work alongside many in our society who also wish to achieve this new perspective on life — a life encompassing sustainability, freedom and justice. We connect with them in rejecting the possibility of the death of birth.

We must give new life to birth: be aware practitioners, practising consciously and knowing what we are trying to achieve, aware of the context in which we work, be canny and sophisticated, open to possibility. We need to accept that because of where we work and how we work, we can lead — not just in identifying the issues and problems of modern life, but in helping to solve them. This is our big picture, our vision. If we could open up to the possible, rather than close down with the risky, we would achieve things that we never thought we could.

'There, I've said it' — as my mother used to say when she got something off her chest.

I have loved being able to theorise midwifery and to share the task with other midwives doing their postgraduate degrees. It has been exciting work. In the School of Nursing, Midwifery and Health Practice at Victoria University of Wellington, I created a postgraduate course called Real World Midwifery — which is still offered today — where midwives in practice identify what they think are the key issues of the time, and think, read, write and share what they think is going on. These midwives are encouraged to choose an issue in their practice and undertake research to explore it further. We invited any midwives in the community to come and listen to their presentations. I thought it was crucial to spread this deeper understanding of our work. I had had the top blown off my head when I was a postgraduate student, and I loved doing this to the midwives coming behind me.

It was also vital that I stayed connected with the 'real world' myself. I continued to offer my services as a second midwife for homebirths, and did the occasional night duty at Kenepuru Hospital. I also used to do short locums for midwives who were going away or who needed relief.

Lecturing at Victoria University of Wellington with Professor Maralyn Foureur (in front). From left: Robyn Maude, Susan Lennox, Jane Stojanovic and me at the master's graduation. We all went on to get PhDs.

One year, Susan Lennox (one of my midwifery colleagues) and I offered to do a locum for the Domino Midwives collective. This was a group of five midwives who worked together and shared a kaupapa of focusing on and promoting natural birth. Every year they all went away together for an annual retreat (code for a very long party). Being off call is a treat. It is the only time we can drink.

There were only a couple of women due that weekend and only two postnatal visits needed, and Susan and I were looking forward to it. We had decided that it would be great to work together. It's special to work as a couple sometimes. You get to see how another midwife talks, touches and helps, how she uses her body and her voice. You can learn a lot. It's also very comforting to make decisions together.

But we ended up being very busy.

My main memory of that weekend was of Susan and me, two slightly rotund (in a good way) but very experienced and capable midwives, lying under the dining room table of some house in Island Bay at two in the morning, with a couple of pillows, trying to get a bit of sleep.

'Is this what we've come to?' Susan whispered at me. We didn't want to wake the heavily pregnant woman who had 'gone off the boil' but, we knew, would be very fast once her contractions started up again.

'Two professional women in their fifties and at the peak of their careers should be in corporate suits and high heels with PAs to fetch coffee, and staff to do all the work,' she added.

We started giggling. Our ageing, child-birthed bladders struggled.

'We need a plan,' I laughed. 'This isn't going to work.'

That weekend, five women took the opportunity to have two of the best midwives in the world at their births. And it wasn't as if they were all close by. The reason we were trying to get a bit of sleep under a table was that Susan lived in Eastbourne, well over half an hour away, and I was in Korokoro, not that much closer. We had been at one birth in Newlands, then one in Karori, then one at the hospital, back-to-back. Apparently, Susan told me later, she couldn't get home to get a change of clothes — so popped into Zambesi for a whole new outfit!

We realised that we needed to split up, especially as we now had postnatal visits to make to those newly birthed mothers and babies. So, at three in the morning, under the table and with our headlamps on (to provide light for suturing perineums), we made a plan. It did make us feel more in control for a minute or two, but was abandoned almost instantly when we were called by a young woman from Porirua whose contractions had started and who was heading to Kenepuru maternity unit, already in strong labour.

The Domino midwives arrived back in Wellington on Sunday evening a little the worse for wear. 'Don't worry,' I said to them. 'We've done all your work for the next week. We'll send you our bill!' Susan and I took to our beds and remained unconscious for some time.

—o—

As I was nearing the end of my PhD in 2005, the joys of full-time academic life were wearing thin, as I was the only midwife at the university. I decided to cut back to working half-time to enable another midwife to work alongside me, as I am not a good lone worker. My creativity comes alive when connecting and working with others. This would also give me the space I needed to do some consultancy work, some writing and maybe even some more births. And it would also free me from most of the administrative requirements of academic life, which I found formidable and life-sapping. In doing so, I let go of the possibility of academic progress. There didn't seem to be a lot of point.

In the back of my mind was also the desire to explore midwifery in low-resource countries. Despite ongoing issues around risk and fear, women in New Zealand had excellent options for maternity care, and midwives had fulfilling and empowering work. This was not the case in low-resource countries, where staggering levels of easily preventable maternal and infant mortality and morbidity persisted, and midwives — even if there *were* midwives — had the lowest status of any health worker, were poorly trained and disrespected.

In 2003 I had spotted a job on the internet that set my mind buzzing. Based in the University of Aberdeen, it was for a researcher in a multinational project evaluating new midwifery interventions in Burkina Faso, Nepal, Papua New Guinea and Botswana. The work involved visiting these countries and supporting the in-country researchers in data collection and analysis. It was exactly where I wanted my midwifery to go, and my heart sang. I applied, even though my only work in what was then called 'developing' countries had been in Tonga some 35 years previously. I made it to the final three. My interview was over the phone from home, at one o'clock in the morning New Zealand time. Peter sat on the floor outside my office listening to my interview. He described it as 'Not your best, Joan'. The first question in the interview threw me.

'What can you tell us about phenomenology?'

Bugger-all, as it turned out. And my lack of development experience showed. Peter reminded me of my very first day of postgraduate study in 1996, when I had come home talking of Heideggerian hermeneutic phenomenology. I still don't entirely know what that is and have avoided supervising any student research that used it as a research methodology.

Luckily I didn't get the job, as I would have been travelling for six months of the year, leaving Peter on his own in Aberdeen, which, bless him, he did say he would do. After an extensive search online, the only job we could find for him there was as the council dog-catcher.

But I kept my eyes open for other opportunities. On a midwifery research forum I noticed a request for assistance from the World Health Organization in Cambodia. They were looking for an experienced midwife with a postgraduate qualification, research experience and an understanding of community development to come and design and pilot a community-engaged, birth preparedness project for remote rural Cambodian villages. There were to be two visits of two weeks each. The first would be to design the pilot project for the local Cambodian staff to put into action; the second would be to evaluate it. It was both well outside my comfort zone and totally perfect. And I got it.

PART THREE

EXPLORING

8

—

Connection and community

The driver of the battered taxi was relaxed as we lurched along what was really a path, not a road. It was an elevated, grassy verge, good for walkers or bikers. On either side it dropped down to the brown rice paddies. Distant figures with colourful krama (scarves) bound around their heads to protect them from the sun were bent over double, rhythmically scything through the stalks of rice. They paused periodically to tie up the bunches and dropped them in their wake. As we passed, the figures stopped in unison and straightened their backs long enough to glance our way. Then they returned to their work. The water buffalo, too, paused in their relentless chewing of the discarded rice husks to look and wonder at who we were and where we were going.

Chanthou, a midwife from the Regional Women's Health Service, and I were on our way from the health centre in Kampong Chhnang to visit the remote village of Koh Keu. We had left Phnom Penh early in the morning on a packed local bus. The driver insisted I sit in the front seat. The bus was designed for Cambodian hips and I didn't fit, nor could I get my legs in straight. Each person who got on after me was forced to step, startled, over the legs of this large white woman twisted sideways in her seat. It was the first of many times during my subsequent work in Asian countries that I would feel like some distorted giant woman. Chanthou and I glanced at each other and got the giggles, which did not last the five-hour journey along the potholed highway. The transfer to the car in Kampong Chhnang township was a welcome relief. The dust from the red-brown road covered my clothes.

This was my second visit to Cambodia. It was June 2005. Chanthou and I were heading to the villages and health centres to do the evaluation of the birth preparedness project we had planned on my previous visit six months ago.

—◦—

The World Health Organization, which funded the project, had wanted strong involvement of the local community. The origins of the project lay in a randomised controlled trial set in the remote villages of Nepal which focused on maternal and infant health. The results had just been published, and showed unequivocally that if a community is asked about what they want and need for their health service and is then given it, things get better and stay better. Well, what would you know? I read the article keenly.

The WHO officer in Cambodia, Pamela Messervy, herself a midwife — unusual in development, where doctors tend to dominate — had some extra funding and wanted to give this shift in activity a go. Although 'community engagement' was a popular term in development circles, in reality it often meant going out into the community and telling people what to do rather than asking them what they needed. Through my work in HUCHS, I had the hands-on experience of working in a community-led health service, and Pamela hoped that this might mean my perspective would lean towards community responsiveness. She needed someone who was not steeped in the culture of international development and who had a strong midwifery focus. That person would also need to have the knowledge base to design and evaluate such a project.

When I read the job description, I had felt my breath shift, just a little, and I knew it was my job. I reassembled my CV, focusing on my community experience with the Hutt Union and Community Health Service, my midwifery background, my political, policy and leadership experience, my cross-cultural practice and my evaluation expertise. It didn't look too bad.

I was so delighted to get the contract. I knew it would be a stretch, but it was exactly right for me. The idea of being with midwives in remote villages, supporting them in their work, was thrilling. I had learnt that connection is the essence of midwifery and that responsiveness and respect are its core values. Was I being patronising or matronising? Was

Two midwives from the local health centre in Koh Keu, Cambodia, talking with a group of young married men about birth preparedness and what they thought was important for their wives when they became pregnant and gave birth.

I romanticising the job and the context in which I was about to become immersed? Possibly, as it turned out.

—o—

Chanthou had helped me with the design of the programme on my first visit. She had also been involved in getting the project underway. Part of the plan we had made entailed midwives getting out into the villages, where previously they had waited for women to come to them in the health centres. There was one health centre for five villages. The essence of the process was that the community needed to be involved. The village health workers found a mixture of people for the discussion groups. There were groups of men and of women, and of different ages, teenagers, old people and traditional healers, village leaders and monks from the local Buddhist temples.

Chanthou and I were now off to see one of these groups in action. This one was a group of young married men. We weren't entirely sure how successful the visit would be, as it was the rice harvesting season — a time for all hands on deck in the fields. Chanthou said that villages were usually empty at this time of year. I was hoping to be able to interview the midwives, the village volunteers and the village leader.

The road to Koh Keu started to widen a little. We passed green ponds with lotus flowers and discarded blue plastic bags floating side by side and overtook buffalo-drawn carts laden with rice. We left clouds of dust to settle on the freshly threshed rice, spread out to dry on mats by the side of the road. The village houses stood high on stilts, and much of the living at this time of year, the hot, dry time, was under the house where the sun didn't reach but any breeze could. Children, bicycles, mosquito nets, mats, rows of clothes and cooking utensils were all spread about. Each home had a wooden plinth under the house where families and visitors could sit above the earthen floor, cool in the hot season, dry in the wet.

As the car pulled up to the house of the local village health volunteer, we could see a group of young men sitting cross-legged on the plinth.

'This is where we are meeting and that is the village volunteer, just on the right. Those two other women are the midwives,' Chanthou explained.

'There are so many. That's more than I would get in a focus group in New Zealand. Fantastic! Where will we sit?'

There were two of the ubiquitous blue plastic chairs beside the plinth. Just as well, as despite many hours of cross-legged meditation on a cushion, I don't think I could have sat on that hard plinth for long. It was also good for us to sit a little apart, as it meant that Chanthou could tell me what was being said without disturbing the chat.

'Chom reap sour,' I greeted them in my best Khmer.

The men nodded and smiled in return. They were dressed in shirts and trousers, much more formal than their rice-planting gear, I surmised. Maybe it was quite special to have someone like me come to see them. They had clearly been waiting for us, as they had not yet started their talk. Who was left in the fields? I felt honoured.

And then the talk began. I settled myself down, amazed that what I had imagined for this part of the project looked like it was working. Even without translation I knew that this was good. Here were two midwives, from the health centre, out of their uniforms and out in the village, talking about birth and asking young men what they needed to help them support the women to birth safely. It seemed pretty perfect to me. I reached for my notebook and bottle of water and settled down to watch, listen and soak it all up. I was deeply moved, appreciative of the chance to be here alongside this community. It was 'pinch myself' territory.

The midwives introduced themselves. The talkers were reticent for a while, then gradually became more engaged. Every now and then, Chanthou would lean over to me and tell me what they were saying.

'They are saying that the problem with the health centre is that they do not have enough money to pay. They say it takes a long time to save up the money. Also, that the women are very shy to go and have antenatal care and there is no motorbike to take them.'

One of the young men spoke passionately and at length.

'What is he saying?' I asked Chanthou.

'He is saying that even if they were to go to the health centre, they have no staff there at night so it's no use to them. They may as well stay at home. Also, if they go to the hospital they cannot roast [a traditional practice of filling the room with smoke] or put ice on the abdomen [where would they have got ice from?]. He says that the women fear the hospital staff and sometimes they can be cruel. At home, relatives can come and help.'

I noticed that the midwife doing the talking (the other was recording in her book) glanced at her notes and then asked them another question.

Talking with the midwives and the Koh Keu village health workers about the project, and what they thought was working well or was problematic.

There was a pause before anyone answered.

Chanthou leant over again to tell me what was happening. 'She has asked them who makes the decision about what to do if there are problems.'

The discussion livened up again and there seemed to be some disagreement.

'They say that the decisions are often made by the old people,' Chanthou told me. 'The old people tell them that if you prepare for birth, it will cause problems, like stillbirth. They think that talking about the danger signs is very bad luck. The traditional birth attendant is there sometimes, and she is very old too. Sometimes the old people surround the house with string to keep the evil spirits away. Some are saying that if there are problems, they go to the traditional healer before the hospital, and some say they would pray first before going to the hospital. The problem is that the hospital is far away, and they have no transport to get there, especially at night. It takes a very long time. At night some of the villagers will not go anywhere because of the ghosts.'

Chanthou paused to focus back on the discussion.

'Some of the others are saying that these old ways must stop and that the midwife with training should help. They should come out to the home just like the traditional midwife does. One says that everybody, especially the first-time mothers, should have check-ups at the clinic. They say that they should listen to the nurses and doctors.'

There was energy in the conversation. It was clear that this issue mattered to them. The midwives then produced the posters that I had prepared. These described the danger signs in pregnancy and things to do to prepare for a birth. The men listened closely, occasionally asking questions. They were especially interested in how to get ready for the birth. They had never heard of some of the danger signs.

About half an hour later, the group disbanded. The young men headed off, with smiles and farewells. They were off to the rice fields, to get back to the harvesting.

I then spent time talking to the midwives and the village health workers.

'What is the thing you like best about the project?'

The midwives both said that it was having the group discussions in the villages. They had never done anything like that before and although they were very nervous, the training was helpful and they enjoyed it so much, and thought it was very important. The two village health workers commented that they had managed to find every pregnant woman in the village, and that they had all had a session looking at the birth preparedness posters. The village health workers had collected all the data on the forms I had prepared on my previous visit. I was delighted. They were all enthusiastic, another sign that maybe the project was going to be successful. Connections had been made. It was looking good.

On the way back to town we stopped, unannounced, at the home of the traditional midwife. In development-speak they are called TBAs (traditional birth attendants), to distinguish them from trained midwives. This one was an old woman, clearly a matriarch in the village, her house full of women and children. She smiled and clasped both my hands tightly and asked Chanthou to thank me for coming to help the women of Cambodia. She asked us to wait a minute and went to fetch her copies of the birth preparedness posters, which the village volunteer had given her. She said she showed these to the pregnant women and told them all to go and see the midwife. Chanthou told me later that all the traditional midwives were getting very old and were not passing their knowledge on to younger women. Things were changing for childbirth in Cambodia.

Back in the bustling town, Chanthou took me for a walk through the marketplace. There were rows of all types of leafy vegetables I had never seen before, enamel basins of live fish fresh from the Tonlé Sap, sacks of rice, bicycle wheels, shoes . . . anything you could ever need. The women fanned themselves and chatted, pausing to smile and greet me as we passed. 'Suasdey, sokhasabbay.'

The men glanced sideways. I was clearly a stand-out object of fascination. A basket of deep-fried spiders was proffered, so I tried one. The legs were crunchy, but the middle was disturbingly gooey. An old, bent-over woman approached, her smile red with betel nut. Chanthou explained who I was; the woman's eyes lit up and then she took off. She found us again as we passed the poultry section, rows of live ducks upside down and tied together by their webbed feet. She offered a small plastic bag of what looked like wood shavings. Chanthou translated that because I was a midwife, these were some herbs for labour that I could take home with me, to help the women of New Zealand give birth.

'Arkun,' I replied, gratefully.

Above: The home of the traditional midwife.

Left: The traditional midwife with the birth preparedness posters from the project.

Searching through my old memorabilia, just weeks into writing this book, I found the notes I had kept during my first visit to Cambodia. My random scribblings reflected my lack of experience and my emotional edginess; there were also a few hints of panic. I was having to understand the complexities of the maternal and child health system in a resource-poor country still recovering from an horrific 30-year war, including one of the world's worst genocides. I then had to design an intervention that might help to reduce maternal mortality there. At that time, it was estimated that 450 women in Cambodia died for every 100,000 births. New Zealand's rate at the time was seven. I had to find and meet with key development partners and NGOs, and work with government staff. Then I had to organise some way to get the data collected and some way of sharing with the midwives what community engagement meant, and work out the best way of putting all this into action.

By the time I arrived, in December 2004, I had read everything I could get my hands on about Cambodia. I knew something of its complex and terrible history, its politics, its demographics, and the status of its mothers and babies. I had spent time with a local Cambodian woman in Wellington, trying to learn a little of the language. The simple greetings were straightforward enough, I thought. But when I was learning to say 'You have a beautiful baby', a phrase I thought might come in handy, I realised that this language was extra tricky.

'Anak meankaun saat,' Reaksmey enunciated, the spoken word having no resemblance to the written.

I repeated it perfectly according to my ear, which I had prided myself as being sensitive and musical. People comment on how good my Tongan, Māori or French pronunciations are. (Except my seven-year-old grandson Mākarā, who corrects my Māori when it takes a wayward drift to Tongan.) Reaksmey made me repeat the phrase over and over, especially the last word 'saat'. But no matter which part of my mouth and face I manipulated, she was not happy. Meanwhile, I could have sworn I sounded just like her. It was a stalemate.

'No, Joan. You are not saying "you have a lovely baby" — you are saying "you have a lovely poo".'

There was some part at the back of my nose that I just could not get to join in. Things didn't look hopeful. I was going to have to perfect a cross-cultural, multilingual smile.

Despite my preparations, I felt I didn't know much. I did, though, have the memory of the culture shock I felt when I went to live in Tonga as a 17-year-old, and I understood the need for openness and curiosity. I had no depth of understanding of the Cambodian culture, no idea how a Cambodian village might work. I had never seen a Cambodian health centre. Nor did I understand how the health system worked, who was doing what about maternal health or what the power structures and political niceties were. I had no idea where to start; I had never travelled to Asia before. On the fourth page of the notebook there is a scribble:

'Find out what is happening in the country!'

It turned out that there was a lot happening. There were over 3500 functional NGOs. They covered every area of Cambodian life: food, agriculture, justice, finance, education, transparency and health, to name a few. By this stage of the country's post-Pol Pot recovery, many of the small NGOs were now Cambodian-led. But most still relied on international funding, as did the government itself. There were a lot of duplicated short-term projects, many with no follow-through and with poor communication. It was a huge effort, mainly on the part of the big development partners, to try to coordinate these activities. It was complex and messy; a sort of semi-organised chaos with activities going off in all sorts of directions for all sorts of reasons. Much like most countries, I suppose, but with fewer resources and fewer external interventions and expectations.

Pamela was keen that I be based in the National Reproductive Health Service office. I would be close to my counterpart, a development term meaning the local working partner. Pamela and I drove together to the office through the centre of Phnom Penh, through traffic that was the most chaotic I had ever seen. There were thousands of motorbikes, trucks, cars, tuk-tuks and cyclos, and the occasional hand-pulled cart. There seemed to be no road rules. Pedestrians wandered into the traffic with not a care in the world. The guidance for crossing the road was to walk out into the traffic purposefully, never changing pace or direction, and the traffic would flow around you. Less trusting people have been known to hail a cyclo to cross the road.

The energy of the place was palpable. I found it both alarming and exhilarating.

We walked through the main atrium of the Japanese-built hospital, all concrete pillars and shiny black tiles. Crowds of mothers, pregnant or with their new babies, were waiting to be seen in the clinic. Doctors or nurses, in scrubs and caps with a distinct Russian flair, waited in the background. We climbed up three flights of stairs, open to the breeze, to find the office of Dr Tung Rathavy, the deputy National Programme Manager of the Maternal and Child Health Service. The office had an ancient computer and a huge pile of papers on the desk, behind which sat a tiny, bespectacled Cambodian woman, her head down in concentration. On seeing us, she jumped up and with a broad smile proffered her hand to shake rather than the traditional sampeah I was becoming used to (where the palms of the hands are joined together at the chest with a slight bow of respect). She introduced me to the two midwives who would be helping, and we briefly discussed the project. I was shown the office I had been allocated — and that was it. I didn't see any of them again, except in passing, for the rest of the week.

I sat at my desk and got out my laptop, plugged it in and sat, motionless, as a rush of panic threatened to overwhelm me. I did wonder what they thought I was doing, day after day, fancy international expert consultant that I wasn't. Maybe they knew as much as I did about what to do.

Each morning, my regular request of Rathavy's PA concerning who I could see that day was usually met with 'I'll see what I can do, but they have meetings all day', or 'No one is in today. They have a conference.'

What I did have was a pile of reports on the current state of maternity care in Cambodia. It made for grim reading. Although all the national and regional health plans looked good on paper, what was happening in reality wasn't good at all. Maternity care was very expensive for families and often still inaccessible. Hard for us in New Zealand to believe, with our free maternity care. Only 32 per cent of pregnant women in Cambodia received care from a midwife or any health professional. Eighty-nine per cent of babies were born at home, but with no skilled midwifery support. The country's caesarean section rate was 1 per cent, indicating a lack of timely skilled intervention. It should have been around 15 per cent; in most Western countries it is over 30 per cent. It was also important for me to know how things happened in the villages. The reports said that during the dry season only 5 per cent of households had piped water, 9 per cent had electricity and only 14 per cent had toilet facilities.

But still no one came to spend time with me and by the end of that week, tears were shed. It seemed that my first job in development might be my last. I was mortified. There was just no possibility of working on a community participation project when not even the organising staff would participate. I Skyped Peter.

'This is all terrible,' I wept. 'I haven't got a clue what to do. It's going to be a total disaster.'

I have since discovered that I would shed tears during every one of my subsequent contracts in low-resource countries. It was always hard work — challenging emotionally, culturally, physically and mentally. My mantra became: 'Do the best you can, never lose your cool, smile a lot. Be ready to be very surprised. Things that look impossible can still work, often in unexpected ways.' Harder to accept was the mantra 'It's okay to fail; sometimes you can learn more by failing. Fail graciously, always.'

At the beginning of the second week Rathavy appeared, announcing that she had time for me that day, but I would have to accompany her to several meetings around town. We could talk in the car, and I could meet some of the key players active in maternal and child health.

We settled into the traffic. For once I was pleased it was so slow. It gave us more time.

'You know, Joan, I just want the women to get to help faster. They need to be told what to do. One of the biggest causes now of mothers dying is the delay in getting to help. We are working hard on upskilling the hospitals, but we need the women to use them.'

This seemed to me a little at odds with the idea of community participation, but I tucked the thought away.

'Tell me a bit about how the health service works out in the villages.'

After her description I don't think I was much the wiser. Another common occurrence I found when working in development is that it is hard for the hosts to understand how little the consultants from other countries intrinsically understand about how things work. I did get better with experience, but the risk of making assumptions about the way things

The project team, with Chanthou to my right, heading into the Kampong Chhnang regional health office to spend a couple of days reading through piles of clinic records to gather outcome data for evaluation.

are can lead one badly astray. This is probably one of the reasons for the reputation that consultants have for going into a country, producing something irrelevant, and then taking off with their fee in their pocket. I so hoped I was not going to be one of those.

Rathavy added: 'The other thing I want is that we accept no help at all from the NGOs in this project. I'm tired of NGOs. They go off on their own and don't tell us what they are doing, let alone ask us if we want it done. Or they interfere. They have all the money. We can do this project ourselves and we need to show people that. We just need help in getting the thing planned. Our staff will do all the work, Joan. They'll do all the organisation and supervision and manage the budget. I need you to come back and show everyone how well we did. We are also on a strict budget, so we won't be putting you up in flash guesthouses and you'll have to travel by local bus. We won't be using the WHO driver.'

All this was helpful, and my mind took off, thinking and dreaming about the possibilities.

'Rathavy, I just need time with Chanthou and Sophea over the next few days. I know you are all very busy, but I don't have much time left here. It would also be helpful for me to have a day out in a village and a health centre, and maybe a regional hospital, to help me get a sense of what things are like.'

We criss-crossed the city, visiting the offices of CARE International, RACHA and ACCESS. In development, I discovered, the overuse of acronyms makes most discussions incomprehensible.

'You will find, Joan,' Rathavy commented, as we entered the white-tiled lobby of RACHA, 'that the local staff who are working in these NGOs were mostly trained by me. It is so hard. I spend a year or so training up the staff in the government offices and as soon as they become good at the job, the NGOs give them jobs at twice the salary and much better working conditions. If they just gave us the money, we could do it ourselves.'

I went on to discover that this was an almost universal experience in development. Development partners and international NGOs in every country I visited had fancier and roomier offices, larger salaries, fatter budgets and many more donors to call on than their national counterparts. For a local to be employed by one of the big NGOs meant a ticket to a secure income, increased status and freedom. There must come a time in development when aid agencies stand back and move on. I never saw this happening. The big NGOs became multinational organisations while their staff and management were mainly local. I was just a beginner in all this, but it was fascinating. I felt lucky to be starting my work directly alongside local staff.

On the way back to the office, Rathavy told me a little of her background. While Pol Pot was in power, she had escaped to Thailand as a refugee. She was just a teenager, and her entire family had been killed. During the 1980s, Russia offered scholarships to 8000 Cambodians. Rathavy was one. She spent 10 years in Moscow doing her medical training, which was taught in Russian. Every Cambodian had a story, and all the ones I heard were horrific. Having said that, few people volunteered the information. Their stoicism amid the impact on their lives remains incomprehensible to me. I sometimes felt like an alien intruder in their space.

There was no time for more self-indulgent tears. That exquisite care that I had learnt as a midwife came into use, and I trod gently into the project planning, trying not to dominate. My discussion with Rathavy had been useful. 'Don't worry about how to get it done, Joan. We'll organise that. We really want your evaluation of it when you come back, because they won't believe it if we tell them we succeeded without NGO help.' But I still had no idea what I was doing and was aware of the gaping hole in my knowledge of the culture and language of Cambodia. It seemed improbable that I would have any ideas for appropriate ways to engage with a community so different from my own.

Once Chanthou and Sophea and I had some time together, we started planning. The dynamic was clearly unbalanced.

'We need to try and do something that engages with the people in the villages, so we can hear what is important for them. How would you usually do this?' I asked. They exchanged glances and laughed. 'This is Cambodia, Joan. We just go out there and tell them what to do.' *Mmmm, this is complex*, I thought, reflecting on all I had read about Cambodia's story.

I suggested a two-pronged approach. The first would be the community-engaged bit, where the midwives would reach as many families with a pregnant woman as possible, and could conduct discussion groups in the villages to talk about what the villagers needed. This would meet the brief of the WHO funders. The second was the educative bit, which Rathavy was keen on. We would make a poster which showed the danger signs of pregnancy, and show this to all the families and at the discussion groups.

I had to hope that I would be able to interpret this in the Cambodian context. With the support of other NGOs who were also working in maternal and child health, I put together a poster and a presentation to help Chanthou and Sophea show the midwives what the project was about. I also created some documentation for the midwives to collect the data I needed for evaluating the project on my return.

At this stage, Sophea commented that the village volunteers would also be helping. I hadn't known there were such people, what they did, or how many of them there were. It turned out that they are a crucial part of the health system in Cambodia. It was just as well it was up to Chanthou and Sophea to operationalise this project, not me!

But I still hadn't seen a village, a health centre or a regional hospital, and I knew that I needed to. It was clearly beyond Sophea and Chanthou's ability to get me there.

I had met up with one of Pamela's friends, a Kiwi called Jan Nye, who was working for VSA on a project to develop Cambodia's disability services. (She also knew Peter very well, and had helped him equip the HUCHS health centre when she worked at Hutt Hospital!) There were (and still are) over 40,000 amputees in Cambodia, one of the highest rates of amputees in the world. Three decades of war had left over six million landmines still in the earth. Good God! Anyway, a day before I was due to go home after my first visit, Jan was heading out to visit a couple of health centres and villages to see how the disability services were being managed. She offered to take me along.

I was imagining a slightly run-down building in the middle of a moderately large village. And I imagined it as very busy, with a lot of patients waiting for a long time to see the nurse or the doctor. There would be some medications on-site, along with the basics needed for everyday care. (I had no idea what everyday care here was.) There would be a room for births, and a space for some postnatal stay.

The first centre we saw was a white concrete square of a building with a veranda and three rooms. It was in the middle of a field, not in a village at all. It was clean — but completely bare. There were no patients there. The nurse we met, or midwife, or maybe both, had an office with a desk on which sat a register of her work and a large erect wooden penis. The room where women could birth had a lithotomy bed (flat, high and with stirrups for the legs!) and a pair of scales in the cupboard. I did not explore further. They had not had a birth there for several months. All visits had to be paid for and, I was told, the staff would need a tip. At the time I was visiting, the government had stopped paying the midwives' wages altogether.

I was surprised and clearly naive, my privileged Kiwi lens to the fore. It was good to be along as an extra with no pressure to do anything. I was also aware that it was Jan's work and I shouldn't be taking time away from her. But she was great. She asked all the questions that I needed answered, even though I was too amazed to know it at the time.

The local hospital was another adventure. I remember that the post-natal ward had a row of women in beds with giant blocks of ice on their abdomens. It was good to see their babies tucked up beside them. The delivery rooms had the flat lithotomy beds, as I learned to expect wherever I went. They also had a CTG, but on enquiry we found it was not used. I was stunned to learn that if any women needed an IV, or any drugs or any equipment, the family would have to go off-site to the local pharmacy to buy them.

I packed my bags and flew home, really struggling to make some sense of it all. People asked me 'Did you have a good time?' Others thought I was 'just fabulous for going to help the poor and underprivileged'. Pamela had warned me that it would be hard to tell people back home what it was like. She was right.

No one emailed me from Cambodia to ask me anything or to tell me how it was going. I had not a clue what was happening. I was afraid it was going to be a complete disaster — which would not have surprised me, given my lack of experience.

Six months later, I got my bags and my passport out again and returned.

—o—

So that's how I found myself in the village of Koh Keu, in Kampong Chhnang, in Cambodia, with Chanthou, listening to young men talking about the problems around getting care for their childbearing women. The project had, apparently, been a success, and I found myself going from village to village, amazed, chatting with mothers, midwives, grandmothers and grandfathers. I even met two of the village chiefs.

Everything we had talked about had worked, even better than I'd

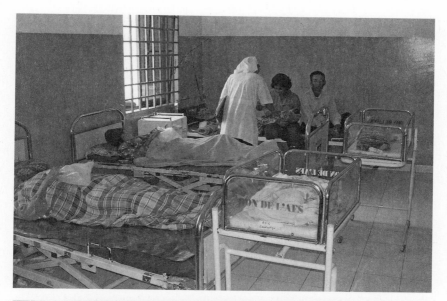

Above: A postnatal ward in the referral hospital in Kampong Chhnang. The midwife in the background is examining a breech baby brought into the hospital to birth.

Below: Meeting new mothers in the community and hearing their stories was always important.

planned. For example, when the village chiefs heard about the project, they wanted to join in the training sessions. Several had since organised that when there was a woman in labour in the village, they would make sure there was some transport close by in case she needed to go to the hospital. The numbers also looked impressive. Fifteen villages had participated. There had been 40 discussion groups with over 300 people. Over 90 per cent (233) of all the pregnant women in the villages, and at least one member of each of their families, had had an interaction with either the village volunteer or the midwife. The midwives and village volunteers had kept great notes, and there were lots of written comments about their perspectives on how things were going. Chanthou and Sophea had kindly translated the comments for me.

My final task before departure on that second trip was to present the findings to the WHO staff, including the Country Representative (the boss), and to other interested NGOs. I stayed up all night analysing the data and preparing the presentation. I even managed to work out the cost of each interaction. It was hot, hard work. Every hour or so I would have a cold shower and then stand, wet and naked, in front of a fan. I can recommend this procedure for anyone in a hot place with electricity but no air-conditioning.

All of the 15 or so people around the table were very surprised at the extent of the positive results. There was an air of scepticism. I felt as if Rathavy were on my shoulder saying 'Told you so'. But the project was clearly viable. I managed to persuade them by showing how carefully I had gathered the results to minimise bias. The WHO Country Representative was, finally, impressed.

'We don't see results like this very often, Joan.' He thought we should find out whether all this interest translated into better uptake of midwifery care and more referrals to the hospital. He suggested that the WHO fund the project for another six months and double the number of villages.

'We would like you to come back again, Joan, to have a look at the data for us. Would you be able to do that?'

So, I did. Of course.

Another six months later, Chanthou, Sochea and I, all now more relaxed with each other, headed out on the bus again to Kampong Chhnang and then on to each of the health centres and hospitals. We buried ourselves in volumes of handwritten records, many of which were written in Khmer script. We tried to find a cool space, but it was a long, hot and tedious process. Often one of the local midwives joined us. There was constant chat and lots of laughter. Every so often someone would translate a bit of what they were talking about, but by now, my third trip to Cambodia, I had become comfortable not knowing the language and so not necessarily being included in the conversation. I loved the sound of it and could usually pick up the tone, enough to know (or to think I knew) when to ask for a translation.

I stayed in a local guest house in Kampong Chhnang. It had a small and very hard bed, a fan but no AC or WiFi, and a tiny bathroom with a hose on the wall for the shower. I always slept well. Chanthou and Sophea stayed with family. Each morning they would collect me and we would find somewhere to have breakfast out — the usual thing to do, I was to discover. They were very particular about which eatery gave the best deal and we wandered through the township hunting for the right place. Chanthou and Sophea chattered to each other. I followed along, relishing the sights, sounds and noises of the town, busy with the morning market. The motorbikes sped past, piled high with bags of rice, or chairs, or children. Old women, ladened with plastic bags full of produce, strode out towards home. The shops were opening and there were loud greetings and exclamations. I did not see another European that whole trip. I loved it.

We would finally find a small shop with blue plastic chairs and tables. Huge pots on the stove bubbled out delicious smells. For breakfast there was rice, and other small things. My requests for clarification as to the contents of the 'small things' were either met with laughter or some generalisation such as 'vegetables' or 'meat'. It was always delicious, but I was a cautious eater — unlike the rest of the patrons who ate with great gusto, depositing left-over chicken bones, fish heads and piles of paper tissues on the floor.

'Joan,' Chanthou commented, 'how come you are so big when you eat so little?'

The numbers we collected during this trip confirmed the success of the project. In the 30 villages there had been:

- a 22 per cent increase in women having antenatal care
- a 32 per cent increase in the number of women who gave birth with a midwife

- a 19 per cent decrease in the number of women who used a traditional midwife
- a massive 281 per cent increase in referrals to hospital.

This was a stunning outcome. I wondered what the Cambodian Ministry of Health would do with figures like that — not that much, as it turned out.

Of course, the project needed more funding. Rathavy could get money from development partners for the birth preparedness posters, but couldn't get anyone interested in funding community engagement. Apparently, she said, no one had community engagement expertise. Seriously?! I was disappointed. But the Ministry of Health did include birth preparedness in their next national plan. The WHO had new staff, and they appeared to be too busy getting a handle on the day-to-day running of the place to take much notice of a slightly quirky pilot project. I wrote a paper on the project, and Rathavy and I had it published in a top international journal. It has had a good number of interesting citations.

By 2017, Cambodia's maternal mortality rate had dropped from 450 per 100,000 births to 160.

—◦—

That year, 2004, was momentous. My contract with the WHO in Cambodia marked the beginning of more international work, something I had longed to do ever since I was that 17-year-old in Tonga. As well, New Zealand midwifery celebrated 100 years of the profession that year. Alongside Pamela Wood, a nurse historian, I curated an exhibition with Archives New Zealand, which honoured our midwifery forebears and showcased how the profession had developed over that time.

Crucially, this was also the year that the government established the Midwifery Council. Until then we had had the same council as the nurses and were outnumbered by them — so important regulatory decisions about how midwives could and should practise could still be influenced by nursing. It had been fraught, and we had relied on skilled and forthright midwifery representation to protect what had been achieved for childbearing women in New Zealand. With the establishment of the Midwifery Council, our autonomy as a profession was complete.

That was also the year I became a grandmother. Peter's Sarah and her partner Richard came home from London to birth Lucy. Nowhere in the UK could they find the personalised and flexible midwifery care that they could get in New Zealand. They lived with us while they waited for labour to begin. We had a birth pool set up in the lounge, where the windows overlooked the harbour and the mountains. We put a hook in the rafters for a sling for Sarah to hold on to; it's still there. She laboured and laboured. Her midwife Liz Brunton, Sarah's mother Cheryl, Richard, Peter and I were all there giving support.

Sarah was wonderful. She had a wee trip down to the hospital to help with the last bit of the labour. Peter, soon to become Papa, went down to the hospital too. At one stage, Sarah was in the bathroom pushing very long and hard. Peter said to me, 'Why is she taking so long?'

'Shut up, Dad,' from the toilet.

Eventually, in her own good time and with mega effort from Sarah, beautiful Lucy decided to arrive. Liz told me to come closer, and soon a granddaughter emerged into my hands, briefly, on her way to her new mother. They stayed with us for a couple of months until Sarah felt it was time to go back to London. How lucky we were.

—◦—

After my second visit to Cambodia, Peter joined me on my travels. It was lovely to have him with me, for him to get a sense of where I had been on the end of all those Skype calls, and to meet all the people who had now become friends. I talked and talked about what had happened with the project and Peter helped me make more sense of it. I showed him around the country like a local. Sarah, Richard and Lucy were safely back in London now, and our other five children were going to be with their other parent for Christmas, so we decided to have our Christmas in Cambodia, just the two of us. We took a boat trip across the Tonlé Sap and took a long motorbike ride into the inner lands of the country. In one place we found a beautiful monastery on the top of a hill, with views of brown rice fields for miles. The monk showed us the caves where some of the Pol Pot killings had taken place. There was a huge one full of human skulls. I had previously declined to go to 'the killing fields' to avoid just such a scene.

We went on, through the villages. We stopped at a wedding and were invited in. Then we found the bamboo railway, the lines built by the

French but abandoned by Pol Pot. We put our bikes on the makeshift trolley, attached to an eight-stroke engine, which a gang of boys lifted onto the old railway line, and rode back to our starting point, through more rice fields, just as the sun set. At dawn the next morning, we watched the Christmas sun rise behind the temple of Angkor Wat.

Travelling between New Zealand and Cambodia, and being with midwifery in both settings, took a while to process. In New Zealand, midwifery's focus was to decrease intervention and to support mothers to avoid birthing in hospitals. But in Cambodia, the caesarean section rate was too low. Midwives were being trained so that interventions could increase, and mothers were being encouraged to go to the local health centres to give birth. The reason for this was that the remoteness of many of the homes made emergency transfers very difficult. There were also no midwives available to staff many of the health centres, let alone provide a homebirth service.

I struggled with this dichotomy, deeply suspicious of what was motivating the development agencies to be against birthing at home. Whenever I suggested that homebirth should be explored, I was dismissed outright. The Western medicalised approach to birth was well entrenched. The now globally accepted idea that having a skilled midwife at a birth was the most cost-effective way to save the lives of women and their babies had been radical enough. The issues of respect, gender equity, women's autonomy or the quality of the relational care — although acknowledged as important — were relegated to being 'not a priority at this stage'. (It was around this time that there was a global push to reduce maternal mortality. In time, I was to get to work in Geneva at the WHO headquarters to see how and why that policy had been developed.)

There was plenty to ponder. I was perplexed about midwifery in Cambodia in relation to my birth stool concept, and how midwives in Cambodia might look at risk. Perhaps my birth stool was irrelevant here. But then again, what sort of model could possibly *be* relevant? In all, I went to Cambodia five times for various projects and in the end these questions remained unanswered. It felt that despite the imperative to save women's lives, the way midwives were to be prepared and utilised had little input from Cambodian women and their families. It was at complete odds with how we viewed our midwifery practice in New Zealand. Yet we shared the human work of birthing. The chasm of wealth, power and privilege that lay between us was both profound and shocking. In the end, Cambodian midwives themselves would need to understand and promote the model of midwifery that would be most appropriate for them. Or was this, too, an abrogation of our responsibilities to act in the face of such injustice and inequity?

My final visit to Cambodia, in 2010, involved helping the Ministry of Health write a direct-entry, degree-based midwifery curriculum. Phnom Penh had become tidier and cleaner, the city hospitals were better equipped, and multi-storey buildings were beginning to dominate the city. Kentucky Fried Chicken had arrived. Despite the traffic lights now working, the traffic — which I thought chaotic before — was now mostly at a standstill. Huge four-wheel-drive cars, tooting constantly, had replaced most of the bicycles and all the cyclos. There seemed to be fewer motorbikes. A pedestrian could easily cross the road now, through the stationary traffic.

It seemed that the tipping point of capitalism had happened here too. There was now a growing middle class, and private enterprise was thriving. Some of the newly established private maternity clinics in Phnom Penh were reported to have caesarean rates of 100 per cent. The gap between rich and poor within the country grew. In the villages it seemed that not much had changed except the exit of the men and the young, who flocked to the cities to work, leaving their families behind, waiting for money. There were still villages with no sanitation or running water, with little access to maternity care. Although by this time the maternal mortality ratio had already decreased, it was still 15 times greater than New Zealand's.

—o—

Each time I returned home, it seemed like I had arrived on another planet: these small, green, safe islands at the end of the world. Wellington felt like the last stop. That's because it was. Although my development work absorbed much of my energy and passion, most of my work was still back in Wellington and at the university.

The summer after my second visit to Cambodia, I finally graduated with my PhD and settled into the life of a full-time academic. I expanded my thinking and my knowledge in ways I had not anticipated, even managing to teach myself, and then the students, the complexities of relative risk, numbers needed to treat, and how systematic reviews of randomised

My PhD graduation celebration. I was one of the first midwives in New Zealand to get one. Debbie Harding, a Canadian midwife but originally a Kiwi, graduated with me. Here we are with our husbands.

controlled trials worked. We started a course called Clinical Enquiry, which showed nurses and midwives how to critically examine research papers from their own clinical environments. It was in this course that we deconstructed the 'term breech trial', the results of which were published in 2000. This research — the biggest ever randomised controlled trial of vaginal birth versus caesarean birth for breech babies — had indicated that the babies were marginally safer if a caesarean section was performed. Almost instantly it was well-nigh impossible to find an obstetrician anywhere in the Western world who would support a vaginal breech birth. No one was trained how to do it, except as part of an emergency procedure. You had to have been a vintage practitioner even to have seen one.

This shift in practice was contentious, and dangerous. Midwives were trapped between medical-led protocols requiring caesarean section and mothers wanting to deliver their babies naturally. Women who wanted a vaginal birth and midwives who were to support them were abandoned and demonised. A whole generation of student midwives and doctors had no experience of, and therefore no skill in, breech birth. Thankfully Maggie Banks, an experienced homebirth midwife in New Zealand, conducted workshops on how to support the vaginal birth of a breech baby while mothers were in different and more active positions. We would meet at her place for a weekend and share and teach each other some of the important skills we needed. We certainly were not getting them from doctors.

The ill-planned and poorly analysed 'term breech trial' was eventually dismissed, but not before the skills involved in assisting a woman to birth a breech baby were all but lost. The study was eventually found to have major flaws, not only in its design but also in understanding of the implications for clinical decision-making in the real world. Despite the study finally being recalled in 2006, vaginal breech birth continues to be a fraught topic. Most women are still encouraged to opt for a caesarean section, an option with its own — and significant — complications.

I remember my father telling me with pride about his last delivery, which was a vaginal breech birth. He was skilled and cautious, as one needs to be. I also remember back to those early breech births I had supported, and the calm skill and teaching that had happened. Breech birth epitomises the tension of the space between normal and abnormal, experience and science, wisdom and fear. It is a curious, uncomfortable place. Within a year, it was to nearly end my midwifery career.

9
—
Battles
of sorts

My Irish friend Eamon said to me, 'There's a fecking war going on there, Joan!'

It was November 2005 and I had recently returned from my second visit to Cambodia. Now I was off to Afghanistan. The Americans and their allies were still at war there, trying to outwit the Taliban and to find Osama Bin Laden.

What was I thinking? Even the planning had been challenging. Apart from not knowing the details of the contract, or whether I could even do the job, I also discovered that I had nothing suitable to wear. I needed to be totally covered, head to toe. This was Afghanistan; burqa country. I sewed a couple of weird neck-to-knee outfits that maybe could work over trousers, and rummaged around in the bottom drawer for some scarves to cover my head and to keep me warm. It was going to be cold, heading into winter and into snow. Anna, Eamon's wife (they were worried about me), had given me a New Zealand flag to sew on to my puffer jacket, which I did. My passport had been couriered halfway around the world and now had a visa for Afghanistan in it.

The night before I flew out, Peter and I sat on the porch looking out over the harbour and had a last glass of wine together. My bag was packed, the lists of things I guessed I might need were all ticked off. I'd read my security briefing about what to do if I was kidnapped. Seriously.

'This time, in two days, I'll be in Kabul.'

Peter, always one to encourage me, and to have a good story to tell, was much more excited than I was.

Over two separate visits, I was to help support five new midwifery schools. This meant I had to travel around the country. How would that even be possible? During the first visit I was to go to Bamyan, Mazar-e-Sharif and Jawzjan. During the second, to Sari Pul and Herat. I googled them, of course, but in 2005 information was sparse. I could just about find them on the map, except Jawzjan; I had no idea where that was. When I look up Jawzjan now, I can even get a detailed weather forecast.

The project was part of USAID's enormous post-invasion billion-dollar support package, and was managed by an American NGO called JHPIEGO. This organisation had been based in Johns Hopkins University and was well regarded. Supporting midwifery schools was a new venture for me, even without doing it in a war zone. I was way out of my depth — again.

I did know that after the Taliban's rule had been overturned, Afghanistan's rate of maternal mortality was the worst in the world. A staggering 1800 women died for every 100,000 births (in New Zealand the number is seven). It was a testament to the fact that poverty, war and misogyny are always a lethal mix for women and their babies. By then, development agencies had begun to understand that the cornerstone for improving maternal and infant health in any country was not building more big hospitals with specialist doctors, but having a workforce of skilled midwives. Countries both rich and poor needed midwifes, and plenty of them. The world *still* needs over 600,000 new midwives, and they must be where the women are giving birth. In Afghanistan, this meant being out in rural communities where most women birthed and too many died.

JHPIEGO had been given the job of setting up the midwifery programme. At the time the Taliban had been overrun, there was no midwifery education. An assessment soon after the invasion revealed only 364 midwives in the whole country — 364 midwives in a country of 25 million people (New Zealand has over 3000 midwives for 5 million people). The hospitals and health centres that had survived the last few wars, and Taliban rule, were not functional — the doctors and nurses were either dead or had fled. I had learnt about this at a midwifery conference in Australia, where Sheena Currie, an Irish midwife working for JHPIEGO, described what they had managed to achieve so far. It was stunning.

They had set up five midwifery schools around the country, and there were more coming. Sheena finished by asking whether there were any midwives willing to come and help. I was captivated by the programme and knew that this was for me. Later that night, at the conference dinner, I made a beeline for her and offered my services.

'You're on,' she said.

—o—

To my surprise, it happened, and within months I found myself in the Dubai airport transit lounge. So far so good. I found my way past glittering cosmetic counters, Gucci bags, and myriad overpriced and brightly lit duty-free shops, to the rather underwhelming exit to Terminal Three. The UN flights (who knew they had their own airline?) left from there.

The bus arrived; only three of us were waiting. It seemed to take us as far away as possible from 'normal people' to a stuffy, dim hangar on the other side of the airport. I could smell cigarette smoke. The shiny shops were replaced by a grimy corner selling cigarettes and alcohol. The hangar was divided by head-high partitions into areas for each departing plane. The place was packed. The departure board was a tour of George Bush's 'axis of evil': Baghdad, Islamabad, Kabul, Pyongyang. The grim, thin passengers were returning to their homes from where, I suspected, they had been slave labour in the houses and building sites of the Middle East. There was not another white face in any partition. No business class or premier boarding here. The airlines on the board were the ones we never normally get to see — if you work for a development agency, you're never allowed to fly them: Pakistan International, Air Koryo, Daallo Airlines, Aero Mongolia, Turkmenistan Airlines, Ariana Afghan Airlines.

Things were getting interesting.

The departure of the UN flight was approaching, and I found the gate and joined the UN passengers. There were only a couple of other women. Everyone seemed very cool, kitted out for rough times. No suits or high heels. All were ominously serious; no chatting. And there I was, in the line, waiting to fly to Kabul.

On boarding the plane, there were cheerful flight attendants in smart uniforms, with impeccable hair and makeup. They offered plastic-tasting egg sandwiches and coffee from trollies. I spent five hours sitting at the alert, not daring to chat with the man sitting next to me lest I reveal my naivety.

Flying low into Kabul for the first time, I stared open-mouthed out the window. Stark, bare, brown mountains with grey-walled houses scrawled purposefully up their sides. There was no colour; no trees, no green, nothing. I had moved into sepia. We taxied past rows of demolished tanks and planes and other military vehicles that had clearly been through a few invasions. Then, even more disconcertingly, we passed rows and rows of sparkling US Army aircraft: bombers, helicopters, mass transport. They were all there.

'Mmmm. There definitely is a fecking war going on here.'

Kabul Airport was chaotic and terrifying. It was small and old. Only one storey, and only one entranceway that I could see. The guard at the gate had a gun. This was my introduction to the AK-47, with which I would become only too familiar. Everyone had one, it sometimes seemed — except the NGOs, and therefore me. As I waited in the immigration queue, a flight arrived; the plane was so close to the terminal that its wing rotated over the roof as it turned to come to a stop. I stepped back, preparing to flee. My co-passengers showed not the least interest. The plane disgorged pilgrims, all in flowing white, home from the Hajj. They seemed hysterical as they poured down the plane's steps, yelling and waving their arms as if some terrible calamity had befallen them. They prostrated themselves on the tarmac and wailed. I was astonished.

Meantime, I searched for my passport and papers to get them stamped, staying close to the other passengers. In the baggage collection area, what seemed to be a battalion of men in pakol hats and kaish (rough woollen blankets) vied to help carry my bags, yelling at me incomprehensibly in what I presumed was Farsi. I was scared that they wanted money and I didn't have any, only my 300 American dollars packed, stupidly, deep in my suitcase. There were no useable banks in Kabul, I'd been warned.

Bags started appearing from the plane, and the squeaky carousel spewed them onto a pile on the floor. But not mine. One by one my flight companions, all seemingly veterans of this airport and this country, grabbed their bags while talking on their phones and headed out to their rides. They were uninterested in the now-terrified woman standing alone in the empty baggage room. The bag-carriers vying desperately for my attention had abandoned me. I found a small office in a corner of the baggage room where a local man hunched over a pile of papers. He took no notice of me. Was I visible? Maybe this was just one of my 'miss your plane and lose your bags' nightmares?

'Salaam alaikum. My bag did not come off the plane. Can you help me?' I hoped he understood English.

Twenty minutes later, and still no bag. It turned out that the UN flight could not board all the luggage and mine was left behind. The next flight was a week away; I'd be in Bamyan by then. Oh God. I needed to get to my ride, so I made my way outside, covering my head with the scarf I'd remembered to put in my hand luggage. It was the first time I had covered my head since being an eight-year-old at Mass. The last traveller was being picked up by a burly, bald, sunglasses-wearing guard in a huge four-wheel-drive. He looked like a trained mercenary, the type you see on TV, gun poised and ready, glancing this way and that. He didn't look at me.

Then everybody was gone. Everybody. How did that happen? Where were the pilgrims? Where were the cool-as expats who might have rescued me? I was completely alone in Afghanistan — no phone, no contact details, no bag, no money. How could I have been so ill-prepared? I sensed a sinister, heavy silence, and I could feel my heart pounding.

My blood pressure medication was in my lost bag.

I am going to die here, I thought.

After what seemed like a lifetime, or what was left of mine, a young Afghan man appeared, swaggering nonchalantly towards me. He grinned, and in perfect English asked, 'Are you Dr Skinner?'

'Yes!' It was impossible to describe my relief.

'I'm Abud. You took a very long time. I've just been talking with some friends. I'll ring the van to come and get us. Where is your bag?'

Abud chatted to me on the way from the airport as if everything around us was totally normal. So, mostly, I tried to act normal too. It helped to slow my overloaded brain and, I hoped, get my blood pressure down. But never has sight alone so overwhelmed me. My hand was white-knuckled to the roof strap. The crowded streets looked like something out of medieval times. There were no women, it seemed. Then I had my first sight of the burqa.

I was dropped off at a walled and guarded guesthouse. There was no loitering at the van. 'This is when the kidnappers get you,' my security briefing had warned. The elderly guard at the gate wore white from head

I visited Afghanistan five years after the first Taliban government had been ousted. Under their rule, the wearing of the burqa (which covers both face and body) in public was strictly enforced. Such was the cultural shift in the country that the burqa was still always worn outside when I was there in 2006.

to toe, even his beard was white. He turned out to be a sleeper rather than a guarder. Unarmed. On querying this, I was told that no aid workers or their security details had anything to do with guns or the military. At this point in the war, it was intended as a message to terrorists that we were not a threat. I was astonished, given that we were part of an aid programme supported by a country where almost everyone has a gun, in a country where there was still a war on. Ironic, too, that I was alarmed to be unarmed. The message was that nothing would be as expected.

I was shown to my room up the stairs. It was spacious and warm. I tested the bed to confirm yet another rock-hard mattress. Why are mattresses right across Asia so hard? I walked out onto my small veranda overlooking the garden. The trees were bare and the shrubs were struggling, covered in grey dust and preparing for winter. I could breathe in the icy air and see the barren hills through smoke and mist as the sun went down. It was still. I remember locking the door and plotting my escape should the kidnappers arrive. It made me feel illogically reassured. The local cook had prepared a meal for us, and I joined four aid workers at the table. We introduced ourselves. They were the hardened experienced types, but were kind to this newbie. The cook, I was told, was renowned right across Kabul. To this day I can still taste his cream sauces and pomegranate salads.

—o—

Four days later, after meeting up with JHPIEGO staff to prepare for our visits, a team of five of us climbed into two four-wheel-drives and headed off in convoy through the mountains towards Bamyan. Looking up the trip on Google Maps now, it says it should take three hours, but I remember it taking all day. We dropped by the airport to pick up my bag, which had, thankfully, mysteriously arrived. And the money was still all there.

Our UN drivers, experienced locals well trained in security issues, weaved their way through packed bazaars in heavy traffic, past shops made from containers and streets of half-finished or half-demolished buildings. The traffic stopped and stood stationary for half an hour; a dangerous security situation. I picked up on the tension in the group and my breathing shallowed. The reason for the delay became apparent when a convoy of fully armed American personnel carriers sped by in front of us. Armed soldiers were at every open top, their guns focused with rotating menace at every face and every vehicle, including ours. In their wake they left a palpable sense of resentment among the crowd, and shock in our car. Strange, we reflected, that we were more alarmed by the conqueror than the conquered.

Back on the move, we drove along the Bamyan River. This land, the fruit bowl of Afghanistan, was now barren and dry, having been destroyed by the departing Taliban. The snow-covered Hindu Kush mountains in the background dominated every view. It was hard to take my eyes off them. Then we headed up on rough roads through the bare foothills. They'd be called mountains in New Zealand. Everything was becoming relative. It was autumn, so whatever trees there were in the lowlands had shed their leaves. It was cold over the pass, and there was already a dusting of snow. The driver called security on the satellite phone every 20 minutes to let them know we were safe and to get security updates. Still good to go. We passed destroyed tanks, left where they had been attacked, and stopped for some photos and a pee. How weird to use a tank as privacy for a pee. There was no sign of whose tank it had been, but we presumed it was Russian.

We drove for hours, around sharp corners and beside steep drops. Hillside villages emerged out of nowhere. My midwifery eyes spied a woman with her baby, sitting in her doorway, and I wondered how she might have birthed. It was a long way from anywhere.

We dropped down into the Bamyan Valley, instantly lulled by its beauty and tranquillity. How could something so exquisite ever have been so dangerous? But then, to our right, stark and horrifying, were the empty spaces where the two huge Buddhas had once stood, carved into the sandstone cliff. They had watched over this valley since the sixth century and had provided spiritual succour to thousands of pilgrims and to travellers on the Silk Road. The Taliban blew them up in 2001.

On the Friday of our visit, the day of worship — so no work — we were able, after security clearance, to drive back to see the area of the Buddhas more closely. I climbed up the crumbling steps that the monks had used to get to their cave retreats, and touched the rough edges where the Buddhas had been obliterated. At the base was a shed containing the remnants, gathered up in some vain hope of reconstruction. Most of it was dust. I picked up a small fragment and held it in the palm of my hand, sending a loving-kindness meditation to the people of Afghanistan. Then I put it back.

———◦———

Bamyan was a perfect place to start my Afghani work. Despite having a violent history over the centuries, it was currently one of the safest places in Afghanistan to be. And it felt like it.

The Aga Khan's NGO had set up the midwifery school the previous year, and the hospital had been rebuilt (by the New Zealand Army) and resourced, albeit minimally. By all accounts, their work had been successful. We stayed with the NGO staff in another walled and guarded compound. In the grounds were large plastic containers with our water supply, which were filled daily from the stream. Beside them were four rose bushes in arid soil and in full bloom.

Our work was to do a thorough review of the midwifery school. This included looking at the quality of teaching in the classroom, and in the hospital, examining whether the school had all the resources it needed, and seeing whether it was being managed adequately. Using a standards-based approach, so that we could make our assessments consistent across all the schools, meant that we would be able to identify gaps. Then we could provide guidance and support about what needed to be done — the most important bit. JHPIEGO had developed the assessment process but had not used it in the community yet, so this visit was going to enable us to see how well it worked.

Apart from being such a beautiful spot, Bamyan was also special for me because the New Zealand troops were there. They'd arrived in 2003 as part of a Provincial Reconstruction Team, one of the first in Afghanistan. Their role was to provide security and to assist with infrastructure development. Any recovery here would not have been possible without them. They had also built trust within the local community, a critical part of peacekeeping and reconstruction. This was such a contrast to how we had perceived the American convoy in Kabul.

The New Zealanders transitioned their role to the Afghan National Security Forces in 2011 and departed in 2013. By the time they left, they reported more schools, more girls going to school, better roads, power to most houses, more wells, improved general infrastructure, and midwives

Afghani student midwives in class.

working in eight small towns in the region. There had been controversy about the participation of the New Zealand troops. Was 10 years of service, eight lives and $30 million worth it? There was also journalist Nicky Hager's assertion that CIA agents were being housed by the Kiwis there. Complex stuff.

Late in my stay in Kabul, I had an interesting chat with a journalist staying in one of the same guesthouses as me. He bemoaned the misrepresentation of the Western military in Afghanistan, saying, 'You know the only reason they are here now is to keep the peace. Without those soldiers, none of you people would be able to be here at all. You need to be safe to reconstruct a country. As soon as they go, this country is fucked.'

As it proved to be.

When the New Zealanders departed in 2013, the Taliban were already waiting in the wings. They had started to bomb the road back to Kabul and terrorise the locals. When I discussed this point of view with people at home, especially those understandably dismissive of ongoing military presence in Afghanistan, they were surprised. The decision to go to war reflects the whole complexity and ethics of intervention, on a massive scale. When you shift the emphasis of the intervention from war to reconstruction, having a military presence in Afghanistan can, paradoxically, make some sense.

On the other hand, we now know that the US alone spent over two trillion US dollars there. That is 2000 billion dollars. One and a half trillion was spent on the military. The rest, 500 billion, went on reconstruction. Keeping mothers and babies alive in a war zone requires interventions at a massive level. This can vary from full-on military attack to educating midwives on how to treat a postpartum haemorrhage. That was part of my job. Even so, the cost is eye-watering.

When I saw the New Zealand flag over the camp by the Bamyan airfield, I was reassured and felt a little bit 'at home'. My interest in having a visit with them was, however, soundly rebuffed. NGO staff never had contact with the military because this was seen as siding with them and increased our risk. My focus had to stay squarely on the student midwives.

They were a delight. Young, enthusiastic and cheerful. They had been selected from outlying villages by local leaders, who had committed to having them back and supporting them in their midwifery practice. All had to be accompanied to the school by males; a Taliban legacy. Even a young boy would do. Those students with babies brought them along and the school provided a creche. They returned home only in the short break midway through the two-year course. Looking at their faces, all startlingly different, I saw the full gamut of Afghanistan's long history: the Eastern eyes of Genghis Khan; the blue eyes of Alexander the Great. I saw Indian and Ottoman faces. I became conscious of the history of this place and how different it was from my own. Yet I could also see that it was a shared history. The lethal combination of misogyny, colonisation and greed is a toxic mess that is still working its way through humanity across the whole planet.

On our first day at the school, Sheena and I spent the morning with students while they were learning the physical skills of midwifery. These included taking a blood pressure, assessing the growth of the baby, and checking the mother's haemoglobin. All this was practised on each other or on mannequins. They also had to learn emergency life-saving skills, such as stopping a postpartum haemorrhage or treating an infection. When we entered the sunlit, slightly cramped room, 15 faces all turned our way. They were dressed for the occasion, rigged from top to toe in surgical gear. A little over the top for a skills lab, I thought. I went over to a group of three students practising something with great focus. One was reading the manual out loud, one was undertaking the procedure and one was watching. The tutor was observing and providing advice and explanation,

'What are you learning here?' I asked.

Without a word, the manual was handed to me. They were learning how to repair a lacerated cervix. This stunned me. It is a complex procedure. In New Zealand, it would be done under anaesthesia by an obstetrician. I have no idea how to do it. The students' manuals also covered all the other interventions needed to save lives: management of haemorrhage, ventouse (suction cap) delivery, management of eclampsia (the fits caused by high blood pressure), to name just a few. It seemed to me that the need to intervene to save lives was dominating their education, but I did understand why. In my own midwifery practice, where hospitals and obstetricians were readily available, the need for assessment and management of risk was balanced by the need both to protect normal birth and to empower new mothers. This was not a priority in a country where death and morbidity were linked with birth, and where the

Three Afghani student midwives with their tutor learning how to repair
a lacerated cervix.

undercurrent of misogyny and trauma was palpable and pervasive. First things first, I surmised.

These students, listening attentively, needed to have a level of literacy high enough to enable them to learn. This was difficult, because there had been a mass exit of millions of people to Iran and Pakistan. The educated and middle classes had left early. For the girls who were left, there was no education under the Taliban, so many of the students and teachers were returned former refugees. The problem was huge. Nineteen years after the US-led intervention ousted the Taliban, two-thirds of Afghan girls still had no education. Despite this, the impacts of the reconstruction had been positive. In their 2017 report, USAID stated that since 2002, around 2500 midwives had been educated in Afghanistan and 51 per cent of women now had a skilled health professional with them at birth. The rate of maternal mortality had halved. It was extraordinary progress.

The sudden withdrawal of US forces in 2022 and the resurgence of Taliban rule was heartbreaking for so many. The impact on women has been horrendous, yet again, and all that progress is almost certain to be undone.

—○—

That afternoon, we visited Bamyan hospital. We needed to see the students learning with real live mothers. The hospital was small, but clean and newly built. Outside, families of the patients waited in small groups, sitting on the stony ground. They had brought Thermoses of tea and meals wrapped in cloth. They would wait there day and night. Only one family member was allowed inside to help provide care. As in most poor countries, families are the main caregivers in hospitals, providing all the meals and linen. They are essential.

Inside, the hospital was dark, as the intermittent electricity was not on. Burqa-clad women hovered in the corridors, withdrawing as we approached. We went to the antenatal clinic first. Pregnant women, their blue burqas now flipped back off their faces, were having their blood pressure checked and their baby's heart listened to by the students. The students were serious and intent on their job as the teachers watched and provided direction. The women glanced sideways at us with anxious, distant eyes. It might have just been because we were present, but there seemed to be an edge of tension in the air. There was no interaction between the women and the students or their teachers. No smiles, no explanations, and no questions from the women. Following the check-up, the women went out to reconnect with their families. As they walked away, flipping the burqas back over their faces, I could only wonder at the reality of their lives.

One of the teachers came to find us. 'We have a mother here who has eclampsia. She came in having fits. She has twins and went into premature labour. The students are with her.'

The young woman lay on the hospital bed in a small, clean room surrounded by masked and gowned staff. There was a doctor at her head, staying close by to supervise the two midwifery students who were helping to monitor her progress. She had a magnesium sulphate IV drip running, so her fits had stopped. She had a mask giving her oxygen. The students, hovering closely, were taking turns to measure her vital signs and record them. On the wall were handwritten instructions about what to do in a variety of obstetric emergencies. Eclampsia was one of them. We almost never see eclampsia in rich countries, because the risks and warning signs are usually identified during routine antenatal care. It is also more common in a twin pregnancy. This woman, I could see, was receiving textbook-quality care. Except that not once did anyone look her in the eyes or talk to her. She looked fearful to me, but I did wonder whether it was a projection on my part. Whose fear was deeper, hers or mine? I wanted to go to her and hold her hand.

'How are her babies?' I asked the doctor quietly.

'She already delivered them. They have gone to the children's ward.'

Her twin sons, born three months premature, both died within hours of birth, and within minutes of each other. There was no neonatal intensive care in Afghanistan. Without help in this hospital, and from these doctors and midwives, this young mother would have laboured and delivered at home, and she too would have died alongside her sons. Intervention, sort of at its best. This was such a contrast from what I had seen at the main hospital in Kabul three days earlier: a dark, hot room with eight women on beds almost touching each other. They all had an IV in, but there were no staff present. All had eclampsia; five had died by the next morning. To see this woman in Bamyan, saved, was a blessing.

We completed the assessment and, after flying to Mazar in the north,

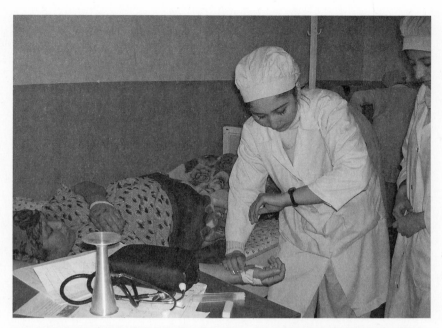

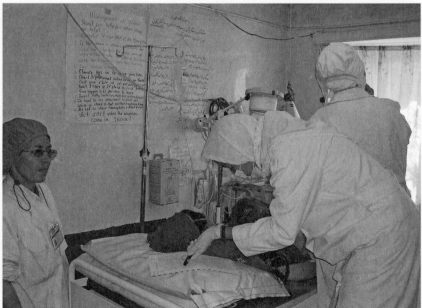

Above: A student midwife doing an antenatal check in Bamyan, Afghanistan.

Below: Students caring for a young mother with eclampsia who has just had twins.

repeated it at two more schools. Then I headed home. The first flight was in a 10-seater plane. After a wait for most of the morning at the tin shack of an airport in Bamyan, the plane took off. We had not been told the exact departure time until half an hour before we left, lest it was leaked. The pilot's safety briefing was perfunctory. But he did warn us that our take-off would be fast and very steep, and that we would veer off quickly to one side so that missiles had less chance of hitting us!

This time I was able to see the beautiful valley of Bamyan from up high. My suggestion to the pilot that we might make a quick diversion over Band-e Amir, the most beautiful blue lake in the world, was met with a perfunctory 'No'. Fair enough. In two short weeks I had developed a strange mixed response to risk, swinging between bravado and terror for no logical reason.

At Kabul Airport, I went straight to the UN flight and on to Dubai, where I again, but in reverse, had the strange transition from Terminal Three to Terminal One. I walked back past the duty-free shops in my dusty boots, my headscarf around my shoulders, and turned my mind towards home.

—◇—

There seemed to be a war of sorts going on in New Zealand, too. Having just celebrated a centenary of the profession in New Zealand and the establishment of the Midwifery Council, we began to think that maybe we were finally being accepted as an autonomous and responsible profession. We had become used to resistance and backlash from both the media and medicine, and were weathering it reasonably well. Women still supported us. By 2004, well over half of all women chose a midwife as their main maternity caregiver, and the satisfaction with their care was high. Karen Guilliland, the CEO of the College of Midwives, did the sterling and unenviable work of defending us in the media.

The following year, though, was arguably our annus horribilis — mine, anyway. Garry Evans, Wellington's District Coroner, had reviewed the deaths of two breech babies, born five years apart and with very different causes. I had worked with Garry reviewing cases for ACC. Although a well-meaning man, he was highly conservative and remained mystified at how midwives had ever been allowed to work without medical supervision. Women's choice and control were not considered.

On the basis of these two deaths — two among the 300,000 babies born over those five years — he recommended that all midwives should be supervised by doctors and have more extensive training — advice that was arguably outside his brief. A frenzy of attacks on midwifery were launched in the media and a furore eventuated, culminating in a front-page article in the *Listener* positioning the development of the midwifery profession as the new 'unfortunate experiment'. It was so deeply insulting as to be hurtful. The cover photo was of a screaming baby being held upside down in the hands of a fully masked and gowned person after what looked like a caesarean section. It was abhorrent.

Despite pressure on the government from many sides, Garry's recommendations were not accepted. However, the Midwifery Council did eventually increase midwifery education by a year and developed a mentoring programme for midwives in their first year of practice.

The assault on midwifery did not end with this coronial report. In that same year, a midwife who had a client wanting a vaginal breech birth transferred her to hospital to labour but concealed from the hospital staff and from the obstetrician on call the fact that the baby was presenting by the breech. She knew that this obstetrician was hostile and not willing to support vaginal breech births. The baby subsequently died at birth and the midwife, at the instigation of the obstetrician, was charged with manslaughter.

I took a call from Karen Guilliland sometime later asking me to be an expert witness for the prosecution. The police would be expecting my support in their prosecution for manslaughter. Good God. Karen's point was that if no New Zealand midwife did it, the police would get in expert midwifery advice from overseas. Midwifery models elsewhere have much less focus on free and informed client choice and are probably more medicalised. I'm not sure why I was chosen. It was either because of my experience or because I'm seen as a 'nice' person. Either way it was clearly my time to step up, so with a great deal of apprehension I agreed.

Over the Christmas period I prepared my statement and had numerous conversations with the police, who were pushing me to be increasingly critical. In retrospect, I really needed to have my own legal advice as I had no experience of the adversarial nature of the High Court and of the implications for expert advisors in that forum. My experience had all been in the Coroners Court, where an inquisitorial process is undertaken.

The coroner is interested in the truth, not in winning.

It was a truly nightmarish experience. I agonised over my evidence and then eventually regretted it. In my cross-examination, where I had hoped to be able to speak some wisdom or give the jury some insight into the complexities of care, the lawyers attacked my practice, my PhD and my previous interactions with the midwife. Thankfully, she was found not guilty. We were all tremendously relieved. But I did feel guilty and complicit. The adversarial process was shocking. If anyone I know ever ends up in court, I will make sure they get the best lawyer possible.

A while later, Karen called those of us who had been involved as witnesses to come together to debrief. She knew how traumatic it had been. She had arranged for a counsellor to be there to help. I have a very vivid memory of the counsellor suggesting we should get a relaxation massage or do some meditation, and the horrified glances we all exchanged. What the fuck! I suppose in the end just all being together might have helped a bit, but I still can't watch television dramas set in courtrooms. I flew home from Dunedin feeling sure that my midwifery career in New Zealand must be over.

—o—

Just a month after the High Court case I was back in Terminal Three on my way to Kabul, joining the ranks of those cool-as-cucumber aid workers. Who could ever have believed it would be a relief to go to Afghanistan? I had some dollars ready for the bag-helpers and my pills in my hand luggage. This time it felt exciting, not terrifying. Luckily, I was again staying in the guesthouse with the cream and pomegranate cook.

I would work with Sabera, a young Afghani midwife. My task was to show her how to evaluate the midwifery programmes. Handing the process over to the local people was a cornerstone of the intervention. For me, it was 'see one, do one, teach one'. Sabera's family had been refugees in Iran for five years, and she had done her midwifery training there. Unusual in Afghanistan, her father had agreed that she could do this work, and he was happy that I would be with her. She was bright and courageous and, once I met her, I felt less anxious about the task. A young Afghani midwife is like gold, and I relished the opportunity to help develop her skills. We might even have a bit of fun.

Overlooking Kabul while watching the kite-flying — the tiny dot in the distance to the right.

Our plan was to visit two midwifery training schools. The first was in Sheberghan, four hours east of Mazar, and was run by Save the Children Fund. The other was a further three-hour drive into the hinterland of the Hindu Kush mountains to Sari Pul. Before we left, Sabera and I spent the first few days at the USAID compound in Kabul preparing for the trip. The planes were organised, security was checked, and the NGOs were expecting us. We were now in winter, so we needed to be prepared to become snowbound.

Before we left, I had a free afternoon at the guesthouse. You're not meant to go outside the gates unaccompanied, but from my window I could see kites fluttering in the sky. What could be dangerous about kite-flying? I managed to persuade another aid worker staying in the guesthouse to come with me to see them. We went to find the cook, as we needed a male.

'Can we go up the hill and see the kites and would you come with us?'

A puzzled look was the response.

'Just for a few minutes,' we promised.

We threw on our headscarves and hustled him along. We snuck past the dozing guard and scrambled to the top of the hill. It was treeless, shrubless and dusty. When they saw us, every kite-flyer (there were no girls) stopped in his tracks and stared. The sight of two Western women was presumably beyond their comprehension, and their fighting kites paused still in the air for a moment. Just behind the boys was an empty and broken-down swimming pool with the high-diving board still intact. Beside it, the ubiquitous demolished tank. The boys carried on running their paper kites in a breeze imperceptible to this Windy Wellingtonian. They hovered over Kabul, stretching out into the valley and over the walled houses. It was so quiet. No rumbles from motorways, no tooting, no gunshots. Just the boys yelling in delight or despair as another string was severed. They did not glance our way again. The cook, looking worried by now, beckoned us back down the hill.

Sabera and I flew first to Mazar, high over brown, rippled mountains. We had to wait a couple of days there for a convoy to be arranged so that we could travel to Sheberghan in a group. While waiting, we ventured out to see the famous blue mosque, the beautiful twin-domed shrine of Hazrat Ali. This was our bit of fun. We walked through the town a little. There were a lot of double-takes in our direction; God knows how long it was since they had seen a European, let alone a European woman, with a young Afghani woman and without a male escort. We came across a shop selling old jewellery and household ornaments. The blue of the lapis lazuli and the grey-brown of the brass and copper filled the small room. These encrusted necklaces, rings and bracelets, battered brassware and dusty blue glassware had, I presume, been pawned for food by the nomadic Kochi women during the waves of war. Sabera and I now have a small but precious collection in our jewellery boxes.

Walking back to our guesthouse, there was a loud and angry call from across the street: 'GEORGE BUSH!' So much for the Kiwi flag on my jacket. Enough venturing out for a while.

—o—

Once our convoy of four four-wheel-drives was gathered for the journey west, we moved fast and in tight formation on wide roads recently built by the Japanese. We sped through fields of ripe hashish, past the remains of one of Alexander the Great's fortresses, overtaking caravans of camels laden down with bushy firewood. No stopping, because the mujahideen controlled this part of the country. Drugs were big here. Even so, our security detail still had no weapons.

We arrived as the sun was setting and were welcomed into the Save the Children compound by Lynn Robson, the programme manager. A slight delight of a woman, Lynn had come to Sheberghan directly from a corporate management job in Washington DC. On hearing, in 2004, that George Bush had won a second term as US President, she was so horrified that she immediately rang Save the Children and asked them to send her to Afghanistan. And they did. It was a huge job, overseeing the health services in the region, and she was the only European resident there. Such stunning but often overwhelming work. Lynn was delighted to have us there, as she was struggling to understand whether the midwifery school was going well and how the hospital was functioning. Despite having a translator, being female in such a place was a drawback. Trying to build working relationships with hospitals and health centres is difficult at the best of times. This wasn't one of them. She had been looking for some support, but also for some company.

The next morning, Sabera and I began our work. After meeting the staff and students at the school, and having started to look at the teaching plans and the curriculum, I felt confident that Sabera was managing well and left her there to go to the hospital. I wanted to spend time with the students there. The quality of clinical experience that students have in the hospital is crucial in determining the quality of care that a new graduate can provide. Students can learn as much as they like in the classroom, but what they see in practice is what they will become. In healthcare education anywhere in the world, there is often a dissonance between what is taught and what is seen. We see this in New Zealand. But in Afghanistan, it was extreme. The high quality of teaching set up by JHPIEGO and enacted by the NGOs in the schools was too often undermined by the students' experience in practice. JHPIEGO acknowledged this as one of their major issues. I was to put my mind to how it might be overcome.

Lynn came with me to the hospital. She was keen to be with me so that she could share my observations, get some of her burning questions answered and check how on-track I thought the hospital was. Not really my area of expertise, but I was happy to look at it and chat out her concerns with her.

The hospital was bare and minimal but, as in Bamyan, was newly built. The bombed-out old one was just beside it, and in the grounds sat a demolished tank that had been painted bright red and repurposed as a children's slide. The corridors of the hospital were clean, the rooms dark and sparse. The electricity was off. The hospital now had medical staff with upgraded intervention skills. There was a small operating room, but no blood for transfusions.

As we turned a corner of the corridor, we saw masked and gowned staff pushing a bed with a girl on it. She looked exhausted and terrified. They were heading to the operating room where, I was told, they were going to do a caesarean section.

'Why are you doing a caesarean?' I asked the doctor, curious about decision-making in these environments.

'This woman has been in labour for three days at home and they have just brought her in now. She is fully dilated but the baby is dead.'

'Have you tried the ventouse?' I suggested.

'It is a very big baby and will not fit,' she replied.

'I think no caesarean for this woman. You must try the ventouse,' I stated firmly, moving to stand in front of the bed — scarcely believing what I was doing.

Caesarean sections to deliver a baby who has died are a bad idea. It can be a death sentence for a young woman who will return to her remote village and have more babies. A scar on her uterus will increase the risk of it rupturing the next time she labours. And we knew that this woman had big babies. We also knew that there was no blood for miles.

I was surprised at how easily they acquiesced, reversing the direction of the bed back to the delivery room without a word. I suspected that the 'Dr' in front of my name gave me this sort of authority. How could a midwife, usually the lowest person in the health hierarchy, make such a decision? I hoped that this doctor's skills extended to ventouse deliveries.

After walking around the wards, saying hello to the new mothers and babies, chatting to the students and looking at their workbooks, we headed to the birth room. I was given a gown and plastic sandals to wear and quietly opened the door in time to see the cleaner throwing a bucket of water over the floor. She had just lit the bukhari fireplace and the room was smoke-filled but still cold. Four women were at various stages of giving birth, with no curtains to separate them. One had just had a miscarriage, one was not in labour but was having her blood pressure checked, and another was the young woman whose baby had died, now surrounded by three staff. Out of the corner of my eye, I saw the ventouse being applied to her baby.

In the far corner, I saw one of the students being guided to deliver a fourth baby. It was not a large room. I gingerly stepped around the cleaner, who was vigorously mopping up the water, and went closer to the student. No way to be inconspicuous here. Both student and tutor were gowned, masked and gloved. I approached with a smile. The young soon-to-be mother was lying flat on her back, pushing — she had no companion, no privacy and now, another stranger. She was silent and composed. The baby's head, dark hair glistening, was easily stretching the perineum. But to my horror, the tutor directed the student to get the scissors to cut the perineum. I made a split-second decision to intervene. I pointed at the scissors and shook my head.

Firmly: 'No cut, no cut.'

The tutor looked at me incredulously over her mask, and they both paused. The mother lifted her gaze and looked straight at me. I should not have been surprised that neither teacher nor student knew how to birth a baby without cutting. Episiotomy had found itself a home in yet another country, I reflected sadly, even here, in what sometimes felt like the edge of the world. But there was no time to brood on this. I moved in. First, to hold the young woman's hand, to smile and tell her how well she was doing.

'Gentle, gentle now. Little, little push.' My tone a universal language, I hoped, while at the same time the other hand was directing the delivery.

'Support the baby's head firmly as it comes slowly. This is good. Yes, yes that's it. It's crowned. Support as the face comes through.'

To the mother: 'Another little push [smile] . . . now pant, pant.' I panted.

All the while, I prayed like hell to the Virgin Mary not to let this woman tear. She surely must be the patroness of intact perineums. Then I decided, while I was at it, that I might as well take things to the next level and insisted that they put the naked, slippery baby straight on to his mother's abdomen. As he took his first breath and opened his eyes, his first contact and his first sight was of his mother. An intact mother. I was relieved and delighted. Perfect.

Everyone else in our little group, though, seemed completely taken aback by what I'd encouraged. What was I on about? Which was more outrageous? No cut, or giving the baby straight to the mother? The joy that I thought I would help to create was absent. In many countries, the episiotomy is still considered to be a necessary, routine intervention for all women. Apart from being taught in those earlier days of medical colonisation, doing an episiotomy also means that the woman and her family can be charged more for the birth services. It's an income stream. But we know now how damaging this intervention can be, and also how important early skin-to-skin contact between mother and baby is. I knew they should have been taught this in class, as it was in their curriculum.

But I couldn't progress to contemplate that anymore, because I heard, from behind, a truly ghastly plop-splash sound. I turned, in what felt like slow motion, to see water slopping over the side of a bedpan on the floor on the other side of the room. In it, a pale and pudgy baby, curled up where she had just been thrown. She looked perfectly formed and could even have been thought asleep. Her mother, the woman who we had stopped from having the caesarean, had her legs hanging in stirrups. Drapes concealed her face from me, but not the bleeding space from where she had just birthed her dead daughter. Seeing her baby thrown into the bedpan filled me with horror and relief at the same time. I wanted to grab a towel and go over and scoop the baby up, so that she might feel the arms of a mother around her just for a minute. But I didn't. I had already done enough.

After some more time with the students, talking with them about how they were, I found Lynn, who had been doing a medication inventory, and we headed out into the icy afternoon, past bearded men waiting for news. Which one of them, I wondered, had the live wife but the dead baby? The driver and the security man were waiting for us, and we headed home. We passed the local market and I longed for a walk through it, just to sense it close-up, and to clear the birth scenes from my brain. I suggested this to Lynn.

'I've never walked here. Always felt a bit scared to, especially being a woman alone.'

'It must be safe enough for a quick walk,' I said. 'Surely no kidnappers would be expecting a couple of middle-aged European women to wander through here. C'mon. Let's go.'

I could see she was excited. We told the driver to stop, and we strolled up and down the dusty, rutted road, taking in everything. Baskets of abundant fresh fruit and vegetables of every colour; peddlers of tins and trays and teapots, bicycle parts, clocks and cutlery; sheep carcasses hanging, the sun reflecting off the butcher's knife. All the stalls were attended by bearded men sitting in the dust. They stared as though we had emerged from a different planet. There were no women. A couple of boys smiled at us.

'Salaam alaikum,' we smiled back.

'What's that?' I asked Lynn, pointing to a horse-drawn buggy which looked as ancient as its driver.

'That is an Afghani taxi,' she joked.

I'd hoped she might say that. 'Have you ever been in one?'

'Never.'

'Let's take it home.'

'Seriously?'

As we approached the buggy, shock emanated from its driver's face. No stopping us now. Lynn asked our security detail to tell him that we wanted a lift down the road. He obliged. The old buggy driver watched incredulously as Lynn and I scrambled aboard. I could see just the touch of a twinkle in his eye. He took his place with his back to us, flicked the reins and we clip-clopped our way all 200 metres back to our compound. Giggling. What a treat. Our car was so close behind that we could read the anxiety in both men's eyes. We had mercy on them, and we did not dally long. I wondered, too, how risky what we were doing was. We hopped out, took a couple of photos, and scuttled through the compound gate, unlocked for us by yet another guard.

'Best fun in ages. You really need to stay a bit longer.'

—o—

Later that evening, we sat around the fire with a plate of pulao, and naan bread with sweet tea, and reflected on our day. Lynn had discovered that the woman with the stillborn baby was only 14 years old — not unusual here. And that during the birth it was a new midwife, trained in emergency interventions at this very school, who had extricated the large baby from her mother's body. So, there was bad news and good news.

Sabera was gutted to have missed the market adventure, but had had a delightful day at the school. We were able to reassure Lynn that it was doing okay and that the students were being well supervised in the hospital, despite its poor resources. We had some suggestions of what could perhaps be improved. However, the clinical setting was, as is usual in poor countries, problematic. The combination of out-of-date practice and inappropriate interventions that become ingrained into the culture of a hospital are tough to shift. We find it hard enough in New Zealand, where we have plenty of resources and access to the latest evidence. We pondered the thorny issue of intervention, both life-saving and life-taking. For me, this exemplifies the stark underbelly of power and authority, of enculturation and of outright colonisation. Or of ignorance. It was an ethical minefield. I did reflect, though, that we in the West do not, in any sense of the word, have the intervention balance right. Why should we expect Afghanistan to?

That day in Afghanistan was the first and only time I ever intervened directly in a birth while I was a development consultant. On their own, out of any context to build on what I had done, my actions felt wrong. I know I made a difference to the outcomes for those women, but I felt that even though I had not been rude (I did smile a lot), my actions had been disrespectful to the staff who were doing their best in difficult circumstances. It was a good lesson for me. I needed to stay with the big picture and focus on the job in hand.

Above: Strolling through the Sheberghan market after a long day in the local hospital.

Below: Taking a local taxi back to the compound, the security car following closely behind.

The thing I found the most horrible, though, was that everywhere I went, birthing women were, to some extent, treated badly by the staff. Staff could be abusive, rough and indifferent, even in front of us. It was normal for them, but painful for us to watch and to hear about. I had to remind myself that within my mother's living memory, birthing women were treated badly, and that even today in the West, they still can be. I also needed to acknowledge that much of this treatment was a consequence of colonisation, medicalisation and hospitalisation, with no acknowledgement of local cultural birth practices. But even so, I found the misogyny in Afghanistan a gaping, painful chasm. A survey conducted in 2002 revealed that three-quarters of all women there were depressed, 90 per cent suffered from anxiety, and over half of all women exhibited signs of PTSD. They so needed kindness when birthing.

The lessons I learnt in Afghanistan were enormous. I started to understand something of the complexities of project planning, developing community engagement, preparation of teachers, selection and support of students and so much more. These lessons proved to be invaluable. I had good midwifery bones and an inquisitive, critical brain, but I lacked relevant development experience. JHPIEGO gave me that, and I was grateful. I used and honed those skills in every country I subsequently worked in.

My respect for the process and for the organisation was tempered only by watching and being aware of the process of recolonisation happening, this time by the US, and by us. But they got midwifery going. They developed a respectful, evidence-based, inclusive, community-engaged, effective midwifery programme. And the maternal mortality in Afghanistan, as in Cambodia, halved.

It was time to sleep. Sabera and I went outside to the toilet block and then cleaned our teeth in the freezing water. Plastic buckets had been set up for us under cover. The staff laughingly promised us a hot shower in the morning. I had absolutely no idea whether they were having us on or not.

We tucked up on mattresses on the floor under a ton of blankets. I woke the next morning to an eerie quiet, and pulled back the curtain to see only white. It was more snow than I had ever seen and I guessed we would be staying a bit longer after all.

10

Going global for local

Snow was falling, too, as I looked out the window from my desk at the World Health Organization headquarters in Geneva. It was the winter of 2009 and I was just beginning a three-month placement as a midwife scholar. It was a strange hybrid — and unpaid — position, another of those interesting-looking jobs I had spotted online. I was very surprised to be offered it, as it was for 'outstanding midwife leaders' and I didn't feel like I was one of those. The placement meant that I could experience and maybe even participate in maternal and health policy-making at a global level. I thought this might help me understand the process of how global guidance is developed and disseminated, the same guidance that I had been using locally, or 'in country' as it is called in development speak. I was to work in the Making Pregnancy Safer unit, which was part of the Sexual and Reproductive Health section. It felt momentous. Once again, I would be far out of my comfort zone.

I also discovered that I was the only midwife in the whole place.

Before I left New Zealand for Geneva, I'd just done some work in Kiribati. I had been contracted by the WHO to develop a supportive supervision process for nurse-midwives working in the extreme isolation of the country's outer islands. Strangely, they were called medical assistants not nurse-midwives, even though there was not a doctor to assist throughout thousands of kilometres of ocean. It was a reflection, I surmised, of the status of nurses and midwives versus doctors, a situation I have found everywhere I've worked. I never did use the term 'medical assistant'.

Visiting with a midwife in a remote outer island of Kiribati. We were piloting a project on how to provide supportive supervision at a distance. Here we are looking through the maternity records for the year with a nurse-midwife supervisor from Tarawa.

The European Union and the World Bank had just rebuilt all the health centres in the outer islands of Kiribati and retrained the staff. The WHO offered to contribute to the programme by providing ongoing support. That's where I came in. It felt good to be back working in the Pacific. It felt more familiar and closer to home.

Even back then, in 2007, climate change had begun to have real impacts on a country already struggling with Westernisation. This was a new issue for me to factor in to my work. The king tides had become increasingly destructive, as had the pollution left by ships that arrived loaded with stuff but never took away any of the rubbish the stuff created. The people's health and welfare were suffering.

The government, supported by the Australians, were in the conflicted position of trying to improve health and social services while at the same time developing an exit strategy for their population. For three years in a row they had diverted the entire graduating class of the girls' high school to Brisbane, to train as nurses. The idea was that the girls would become settled in Australia, help alleviate the nursing shortage there and be granted citizenship. Eventually, their entire extended families would be encouraged to join them. It was seen, strangely, as a win–win! But the Kiribati people have a strong bond with their islands, and to imagine abandoning them as they became uninhabitable would have been horrific. It was not a topic I ever heard any of the locals talking about.

My work in Kiribati, my contracts in Cambodia and Afghanistan and of course my work in New Zealand provided me with a reasonable backdrop for considering global maternal policy in the field. The university granted me paid leave to go to Geneva and the Ministry of Health provided me with a small contribution to help finance the trip. By then, all three of my children were working or studying overseas. It was time for me to join them.

—o—

I was getting settled into my work at one of the rare spare desks that the WHO staff had found for me. My initial task was to gather up all the resources that WHO had accumulated in relation to maternal health so that they could all be put onto a CD. This would make distribution out to the regions more efficient. It was a step up from paper copies. It was the perfect

Above: At the World Health Organization (WHO) headquarters in Geneva. Behind me is the iconic sculpture commemorating the eradication of the parasite causing river blindness in Africa, WHO's first major success. I found it deeply moving and even today it radiates hope for what is possible if we work together.

Below: At my desk at WHO headquarters with one of the Making Pregnancy Safer unit staff.

starting task for me, as I was able to get a picture of how the organisation was structured and see the extent of their work. Having full access to the WHO library was a thrill. (Only an academic would say such a thing.)

Sitting in the desk opposite me was Annika. She was from Bosnia. Her background was in medicine (as was almost everyone's there) and her passion had been public health. She also had a PhD and a young daughter.

'Joan, come with us to the meeting we are having with the two DDGs. They want to plan WHO's response to the UN's call to act on MDG5. Bernard from MPS and Kirsten from HRH are coming too. It would be good if you could come and give us a midwifery perspective. It's in half an hour. Let's go and grab some lunch first.'

Sometimes the acronyms in the development world made it seem like we were speaking another language. What was about to happen at the meeting, I worked out, was that the head of the Making Pregnancy Safer unit and the head of the Human Resources for Health unit were meeting with two of the Deputy Directors-General of WHO to plan its approach to the UN call to action on the fifth of the Millennium Development Goals (MDGs). This goal had been to improve maternal health by reducing the number of women dying while giving birth. Most of these deaths are preventable (infection, haemorrhage, eclampsia, unsafe abortion), and in rich countries very few deaths occur from these causes. Theoretically, a reduction in maternal mortality should not have required too huge an effort. Yet an evaluation undertaken halfway through the MDG timeframe, just before I arrived in Geneva, had found no appreciable decrease in global maternal deaths. It was the only one of the UN's eight goals not to have improved.

Unlike the sparse 1960s furniture and way-out-of-date computers of the office space, the cafeteria at WHO was a surprising culinary delight. I got the impression that most of the staff had their main meal of the day there. They were often on short-term contracts or visiting, and many had no family staying with them. There seemed to be a massive array of food types, perhaps reflecting the variety of ethnic backgrounds. Sitting over my chicken fricassee and salad, I felt so out of my depth about the upcoming meeting that I didn't even know what questions to ask of Annika.

We ploughed through lunch, then strode through the long corridors to the meeting. The faces coming towards us, chatting, greeting, in intense discussion or simply at ease, were a collective picture of the world's diversity. As I started to get to know just a few of them, I was always impressed. They were a stunning group of people: intelligent, curious, bright, quick, pragmatic and so hard-working. I don't think I ever encountered a single person with an over-inflated ego.

At the small meeting table in one of the DDG's offices I was introduced to everyone. Both the DDGs were women, one from Nigeria, the other from Cameroon. The two unit directors were from Sri Lanka and the UK, both male. The conversation went something like this:

'We have to sort out our response to the UN on this call to improve maternal health.'

'We need to find out what the others in the H4 are doing.'

(Thankfully someone explained to me that the H4 are the four major development partners: WHO, UNFPA, UNICEF and the World Bank. I never did find out what the H stood for.)

'Does anyone know anyone in the World Bank who might be working on this?'

'I've got a contact at UNFPA headquarters in New York, and they will probably be in contact with UNICEF.'

Suddenly, unexpected though this was, the discussion felt like it could have been happening around just about any meeting table.

The informality of making high-level contacts based on who you knew felt surprisingly like home. I relaxed a little.

'We need to stick to our core business, which is the development of normative tools. What do you think we could offer?'

(I eventually discovered that normative tools consist of the written guidance for action or change which has been based on worldwide consultation and consensus and on the available best evidence. It is indeed what WHO excels at.)

'Well, Joan is doing some work bringing together all the WHO tools in relation to maternal health.'

'And I have some expertise in outcomes-based evaluation, so I could develop a tool that could be used in either needs assessment or programme outcomes measurement. If I make it flexible enough, it could work well alongside any programme work that the others in the H4 might be working on.'

I could hardly believe that those words came out of my mouth. I thought I might as well go for it then.

'Why do you have no midwives working here at WHO?' I asked as the meeting was coming to an end.

'Oh, yes, we know. It's been one of those things we just haven't got around to. But we need to.'

The next time I went back to work at WHO, three years later, there was a midwifery advisor.

After that meeting I had to produce something. The 'some' expertise that I had in evaluation was not extensive. Fortunately, I knew someone who had a *lot* of expertise — Paul, my former husband. Using software that he had developed, and with his input, I came up with what I thought was an excellent evaluation model. Not long before my departure, I presented it to the MPS staff meeting. They were impressed with what I had produced. I headed home feeling quite pleased with myself. I was also very aware of what I had learnt and what I had become.

—o—

That first morning home I woke early, still jetlagged, and turned on Radio New Zealand for the news. The opening item was about the Minister of Education. It was alleged that 30 years previously, when he had been a young teacher, he had put a tennis ball in the mouth of one of his wayward students. Even though the claims were unsubstantiated, he eventually resigned. The fact that this was the leading item on the national news, given all that was happening in the rest of the world, shocked me and has been imprinted somewhere prominent in my memory. Was this what New Zealanders really wanted or needed to hear about?

New Zealand was beginning to seem a long way away, in more ways than just physical distance, and reintergrating back into the community was challenging. The country seemed to be a strange contradiction between being an innovative world leader and a small-minded backwater. In Geneva, I found that New Zealand's health system was seen as leading the world in how it was progressing in both primary care and maternity care. I felt proud to be a Kiwi midwife.

My report to the Ministry of Health on my return focused on how maternity services in New Zealand might be integrated more fully into a primary care model. This was built on the most recent World Health Report, which had focused on primary healthcare. It was called 'Now

More Than Ever'. One of its recommendations was to integrate primary care and maternity care. I had examined the primary healthcare model in relation to New Zealand maternity care in detail, and wrote the following recommendations to the Ministry in New Zealand:

- There needs to be a conscious protection of what New Zealand has already achieved in its development of maternity care as a primary healthcare service.
- There needs to be a clear articulation of the different models of integration (e.g. marae-based services, rural services, Union Health Services) already being provided so that others can develop similar models as able or as appropriate.
- There needs to be the provision of primary health birth facilities for all women who have uncomplicated pregnancies.
- Midwives should not be required to provide care within medically and illness focused primary healthcare services with no proven record of collaborative practice.

Years later, I was shocked when I re-read this (I'd found it tucked away in my 'old jobs' folder). Looking forwards to our maternity service 13 years later, none of these recommendations had ever been considered. Not that I expected them to be.

At the time, 2009, midwifery in New Zealand was beginning to really struggle. The 10 years after St Helens closed, during which we had trained very few midwives, was beginning to impact on the numbers of midwives both in the hospitals and in the community. In spite of this, the regulatory and professional midwifery bodies were both functioning well. Sound processes for the education and support of midwives were all in place, and accountability was an accepted part of our practice. But despite all this and despite impressive individual consumer feedback on how satisfied women were with their care, there remained a strange resistance in the community to fully supporting a model of physiological (normal) birth provided by midwives. Public discourse remained mistrustful, and the media was still quick to take us to the front page. Individual midwives still felt fearful. Meanwhile, the Ministry of Health did little, if anything, to ensure that the model of community-based, midwifery-led maternity care was sustainable.

Over the next few years, I maintained my role as half-time senior lecturer at the university, continuing to teach and support midwifery postgrad students. Peter's children produced some more beautiful baby girls for us, and by then we had seven granddaughters. Enough for a netball team. Life could be chaotic, noisy, messy and utterly joyful, especially when we all got together for our regular Sunday night family tea.

Grandmotherhood was, and is, a very hard-to-explain state of being. I watched in fascination as these wee girls grew and learnt. It was something I don't remember focusing on as a mother myself; I suppose I was too busy. Then there is the amazement at how differently our children come to parenting. My guiding principle as mother/mother-in-law followed how I was alongside new mothers as a midwife.

'Wow, you are doing an amazing job!'

And they were. They are.

—◦—

Before my next visit to Geneva, in 2012, I fulfilled contracts in Vietnam, where I assisted the University of Hanoi to evaluate the government programme to educate ethnic minority midwives, and in Nepal, where I helped to develop a direct-entry midwifery curriculum. I also had another contract in Cambodia. By now, every country I visited had an overt commitment to midwifery as a way of reducing maternal deaths. I never once talked with anyone in those countries who was less than totally positive about the important role that midwives could play. I found this remarkable, although I did begin to worry that other parts of midwifery were being disregarded. The protection of normal birth, now seen as an important part of the New Zealand midwife's role, was all but disregarded in the development world. All the WHO training manuals on the management of the complications of pregnancy and birth had been upgraded, but the module that provided advice on care in normal pregnancy and birth was left on the shelf.

I also became aware that the most difficult thing to overcome in any of these countries was the lack of midwives who could teach. If there are no midwives in practice, there is no pool of possible teachers. And there

Above: Saying goodbye to the midwives in Nepal, where I had helped write a direct-entry midwifery curriculum.

Below: With midwives from the hill tribes of Vietnam. I had helped to evaluate a midwifery programme which focused on the lives and needs of the country's minority tribal groups.

is no quick fix for this. Different countries tried to solve the problem in a variety of ways. In Afghanistan it was female doctors, newly returned from having taken refuge out of the country, who started off the teaching. In many countries, though, it was the nurse teachers who took over teaching midwifery, with varying degrees of success.

In some countries the nurse teachers had a short training course to introduce them to the curriculum. These curricula contained a lot of new material, were competency-based and usually had a very different teaching methodology. It was a stretch for the nurse teachers, who had well-established and mostly didactic teaching approaches. In other countries, nurse teachers were sent to a neighbouring country for training. Sometimes midwifery schools from universities in the West invested heavily in supporting teaching.

In the worst case I saw, existing nurse teachers — already working in extremely poorly resourced nursing schools — were sent a curriculum along with 50 new students that they had to feed and house, with not a single extra resource. My heart went out to these teachers, who were struggling and were often overtly distressed. In several countries I advised that no more new students should be accepted into a course until the quality of teaching could be improved.

When, in 2012, I received an invitation from the WHO to lead an international consultation on the development of core competencies for midwifery teachers, I was both shocked and delighted. I was not sure exactly what they wanted — not an unfamiliar feeling when taking on these jobs. But I was going to get paid for this one. They must have been pleased with the work I had done for them previously.

The job was extensive, and I was glad that I only worked half-time at the university. The first part of the task was to do a literature review of research and other documents that might inform how and why core competencies for midwifery teachers are needed. This background paper would be included as an annex to the competency document itself. Then I had to draw up the draft competencies that would be taken to the global meeting for discussion. It was perfect work for me. Having spent so much time with midwifery teachers all over the world, I had a good sense of the competence gaps. My skills as an academic made the search through the literature stimulating; I enjoyed it. I arrived in Geneva a couple of days before the meeting. The WHO staff had done all the planning and preparation. They ran over the agenda for the two days, and then let me loose.

If there is ever a time to heed my mother's advice to summon my mad McGrath, it is now. I am in the conference hall at the WHO. This time I am at the front, by myself, chairing a global consultation. Waves of terror sweep over me and I seriously consider that this time I might have pushed myself one step too far. There are nearly a hundred faces looking up at me. They are from all over the world and are all experts. They are from government health ministries, universities, professional associations and partner organisations. I *think* I am well enough prepared but am not entirely sure.

I smile at the participants, take a very deep breath and reassure myself that by now I do know (I hope) what I am talking about. 'Enjoy yourself, Joan,' I hear my mother say.

The first part of the morning session is for WHO and the International Confederation of Midwives to give their perspectives on midwifery teacher development. Then it is my turn. I present my work on the background research I did, and then describe the draft competencies I have developed. I use Paul's programme again to describe, using an outcomes approach, what a competent midwife teacher looks like. It is such a useful tool and I use it in most of my consultancies now.

Over the next two days, the participants break up into groups to discuss and comment on the draft competencies. I work my way around the groups, listening to the comments and answering any queries. It seems to be going well. I am relaxed now and am finally able to enjoy the discussions. The workshop ends with feedback from the groups and recommendations for change. There aren't many. I am gratified.

I return to New Zealand and go straight into a very heavy teaching workload at the university. My brain feels a little fried. I make time to do the amendments to the draft competencies and it gets sent back to the participants and around all interested parties globally. The feedback is daunting, but I make further adjustments, and draw up the final draft which goes to a core group in WHO for penultimate sign-off. The final part of the process is validation in country. This is done in Rwanda and Bahrain.

The document is finally published at the end of 2013, and the competencies are almost identical to the draft I had prepared a year earlier. I went on to see this guidance used in all my subsequent work. It was in every midwifery school I visited and in every organisation that was supporting the development and teaching of midwifery. One of my best jobs ever. I am very proud of it.

PART FOUR

TO THE EDGE

11

—

A space
for birth

It was pink. It was stunning. But not in a good way. It wasn't even so much what it was, but what it *represented* that was confronting. It gleamed at me: a humungous, pink, plastic-covered delivery bed. It had metal poles with pink Velcro straps to keep women's legs apart. The armrests also had pink Velcro straps. They could be rotated 360 degrees, like some medieval instrument of torture — only pink. It was high and hard, and it was in the middle of a health centre in remote, rural Laos.

At first, I could not believe what I was seeing — that momentary brain flip of split-second sense-making. Then I got it: that same feeling I'd had when I'd seen the dungeon prepared for the birthing women of Wellington 25 years earlier. Only this time, I also felt complicit.

The health centre manager, a shy young man, smiled wryly. 'It is just new, Dr Joan, but we can't use it. It's our women. They are too small. Even if they can get up, their legs do not reach the poles.'

'What do you think you might do with it?' I asked, my voice flat, trying to appear as non-reactive as possible.

There was a pause in our conversation. Both of us were speechless. Me, from shock. For his part, I suspected that he might have wanted to seem grateful, polite or compliant. He knew I had been sent here by the same agency that had been buying all this new equipment. It might well have been difficult for him to complain. And I thought he might not know what I was thinking, either.

What I wanted to say was, 'Well, you know, this bed is the perfect representation of the medicalisation, institutionalisation, commodification, colonisation and recolonisation, poverty, war and misogyny that are really at the core of the whole bloody problem in the first place.' But I didn't.

We exchanged glances, unsure of what the other was thinking or expecting. I rescued us both.

'Well, let's just carry on with having a look at the rest of the centre. What else would you like to show me?'

He was still hesitant, looking around to see where he might take me. Maybe he thought I should be directing him. Ket, the young Lao doctor who had been assigned to work alongside me, suggested that we might go and see the water supply.

—o—

Just getting to the health centre with the pink bed had been a challenge. It was in a remote part of the north, a three-hour drive from Luang Prabang, a small provincial town at the juncture of the Mekong and Nam Khan rivers. They were brown and slow; no brisk, braided New Zealand rivers here. At dawn we drove through the town, a Buddhist temple at every turn, past the morning vegetable market, past the line of orange-robed monks with their supplication bowls, receiving their daily food (and rows of tourists taking photos of them). We drove past fields of rice, still green and wet, through villages with children in crisp white shirts, hair in ponytails, walking hand-in-hand to school. Soul-soothing stuff for me. Then, the last hours — my romantic reverie interrupted — on potholed tracks and through uncertain fords, the car sometimes lurching through mud at an angle of 45 degrees. It was hard going. Thank goodness for the driver. He was slow but never hesitated, and looked like he had done this many times before. How the pink bed had got there was incomprehensible; how mothers needing help got out, even more so.

The health centre was small and bare, but well maintained. There was a front veranda to provide shade from the hot sun or heavy rain, and where patients waiting to be seen could gather. Lush trees surrounded it. The walls of the centre were covered in health posters, a little the worse for wear. Otherwise it was sparsely furnished and equipped. The midwife, a tiny woman (compared with me), was there to meet us along with her husband, who was the centre manager. Smiles, introductions and a nop (palms together with a bow) were exchanged.

Above: Arriving at a health centre in northern Laos after a long, slow, muddy trip.

Below: Ket, the Lao doctor working with me, and I chatting with (interviewing) the midwife from the health centre.

'Sabai dee,' I had learned the Lao greeting. It means 'It goes well'.

We made our way onto the veranda and settled around a small table. Bottled water was offered. We took the conversation slowly. I was getting good at just 'being' in these environments now. Pausing to take it all in, spending time getting to know the staff, smiling a lot. I especially loved being with the midwives. I was relaxed enough now to be shown around without giving too much direction, and experienced enough to be appreciative and encouraging of the work being done. I had really found my confidence in these settings. No checklists for me. Just some gentle probing. Ket helped with the translation.

We had spotted solar panels on the roof as we arrived, so we broke the ice by talking about those. We were told that they had been installed by a different aid agency as part of an immunisation programme. There were only enough of them to power the immunisation fridge, and the wiring had been made inaccessible. The effort and resources needed to set up solar power here must have been immense; not to have put in a few more panels to power the lights and cellphones for the centre seemed absurd. That's how parallel development programmes function; coordinating funding and supporting primary care in remote communities has always been fraught. But let's not go there. It's a long and tortuous story.

After we had finished looking through the centre and talking to the staff about what they thought they needed, it was time to start some storytelling. I've learnt that the best way to find out what is going on is to listen carefully to the stories that are told. We sat back on the veranda and the bottled water came out again. The day was hot and humid, so the water was very welcome. The midwife told us about a 14-year-old girl in the neighbouring village who had given birth at home the night before, with just her family for help. She had started to bleed heavily after the birth and her father had come to find the midwife for help. Later in the day, we visited her in her home. She was lying on a mat on the floor in a darkened, smoky room, breastfeeding her baby, with an IV drip still in. The young midwife checked her and the baby over, and removed the drip. They were all doing well. I attempted to ask some questions about how the labour and birth had gone, but they were too shy. It wasn't appropriate to pursue it.

But despite that, being there, with a midwife who had likely saved the life of this young woman, was one of those magic moments. It was exactly what the whole programme was about: life-saving stuff. I surmised that maybe pink beds might just have to appear every now and then as we all fumbled about trying to make a difference to women's lives.

The general view in global development policy is that births should happen in local health centres, not at home. I still found this a difficult policy to support, until I understood that the priority was to have skilled midwifery support at every birth. To push for birthing in the home was all very well in somewhere like New Zealand, where we have plenty of midwives. But Laos had only 100 midwives for six million people.

Whenever I have mentioned supporting homebirth in low-resource countries, it has been met with horror by the development agencies. I am pretty sure that there is a strong undercurrent of being against homebirth in any form, in any country. However, I was conflicted. The institutional birth spaces that have been created in low-income countries, by the colonisers, over the past couple of centuries are in my experience horrific. The hospitals I have visited in these countries have been intensely over-crowded and desperately under-resourced. The primary health spaces were underutilised but equally under-resourced. The maternity carers seem to have modelled their practice on authoritarian, uncaring medicalised birth — a colonised response I suppose. Every single birth space I saw, whether in a remote health centre or city hospital, had the delivery contraptions that I won't dignify by calling beds. I have often wanted to go into the waiting rooms and tell all the women that they would be better off at home. The ethics of trying to persuade birthing women to go to these dreadful institutions bother me. The ubiquitous pink bed shows that we, the development agencies and now the recolonisers, are far from doing it well.

We left the young woman with the new baby and returned to the centre. Eventually, we got to see the water supply. And it was just as impressive as the pink bed, but in a different way. The water was in a concrete tank a few minutes' walk from the centre. It was someone's job (probably a woman's) to carry the water to the metal drum sitting outside the birth room window.

'How do you wash your hands?' I asked, puzzled.

The midwife leant out the window and pointed to a plastic bucket floating in the water.

'She has to call someone to come and scoop the water up and pour it over her hands,' Ket translated.

The midwife and I visiting a young woman who had birthed at home and had
had a big bleed. We were checking that all was well and removing the IV.

So what was I doing here? At that time, in 2014, Laos was still the poorest country in Southeast Asia and had the worst outcomes for mothers and babies in the region. The United Nations Population Fund — UNFPA, the organisation I was funded by — was Laos' lead maternal and child health partner. Together with other NGO support the Laos Ministry of Health had developed a five-year plan to work towards having a midwife at every birth. Global funding had recently been earmarked for this to happen in all countries with high rates of maternal death, as part of the drive to meet the UN's Millennium Development Goals.

In Laos this global policy informed and supported the establishment of midwifery as a new profession, so all the hospitals, health centres and clinical schools needed to be updated. Policy changes were needed to enable midwives to be educated, regulated and deployed to the right place. It was a big job. Their planning had been broken up into measurable five-year chunks. Now their first five years were up, and it was time to see how successful they had been and to work out what to do next. That's where I came in.

My skill-set matched what was wanted, and I knew the staff member running the maternal and child health programme from my time in Cambodia. My work there, as in Afghanistan, Vietnam, Nepal and Kiribati, had been focused on midwifery education and how new midwives could be integrated into the community. I'd also done those two short stints at the World Health Organization in Geneva, again focusing on the role of midwifery and midwifery education.

By the time I arrived in Laos, my expertise had moved from hands-on clinical and teaching skills to providing policy and practice advice. It had been eye-opening to see how global organisations worked (and sometimes didn't), and to realise the implications of the MDGs. When the goals were agreed on at the UN, it was the first time ever that global organisations and the UN-affiliated countries had agreed to act collaboratively on trying to solve world problems. The goals came with agreed measurable indicators, collaborative planning, regular feedback and a lot of money. The World Bank, the International Monetary Fund and the Asian Development Bank all opened their purses. And here I was in Laos, putting all that global research, all those days and months of meetings, and some of those resources, into use. I felt like I was at the coal face of the best attempt that humans had so far made to look after each other. I knew I was at my best, too. Every cell in my body felt fully alive. I was riveted.

My job in Laos was to understand as much as possible about the context and what they had planned. I needed to get a feeling for the politics and the key players. There is always subtext, even if the people themselves can't articulate it. By now, I understood that the people I talked with did not know how much I didn't know. This was usually a lot. It was my job to fill in the gaps. The cliché 'hit the road running' was all too true.

My first few days in the capital, Vientiane, were spent planning the evaluation, which meant a couple of days around a conference table at the UNFPA office with members of the Ministry of Health and UNFPA staff. A lot of my development work was spent around tables talking. Not so riveting for the reader, but crucial to getting the work right. First, we had to finalise what I would be aiming to do. The scope of the contract was huge. They could have sent a team of 20 to do it, but they just had me and Ket. It was vital that I set boundaries — not just around what we could do but also what we couldn't. This is a basic rule of evaluation projects. It ensures that there are clear expectations of what the final product will contain. This is where the size and scope of a project are important. I sat down at the table with not a little anxiety and listened carefully to what they had planned so far.

We settled on a scope that I believed would allow me and Ket to do the job, although it was still enormous. I would limit my focus to midwives, not all health workers. Unfortunately, we also had to dispense with talking with the mothers, the consumers of the service — which went against my Kiwi midwife heart. We did try to put this into the evaluation plan, but realised that doing it properly would have used up too much of the two weeks of fieldwork available. I did manage to include in the plan that whenever we went out to the villages, we would take every opportunity we had to meet with new mothers.

The evaluation was to be undertaken in two districts of Laos: Luang Prabang in the north and Savannakhet in the south. In both areas we would spend time in the regional offices, the midwifery schools, the referral hospitals, and as many village health centres as we could get to. We would interview managers, teachers, students, doctors, midwives

236

and women. We would also do some observations of hospitals, schools and health centres. Then Ket and I would have to figure out what was working well and what needed more work. All this had to be done in two weeks. It was massive.

We were also heading into the monsoon season, which would make roads impassable and flights unpredictable. UNFPA had done a lot of the logistics work, however, and was well organised. Flights, accommodation, drivers and all participants had been alerted that we were on the way. People would accompany us at every point, preparing ahead so that minimal time was wasted. It was impressive, so I felt I needed to be impressive too. I worked late into the night before we left, planning and preparing. I could almost smell my brain burning.

The next morning, we flew to Luang Prabang. I felt excited.

For me, the birth space is always the most crucial part of an evaluation; the endpoint of all the planning and preparation. Everything should come together there. As I've already mentioned, in global development policy there has long been the strong belief that this birth space should be institutionalised. This means that women are expected to leave their homes in labour and travel, sometimes over terrible terrain and for great distances, to give birth in one of these birth spaces. Sometimes it will be a hospital, sometimes a small health centre. The community needs to trust that the women will be physically safe and well cared for. For this, kind and skilled midwives are needed. I almost never find a birth space like this in poor countries. It seems that if you want to see how well a country is doing, just look at how it supports its women to give birth.

So why should I have been surprised at the pink bed? Maybe I was horrified and disappointed rather than surprised.

—o—

Before heading down to Savannakhet, we had a day off in Luang Prabang. I was relieved that the first week of the project had gone well, and I was able to sleep easily for the first time. My body had lost its tension. No monsoon had arrived to shut us down, and the travelling and the meetings had happened as planned.

I opened the door to my veranda and stepped out. It was just wide enough for me to do my tai chi. The town was green and lush, and despite the passing motorbikes had a tranquillity I had not found in Southeast Asian towns before. The Mekong was just over there; I could have thrown a stone into it. But I still couldn't hear it. The finials on the temple rooves showed themselves above the palms and Bodhi trees. I planned to spend the afternoon exploring some of the 22 temples in the town, but for now I climbed back into bed to rest. My mind was relaxed enough now to read, and I disappeared into my copy of *The Vintner's Luck*. I stretched out my body and read till hunger reminded me that I had missed breakfast.

I dressed, then strolled along the main road, finding a café with perfect coffee and pastries. It was the middle of the day so the heat was sweltering, but it meant that the tourists had gone. I wandered from one perfect wat to another, sometimes lighting incense to pause, take in the beauty, and cool down. Whichever temple I entered, a large Buddha dominated, in one of the 49 positions he is said to have used. Each Buddha was adorned with silk, always a little differently. The inside of the wats featured dark, lacquered teak decorated with gold stencils. Every wat had fresh flowers, in all varieties. Some had pools coloured yellow by turmeric and frangipani. I had most of them to myself. The monks must have been resting in their quarters and the tourists in theirs.

—○—

Ket and I had proved to be a perfect match. I think the biggest challenge for him was that my interviews with the participants were very conversational, as opposed to working through a list of questions in order. My approach gets a much better story out of the interviewee but is almost impossible to do well when working in another language and culture. Almost all our interviews were in Lao, and Ket's translations for me were clear. When we went over the interviews later, he could see that all the planned questions (or most of them) had been answered. We gelled as a research duo, two brains working in tune with each other. By the end of our two weeks, Ket was doing most of the interviews with little need for me to prompt, and not much need even to translate. I could see his interviewing and research skills developing and realised that I wouldn't be needed in Laos again. Excellent!

The road followed the Mekong down to Savannakhet, and I'd swear we arrived before it did. Central Savannakhet was another old French

Chatting with the wonderful but very young student midwives in Savannakhet.

colonial town, but there were no tourists except the odd backpacker. The town was surprisingly busy, but not touristy. There was a bridge over the Mekong to Thailand, so it had developed as a centre of commerce. Before setting out to the villages I had to go over this bridge to get my visa renewed — just a little nerve-wracking, as always at border checkpoints. I had to walk over alone, as no one could be assured of either being allowed in or allowed back. Laos is a communist country, so control of the population, although not particularly obvious to Westerners, was clearly evident to the local people.

The next day, Ket and I visited the school first. After talking with the school's director, we went off to have a group chat with the teachers. As we passed the classrooms, I spotted six girls sitting outside under the veranda and hoped they might be the midwifery students. And they were. I asked Ket to see if they would be happy to talk with me and sent an apology to the teachers for being a little late. Our timetable would be disrupted, but I couldn't resist. Here they were, petite, in pink smocks over traditional sinh (calf-length skirts of folded silk). They giggled when we were introduced and were keen to talk.

The students were enthusiastic about their course. When I asked them if there was anything they found hard, they all shook their heads definitively. I was struck by how young they were, though my Western lens has often been wrong about age in Southeast Asian countries. But I was right this time. They were all around 17 years old. It was this group of new midwives that the Ministry of Health was planning to send directly out into remote villages the following year. They could already tell me where they were being deployed to, and seemed excited to be going there. I was worried. In my view, it should always be the most experienced midwives who work remotely. I felt that these young women needed to be mentored to practise in sites where others could support them. I was also unsure of the cultural impact of sending young and inexperienced women to work and live alone in remote health centres.

Ket seemed to feel the same as I did, and others that I interviewed from the NGOs were similarly concerned. I added this question to the items we needed to discuss with the Ministry when we returned to Vientiane. Eventually, one of the urgent recommendations in my report was that these young women should not be sent directly to remote and isolated work settings.

In the first few years of the new millennium, the Lao government had pledged to train 1500 new midwives by 2015. According to the data they gave me, it looked like they might achieve it. It was time to talk with the teachers to see how they thought the education of midwives was going. What I had learnt from evaluations in other countries was that there was a severe shortage of people able to teach midwifery to a standard that would prepare students to be competent. It was a bottleneck everywhere I had been, except in Afghanistan where JHPIEGO had understood the need for midwifery teachers who were skilled, and had built the development of a cadre of teachers into their plan. All other countries I visited had given the existing nursing teachers a little training in maternity care, and a curriculum, and had set them to teaching midwifery.

I had become more and more concerned, not only about the skills of those who were teaching midwifery but also about the extreme pressure they were being put under, teaching something they didn't understand and had limited experience with. We found things to be the same in Laos. The teachers in every group we spoke with were in various levels of distress. They felt overworked, under-resourced and ill-prepared. Most hadn't worked in the maternity context for many years — if ever. There had been a six-week training-of-trainers programme, but they had felt it insufficient. I found it all very distressing myself, and completely unsustainable.

On our second day in Savannakhet we headed out to Seponh, a village across the other side of the country. Halfway there the road started to rise, and we weaved our way slowly towards the border with Vietnam through deep, dense forest. We stopped at a suspension bridge that Ket said had been built by the Vietnamese to mark their friendship with Laos. We walked almost reverently over the bridge while Ket explained to me the close relationship Laos had with Vietnam during the American (Vietnam) War. Far below in the muddy brown water we could see two men in a silver canoe, moving their wares downriver.

'That canoe is made from the shells of unexploded bombs. You will see them used for all sorts of things in this area.'

I had read something of the history of Laos before I arrived. It remains to this day the most bombed country on the planet. During its war on Vietnam, the United States dropped the equivalent of a plane-load of bombs on Laos every eight minutes, 24 hours a day, for nine years. Eighty million of them lay unexploded in the landscape when the war ended.

In 2014, the year I was there, the US spent $12 million removing some of them. That year, they also spent $145 million on their new embassy. In total, fewer than a million bombs have been cleared. The Lao people are still being killed and maimed by that war.

We drove on, but soon Ket asked the driver to stop again. We had been driving alongside a 3-metre-wide strip of grass which was bordered on one side by a small cast-iron fence. There was a gate with a sign, wrapped in faded Buddhist prayer flags.

'This is the Ho Chi Minh Trail. Would you like to visit?'

The trail was how the communist North Vietnamese sent their supplies to the south during the war. Most of it went through Laos. The area had been thick with CIA agents, who were reported to have manipulated cultural differences to co-opt the locals into collaboration. The ground under my feet was muddy. Here I was, in yet another country existing in the aftermath of war. I felt out of my depth, understanding my own inability to grasp, in any way, the horrors of how it must have been. What was I doing while the war was raging here, in this mud? I had been a teenager living in the prosperity and peace of New Zealand, learning about life while wrapped up in love and privilege. But it was too hard here, on the actual trail, to make any link with my 18-year-old self. I walked a few steps, then paused, closed my eyes, and attempted some sort of respectful moment.

'Shall I take your picture, so you can show everyone at home?' Ket called to me.

—o—

The health centre we visited was on a small rise overlooking the village. We had moved into the land of the Mon-Khmer people, who make up 11 per cent of the Lao population. The Mon-Khmer grouping encompasses 33 different ethnicities and a variety of languages. Laos is the most ethnically diverse country in Southeast Asia, having over 80 ethnic groups. Yet it is also the most sparsely populated, giving rise to challenges in providing services, including health and education. These remote areas were where most mothers and babies were dying and where skilled midwives were needed. It was important for us to visit one of these areas to get some idea of the challenges there, and to see how new midwives might be able to work so remotely and so immersed in a different culture.

The clouds were low and mist was suspended in the trees, threatening rain at any minute. The village was noticeably poorer than many we'd seen, the houses less well constructed and the gardens untended. The health centre was bare and empty, so Ket called out to find someone. Tula, the nurse, was in her room behind a curtain at the back of the centre. She was a tiny woman, and not young. Her long hair was piled up in a bun on her head, but even this did not help her reach the height of my shoulders. She had been living and working here for the past five years, although her family were from the other side of the country. Tula was ethnically Lao Tai, the majority ethnic group in Laos. She had learnt enough of the local dialect to be able to communicate with the families.

We chatted to Tula about her work. She had been trained as a nurse and had done some maternity training. She was the only health practitioner for miles around. There were many ethnic 'hill people' in this area, and she would spend a few days every week travelling around the villages, sometimes on her motorbike if she had petrol, sometimes on foot. When she was away, there was no one in the centre. We talked about the births. Only about one woman a week birthed in the centre. Most mothers in the area stayed at home.

We strolled into the village and greeted the families, pausing occasionally to talk when we saw a young baby. Tula had to translate for Ket, who would then have had to translate for me, so I encouraged them to talk freely without me. I could catch up later. I was also getting good at picking things up without understanding the language. Tula was clearly welcome in the villagers' homes. They chatted and laughed as she asked after the children, some of whom were themselves carrying babies on their hips. We moved on, but not before taking photos of all the children, who had never seen anything as funny as each other's photos. It took a long time. The cheekiest of them would reach out and touch my hair, shrieking with delight. I longed to be able to sit down and have a natter with the grandmothers. I missed Mākarā, my first grandson. It had been hard to leave him. And as so often in these travels, I wished my kids could be along to share some of these experiences.

Tula took us to meet a young woman who had come down from the mountains to give birth in the health centre, but her brother had

Above: Popping in to visit with a local family who had recently given birth at the health centre with the midwife.

Below: The midwife, me and two new mothers.

forbidden it and he had delivered the baby in his house. The baby was now about three months old. The house looked unkempt. We followed the nurse up the rickety ladder. Ket and I waited at the door while Tula went over to talk to the young woman. The large room, which looked like the main internal room, was empty and bare except for a worn mat on the wooden floor. A little light shone dimly across the room. The young woman was seated in the middle of this room, cross-legged on the mat with her sleeping baby in her lap and a bottle of water beside her. It was as if she was unable to move. Her face seemed flat and expressionless. There was no obvious recognition of the midwife. The talk seemed serious, and Tula started to look at the baby, undressing him a little to look at his chest. Something looked wrong. She turned to us.

'This baby has been sick for three days and the family have left her here to go and work in the fields.'

She carried on asking questions of the woman.

'He stopped feeding two days ago and now she cannot wake him up. Come and have a look at him, please.'

I let Ket go in first. He was the doctor, after all. We neglected to take our shoes off. We realised that the baby was not asleep. He was unconscious, floppy and unresponsive. I felt dread. My mind did a split-second reach for 111, the ambulance, the well-equipped hospital. Nowhere here, of course. Ket seemed paralysed, too. We exchanged desperate glances. Ket had no medical equipment with him, so all he could do was feel the baby's pulse, look in his eyes and try to rouse him.

'I think this baby has nearly died, Joan.'

'What should we do? Can we take him back with us to the hospital?'

There was talk between Ket, Tula and the young woman. I watched horrified as the young woman replied to their questions in a passive monotone.

'Joan, she will not come to the health centre as her brother has forbidden her.'

'Will she come with us in the car to the hospital in Savannakhet?' I was frantically thinking of something we could do.

'No, she can't.'

'Why not?'

'If she comes, her brother will disown her. They never go to Savannakhet and they could not afford it.'

'What if we take the baby for her?' I had no idea how that would be managed.

'No, Joan. Even if he survives, he will be abandoned.'

'Oh God, Ket. Are we just going to leave him here to die?'

'I think we must, Joan.'

Ket and I walked slowly back to the car. Silent. The rain that had been threatening arrived, and the sky darkened even more. In the rear-vision mirror, I watched Tula walk slowly back to her lonely health centre. We had a very sombre ride to the city. The mist came down lower into the forest. I did not notice the winding road or the villages. The bridges and the rivers passed us by, unremarked.

Three days later, after completing our interviews and visits, we headed back to Vientiane. Ket and I had interviewed 96 people. I was exhausted, hoping for a day off. But there was no time to rest yet. I presumed, as in other countries I had worked in, that I would have a debriefing meeting with some of the UNFPA staff and the Ministry of Health before I flew home. These meetings had usually been relaxed and preliminary. But not this time. Unbeknown to me, the government had hired a hotel conference room and invited everyone. There would have been some political message in that, but these things often went over my head. They had made a huge poster for the conference room which said, in Lao script and in English:

Evaluation of the Midwifery Component of the SBA
Development Plan
Presentation of Preliminary Findings
12 September 2014 Lao Plaza Hotel, Vientiane Capital

The room was full. The Minister of Health came with four heads of department and some of their staff. All the directors of the development organisations were there: UNFPA, WHO, JHPIEGO, CARE, Save the Children. They had all brought some of their staff. We had a translator and headphones. Even a big lunch was provided. It was to be formal, and would take all morning.

I had half a day to bring all the findings together and make up a presentation. By this stage I was too dazed with tiredness to worry, so was relatively philosophical about what would happen. I had to trust my experience and my expertise and just get on with it. I thanked my lucky stars that Ket and I had deliberately discussed our findings at the end of every day together. As I had also done similar work in Vietnam, Nepal and Bangladesh, I was getting used to having little idea of what to expect, and to trust my instincts and my energy. I was also getting to the stage of trusting my expertise. That's a grand feeling.

I summoned my mother's mad McGrath, her knack of making a good show of things, and joined Ket with a smile and a more confident appearance than I was feeling. My presentation was short and clear. I spoke authoritatively about what we had found. Ket was great in backing me up in describing the issues and challenges.

Laos had been such a delight to visit and to work in. It was thrilling to see and hear about their commitment to developing midwifery as the cornerstone of maternal and infant health. What Ket and I found was that in the interest of building a midwifery workforce as fast as possible, they had neglected to build in quality. We recommended that they pause in increasing the number of students, and instead work on improving the quality of the education and the preparation of the work environment. The two most urgent things they needed to do were to ensure that the teachers were better prepared and resourced, and that new young midwives would not be sent alone to work straight away in remote rural health centres.

We found that the midwifery teachers were being poorly prepared and supported. They were stressed and distressed, knowing that they were not doing a good job. Laos needed to ensure that the vision they had was sustainable in the long term. The community needed to feel confident that if they were to use midwives to help with their birthing, these midwives would be skilled and kind. It was time for the authorities to pause and build in some quality measures, especially in midwifery education.

There was lots of discussion and questions, and by the time we had finished the room was energised and positive. They agreed with us. The following year, I heard that there had been a big push to prepare teachers better, mostly in neighbouring Thailand. The midwifery programmes had been reduced to one, and the new young midwives had gone to regional hospitals for their first year.

On the way to the airport the next day, I had lunch with Ket and his family. We had built a lovely friendship. For him, the experience was an important step in his career. He had recently returned from the Karolinska Institute in Sweden, where he had completed a master's degree in public health. He was keen to work in the evaluation area — a growing need in development, as accountability has become more central to project planning. He was good at it; I was sure now that I wouldn't be needed again. The perfect outcome!

I slept all the way home.

—◦—

Sitting around the dining table back in Wellington, reunited with Peter and the kids and with my baby grandson on my lap — who was the same age as that dying baby — I found it hard to express in any meaningful sense what my time in Laos had been like. I didn't have the words. I passed out the gifts of woven bags, and silk scarves from the market in Luang Prabang, and showed my photos. Then I showed them the silver chopsticks made from bomb casings.

12

—

Can you tell me where you are?

Two weeks before my sixty-first birthday, and a week after I returned from Laos, I had a stroke. It was a left, peduncular, cerebellar stroke, the kind that wipes out balance and proprioception rather than the kind that paralyses or affects speech and cognition. I had been up all night finishing the writing of a paper about my research on risk and uncertainty. The irony was not lost on me.

The paper had been accepted into a top international journal, and getting it in by the deadline was important academically. I was sitting on the back deck later the next day, having a wine and reflecting on how lucky I was. I was at the peak of my career, having just nailed a tough contract in Laos and submitted a good paper for publication. Suddenly, my vision doubled. My body's understanding of itself in space and time evaporated and I slid, fully conscious, to the ground.

Eventually, after the ambulance trip, ED, brain scans, heart scans, intensive monitoring, consciousness checks every two hours day and night — 'Can you tell me where you are?' — and after I stopped vomiting, I made it to rehab. This was not drug-and-alcohol rehab. No trendy youngsters getting over a cocaine habit. In this rehab, no one except me was under 80. Most of the time I was strangely calm, like an external observer of myself, unattached and non-reactive. I imagined that this might be what it felt like after ECT, or when meditators have achieved enlightenment: a brain wiped clear. Language flowed through me and I managed to capture some of it, suddenly writing poetry.

This equanimity was annihilated by the physios when they arrived at my bedside one morning with a walking frame. I cracked.

'No, no. Please. I can't do that. Take it away,' I pleaded.

'Joan, this is just to get you started. I promise, you won't need it for long.'

It turned out that the physios were my saviours. I wished for a time that I had done physio instead of midwifery. They were so much better than the nurses, who, without exception, were good at doing my vital signs but seemed uninterested in me. The nurses gave me a large towelling bib with my meal trays. One of them suggested that I join the other patients for lunch in the dayroom. I've worked in stroke wards. A room full of old, moaning, drooling, dribbling, half-sided diners was not my idea of a congenial dining space (I know this is ageist and ableist and shows my true colours). No way.

'I would rather gnaw my own arm off,' I thought to myself, in a very non-Buddhist fashion.

The physios pushed me harder and harder. I both hated them and loved them. They made me do things that terrified me. 'Joan, I won't let you fall. I'm going to throw this ball to either side of you and you need to move fast and try to catch it.' Another physio had a belt around my waist so she could stop me falling. I felt like a decrepit old woman. It was hard and frightening. There was a lot of swearing and deep breathing.

Once I had mastered the walking frame I walked round and round the ward, trying not to look at anyone. There was one old lady who had no teeth and was bent right over. She couldn't speak, but every time she saw me she would give me a wave. 'Please, God, no,' I thought, terrified. Was she my future?

After weeks of this, on the day I turned 61, I made it around the ward with no walker, no stick, just by myself. On the way back to my room, the old toothless woman spotted me. Her eyes lit up. They even watered a little. She gave me the biggest smile, shuffled towards me, and wrapped her arms around my middle. Her joy at my recovery left me feeling ashamed of myself. I can still see her eyes, and I try to bring her closer when I get self-important and am hopeless. The whole stroke thing was pretty humbling. I still didn't go and eat in the dayroom, though.

Tai chi from a wheelchair while in stroke rehab at Hutt Hospital.

Once home, I was into anything and everything to recover. 'The brain is plastic', was my mantra. Turns out it's harder than it sounds. Over the next few years I tried physiotherapy, osteopathy, hypnotherapy, Feldenkrais, acupuncture (65 needles from head to little toe, which I kept finding in my knickers for days), Pilates, tai chi, qigong, swimming, gyming, meditation, massage, walking and talking. It cost a fortune. I found a neuro-physiotherapist in Auckland and would fly up every three months to see her. She would push me so hard. 'You need to do everything faster, longer, harder, Joan. Neuroplasticity takes huge effort.' So, I put in huge effort. Then I would strain a knee or trip and fall over, and it felt like I had to start over again. I was a mess, although a high-functioning one, apart from the times I despaired and would take to my bed with a box of tissues and cry for a whole day. I lived a yo-yo of hope and distress, completely out of character and out of control.

The tiredness after a stroke was also disabling. For the first time ever, I experienced what it was like to 'hit the wall'. It was usually when we had a household of visitors or noisy grandchildren. I had no inner resources to push myself with. I would just suddenly stop, and realise that I had to escape. I did not even have the energy to tell anyone; I would just go upstairs and climb into bed. That was not the old me. I used to be the perfect hostess, and the matriarch, running the house and the kitchen with competence and assurance. It was my realm. Nothing was too much. Letting go of this role was excruciatingly painful; it makes me cry just to write about it. I felt like I was in my eighties, not my sixties, and I hated it.

I missed walking, just ordinary strolling along the beach or into the bush. Every step since that day has been a conscious one, taking effort and concentration. Our lovely and lively border collie missed it, too. Overall, I found that the process of becoming disabled was profound, long and dark. I still have moments of terrible rebellion, refusing to accept it. But then my left leg reminds me, refusing to join in with the plans for the day and making me look crippled or as if I had been into the wine. 'Breathe, Joan,' I tell myself. I got some strange stares at Pak'nSave, doing this. I was still self-conscious about it and was reticent to engage with anyone when out.

'Hey, Joan!' There was a roar from frozen veges and a trolley hurtling towards me pushed by a large woman with a huge afro. She abandoned her trolley at the milk and cream section and wrapped her arms around me in an all-encompassing embrace. 'Oh God. Who is this?' I thought. I must have delivered her baby. This was not an uncommon occurrence at Petone Pak'nSave.

'Oh, it's you, Lizzie.' Whew, I'd remembered. Here was my Christmas morning companion the first year after my marriage with Paul ended.

'You look just the same. How are you? How's that baby?' I had no idea of the name or gender of her baby. I'm not good at this.

'He's not a baby anymore. He's twenty-three.'

'Oh my God. That's too old. What's he doing?' I hoped he was okay. 'Is he okay?'

'Yeah. He's doing good. Just got a job at Mitre 10 and he moved in with his girlfriend on Saturday.'

'Ha! You're going to be a gran soon?'

'I hope not. How about you?'

'Seven granddaughters, three grandsons. One more on the way.'

'Cool. How are you anyway? Jeez, you look like shit. What happened to you?'

—o—

I needed to do something. It was time to go back to work.

It's hard to go backwards, especially when every bit of your being is trying to go forwards. Heading back to the university didn't really work. I could have stayed on, as my brain was just as functional as ever, but my heart wasn't in it. That stroke experience had shifted something in me. Life was different. So, I quit. I had a farewell celebration at work, which was disturbing. I think word had got around that I'd had a stroke and was retiring. I so hate any hint of 'poor Joan' — and I wasn't retiring, more re-tyring, I told myself.

Thankfully, I could carry on doing some PhD supervision and a little teaching, which enabled the sudden gap to be cushioned. Supervising three beautiful and very clever PhD students who I had pushed hard to undertake difficult projects really helped to ground me. Bec's PhD was an action research project to work with neonatal intensive care staff to increase the amount of skin-to-skin contact for premature babies; Tosin, a nurse-midwife from Nigeria, interviewed women who had experienced stillbirth to see where they got their social support from; and

Isaac, another African nurse-midwife, evaluated opt-out HIV testing in antenatal clinics in Ghana, focusing on whether the process was being undertaken ethically. They were all complex and challenging projects. These three may have thought I helped them, but I don't think any of them understood how much they helped me. I discovered that my brain was okay. Maybe it was even a little better.

The midwifery profession was also still struggling, and it was painful to watch. Since that first contractual change after the Maternity Benefits Tribunal in 1993, attempts by the College of Midwives to maintain the working conditions and pay of midwives in the community were to no avail. Pay experts had estimated that by 2015, midwives earned 60 per cent less than male-dominated professions requiring a similar level of qualifications, skills, expertise and responsibility. The Ministry of Health ignored their requests. We protested at Parliament, lobbied whoever we could, and even managed to get some support in the media. But nothing worked.

At issue was Section 88, which specified the contract for services that the midwives had with the Ministry of Health. It was a one-sided contract, leaving midwives powerless to force action. Midwifery care was unvalued; arguably, there was systemic institutional misogyny. By that stage, midwives had been forced to take bigger and bigger case-loads just to maintain their standard of living. At the same time, more and more requirements were placed on them. They had to do family violence assessments, extra screenings and tests, comply with complex reporting mechanisms, carry out reviews of practice, and mentor students and new graduates. Media scrutiny of their practice continued. Many left, especially new young midwives, shocked at their poor remuneration. One rural midwife related a call from her accountant: he had estimated that after expenses, her earnings were eight dollars an hour. So the College of Midwives took the ministry to court. Eventually, both parties agreed to go to mediation.

The first mediation meeting was on The Terrace in Wellington. I remember that day well. Wellington midwives marched up The Terrace, banners flying, calling out to support our College representatives going in to bat for us.

I didn't know what was going to fill the rest of the gap left by quitting the university, I just knew I needed to make space for something else. Maybe volunteering would be it. I tried being a Red Cross refugee support worker, which I loved, but I found that I really needed to be able to walk properly. I joined up with Good Bitches Baking, but baking cakes to give joy wasn't giving me any. I briefly took up ventriloquism, making strange diaphragmatic sounds in the shower every morning and looking for 'vents' on Trade Me. I thought about teaching reading in prisons, cuddling babies in the neonatal unit and helping at the Women's Refuge.

Over this time, two of my brothers died. My little brother Mark died at 57, of glioblastoma, the same brain cancer that had killed Dad. He was my childhood friend, my co-adventurer. He was so full of life and was starting to see the end of the Sydney corporate lawyer slog which he didn't enjoy. I hated watching his lovely brain rot away. I still miss him. My big brother Chris died of desperation and loneliness in his seventieth year; he was found hanging in the bathroom of a hostel in Ōamaru. Chris had a brilliant mind with a photographic memory and knew everything about everything. But his Asperger's, which was diagnosed in his later years, was significant enough to make social interactions almost impossible, and he became a hopeless alcoholic. Peter and I had become his main source of support, but it was eventually unsustainable. My guilt at his suicide was, and still is, profound. That is what suicide does to families, so they say. It pretty much tore us apart for quite a while.

So it was loss upon loss. In my characteristic tough 'daughter of Ro' style, the shell protecting me did its job — mostly. Cracking up was never really an option. Alongside of all this death, there was a cascade of major and minor disasters, like floods and rats. Oh, yes, and our dog got run over and killed. By then, I couldn't even process a dying pot plant. I mourned the loss of long walks by the sea, of planning adventurous overseas trips, of walking in the bush, of being able to look after my young grandchildren on my own. The mourning became bitter instead of sad, and I felt alone.

I projected all my grief and fear onto poor Peter, my resentment and criticism oozing all over him. He could do nothing right. I thought he didn't care about me and was selfish and lazy. His cooking was horrible. He was messy. He didn't understand my pain, and on and on and on. I was convinced of it; eventually Peter was, too. Not one to often tackle me head-on, he announced one night, 'I can't do this anymore, Joan. It is too horrible. I am a good, kind person and you are not going to make me otherwise.' And off he went into the night (but just for a couple of hours).

I was numb, and done. I had enough nous to know that too much grief, guilt and trauma would be a big part of what was happening. I made a loss list, found a good trauma therapist and headed back to the couch. It helped. I still feel those losses and I still grieve, but it doesn't incapacitate me. And Peter and I reconnected, which was important. But I still hadn't found out where I was. Was I functional or not? Did I still have any purpose, did I matter? Were there any adventures left for me — could I still grow, or had I 'had it'?

So, I went to North Korea.

—o—

On one level, I knew what I was doing was insane. I'd opened my emails one morning in March 2017, expecting the usual sort of thing. I worked through them methodically. Maybe one of my wayward students had at last produced some writing for me. Then I spotted it: 'Greetings from Pyongyang! You may not remember me, but . . .'

Sometimes one sees things that are so unexpected that there is a pause while the brain turns it over. Isn't that in North Korea? I thought. I had to Google it to be sure.

I went downstairs to tell Peter. He was in the kitchen, chopping carrots for a batch of pea and ham soup. In the background the latest podcast on Trump was playing.

'Peter, UNFPA want me in North Korea!' That got his attention. He turned to look at me with wide-eyed excitement.

'What do they want you to do?'

'It's from the Country Rep there. She was deputy in the Lao office when I worked there and wants me to come and do the same thing in North Korea. Who knew UNFPA had an office in North Korea?'

'Fantastic. Can I come too?' He is well known for his enthusiasm and has led me astray several times. 'It's perfect, Joan. It's right up your alley.'

'I know. But I've had a stroke and my hip has gone. I can't walk, in case you haven't noticed,' I commented, crestfallen, and with a touch of bitterness.

'There'll be wheelchairs there,' Peter said, relentlessly positive.

'I cannot do an international consultancy in a fucking wheelchair,' I replied, contemplating both the practicalities and the humiliation, but surprisingly, even to me, not really worrying about impending war.

'Why not?' Peter asked.

In light of the therapist's advice to be gentle and kind to myself, going to North Korea looked like a terrible idea. But the thought of turning it down was too sad to contemplate. It was highly likely that this would be my swansong, and a very impressive one. The risk of my *not* going was that I could turn into a wine-swilling, bitter blob of nothingness, with only death to look forward to. There was enough of the 'get out of your comfort zone' left in me, along with a healthy dose of 'fuck people pitying me', and just a little bit of ego polishing, to get me to go.

'Okay,' I said. 'Let's do it! But you'll have to come with me.'

13

There and back

Getting to North Korea was much more difficult than being there. The major issue for us was our family and friends, most of whom thought that Peter and I were out of our minds. My kids were the worst. The boys were impressed but very concerned, maybe even a bit horrified. Kena hated the idea. She also was freshly postpartum, having birthed her beautiful Kahurangi at home (my last ever birth, I think — I hope!), so was vulnerable. She begged me not to go and was furious when I did.

Everyone we told was happy to offer an opinion. It felt a bit like telling people you were planning a homebirth; some were horrified, others delighted. Peter and I had friends who had worked in the Ministry of Foreign Affairs, who told us to go as it was the chance of a lifetime. Others said it was too dangerous. My risk lens was fully engaged.

I was less sure about this job than any I had done before. Would I achieve anything? I didn't know. I just had to trust that the people there knew me, knew my work, and had invited me because of it. But I think in retrospect that my going on this trip was just for me. Others might have gone on a holiday in the sun in Fiji, or stayed at home with a pile of good books. Both did have their appeal, and I had plenty of time to consider them in the seven months between being invited and finally getting there.

During that time, a lot happened. It was 2017. In April, North Korea tested an intercontinental ballistic missile. The US, led by Trump, responded by moving its naval strike capacity into the Pacific and setting up a missile defence system in South Korea, alerting the world to the possibility of major conflict. Meanwhile, my disordered walking following the stroke had worn out my hip and in June, three months before we were to leave, I needed a hip replacement. Things were not looking positive. That same month, an American student, arrested and tortured in North Korea for trying to take a poster of Kim Jong-un out of the country, was released but later died without recovering from the coma he was in. Trump banned any American from entering North Korea; Kim Jong-un responded by proclaiming that North Korea's missiles could now hit any part of the world. Trump came back with a promise of 'fire and fury'. Meanwhile a new grandson for us, Maxime, was born in Seattle, now within reach of North Korea's missiles.

The escalation continued and we all watched. North Korea released plans to attack Guam; Trump replied that the US was 'locked and loaded'. North Korea fired more missiles, one over Japan. In early October, just as the United Nations held an emergency Security Council meeting and placed even more stringent sanctions on North Korea, I got confirmation that my contract there would begin on 20 October.

North Korea continued to test nuclear weapons and fire ballistic missiles. China got worried. Russia joined in, sidling up to China, and NATO joined in too. Apparently, China rang the US and Trump backed off a bit. However, North Korea then threatened to 'sink Japan' and fired even more missiles. In mid-September, Trump addressed the UN, calling Kim 'rocket man'. Kim then called Trump a 'mentally deranged dotard' and announced that the US had declared war. On 18 October, the day before Peter and I were due to leave for Pyongyang, the CIA announced that war with North Korea was more likely than ever.

Peter and I (and our family and friends) had watched these developments closely. It looked like there was a risk of getting killed in the crossfire of a nuclear war. However, Peter and I figured that if the world was going to explode, we would prefer to be under the first bomb that went off — likely to be in Pyongyang. I did recheck the security risk with UNFPA in North Korea several times, who stated, quite calmly, that they had no indication that there were any extra security concerns! I knew I was going there as a guest of the North Korean government and the UN, so I would have minders. I would not be going anywhere except for work and so was at low risk of getting myself into trouble. Peter was the worry here — his extreme extroversion was going to have to be curtailed. Peter needed to come with me just for the physical support, but did I trust him not to overextend himself? His natural exuberance and curiosity, usually a total asset in our lives, might not work in North Korea. He was the children's biggest worry too, as it turned out.

The real problem for me, though, was my leg. After my hip replacement I had presumed that with lots of exercise it would be better than it was before. It wasn't. My leg remained weak and non-functional no matter how hard I pushed it. I contacted an Australian midwife who had been to North Korea for three weeks the year before to get her advice. She had been training the teachers of midwives (or so she had thought).

'Of all the places in the world to go with a crook leg, North Korea is probably the best,' she said, surprisingly but reassuringly. 'You won't be allowed out of your hotel room, and when you do go out, they will take you everywhere by car. There will be no walking about. Do take Peter with you, because it's incredibly boring in the evenings. I went from my hotel room to the classroom and back again, for three weeks. But I tell you what, the place is so weird that it is hard to explain to anyone. Ring me when you get home, for a chat.'

She was also very helpful in giving me some sense of what I might be going to, although it did look like I would be getting to see more of the country than she had. 'I could never work out who I was teaching,' she told me. 'And there were clearly people in the room who were watching everything that was said, not really by me, I think, but by the people I was teaching. It was slightly sinister. But you'll be perfectly safe so long as Trump pulls his head in. Also, assume that your hotel room is bugged.'

The next problem was the logistics of getting flights, visas and travel insurance. We planned to visit our new grandson in Seattle on our way home, and we needed to go through Beijing to get our visas. We worried a little about how we would be received at the US border with newly used North Korean visas. Peter found some cheap flights on a Chinese airline that was new to New Zealand. Getting travel insurance, though, was nearly our downfall. Peter spent hours trying to find a company that would insure us for North Korea. Finally, someone suggested World Nomads, and we filled in the online application form. Later we suspected that they had just forgotten to take North Korea off their website; sure enough, they took it off the instant we applied, and did try to deny insurance to us. We were probably the last people on the planet that year, and for some time, to get travel insurance for North Korea.

The terms of reference for my contract were 'to provide technical assistance to the Ministry of Public Health for developing the National Midwifery Strategic Plan 2017–2021'. UNFPA was supporting North Korea to develop a midwifery profession, and it was in the second year of the programme. My job was to assess how they were progressing, and to identify their next steps. They had plans to take me to two regions of the country to visit midwifery schools and hospitals. Then I was to run a three-day workshop. It seemed that I was going to be doing strategic planning with, and for, the North Korean government.

By departure time I knew, deep down, that I should not be going. I wasn't fit enough, and I couldn't walk. I packed my bags in a daze; a far cry from how I had felt before leaving for my previous jobs. It took a long time, and Peter had to help me. I felt on the edge of panic, but it was now too late not to go. At Auckland Airport, I only had to walk the 300 metres from the bus to the check-in area, but I was already exhausted by getting this far. I could manage four or five steps before having to stop and rest. Every left step was an enormous effort and each one was harder and harder. I panicked and lost it, in public.

'Peter, Peter — I can't do this, I can't.' I was bent over my walking stick, looking pleadingly up at him.

'It will be okay. Here, take my arm and just take it slowly.'

Since my stroke, any emotional distress I experience, conscious or unconscious, stops my leg working properly — even to this day. By this stage of the journey, I was both consciously and unconsciously distressed, on top of being exhausted. Even Peter was beginning to worry. His jollying me along now had an edge of desperation and I could tell he was worried. I don't think he had ever seen me like this before.

'It's all right, Joan. Just stop for a minute and catch your breath and then have another go.'

'No, no. I really can't do this. What am I going to do? I can't do this. Please, help me, help me. Please. What can we do?' I looked around desperately and uselessly, trying to see something or someone that might help. All I could see were other travellers, striding past, staring.

I took Peter's arm and carried on in this vein until we got to the airline counter, where I recentred myself a little. I was wheelchaired to the plane.

I held myself together, summoning the last of my will, until I was in my seat, and then cried almost all the way to China. I regret now that I did not make the most of my first, and probably last, business-class travel. When it had become obvious that my leg was not getting strong fast enough, we had decided that I would travel business class even though it cost my entire consultancy fee. Peter was back in cattle class.

The concerned flight attendant tucked me up under a puffy duvet. I took a sleeping pill (I could have done with something stronger), and eventually slept for a couple of hours, trying desperately not to think about what was coming. I know that a lot can be learned from mistakes and failures, but this was going to be a cataclysmic one. Finally, I had pushed myself too far.

In Beijing, our hotel was in the block right next to the North Korean embassy. The puzzled taxi driver we had summoned to take us from the hotel to the embassy pointed out, in sign language, how close to us it was, but took us anyway.

The embassy took up the whole block. It seemed menacing, dark and deserted. The high fence was topped with barbed wire, and the armed guards in their oversized hats, which would look ridiculous if they weren't so sinister, were completely still. I wondered if they ever felt like making a run for it. Apparently, a few do. There was a small entrance into a cold, dark, enormous marble hall, empty but for one other woman. The lights were not turned on. At the reception desk a smiling man took our passports away, and returned a few tense minutes later with them now proudly supporting North Korean visas. By this stage, even Peter was anxious. He had stopped smiling and talking. We exchanged glances. Without a word, it was obvious that the implications of what was coming were uppermost in our minds.

There was no way to call a cab back to the hotel, so I would have to walk. As we rounded the first corner, me hobbling along a few steps at a time, there was a group of men chatting together by the side of the road. One of them was in a wheelchair, and when he spotted me and my hobbling, he hopped out and strode effortlessly towards me, signalling for me to use the chair. I was reluctant. Peter was keen. He pushed me back to the hotel while the man, clothed in a singlet and shorts, walked beside us. All we could do was smile at each other. It was hysterical. I remember feeling as if I had moved into another realm. Hysteria was better than terror, I hoped.

We flew from Beijing to Pyongyang on Air Koryo. The check-in induced more fear in us. By now, anxiety about my walking was replaced with anxiety about my life. Surprisingly, my walking improved a little. Our luggage was scanned, and Peter was called over as they had a problem with his bag. 'Oh no, Peter, what the hell did you put in it?' The problem was two spare AA batteries. Peter tried to smile and chat as if we were at an Air New Zealand counter, but nobody smiled back. The Korean passengers all seemed to have enormous numbers of purchases to return home with. There were television screens, a baby's cot, electronics of all descriptions. We presumed that the international sanctions, which were by now extensive, meant that they could only purchase such things when they were out of the country. I can't tell you what else they were taking home, as by now we were both, even Peter, keeping our heads down and trying to be as inconspicuous as possible. This was hard given that we were the only Europeans on the half-full plane.

The sombrely dressed and suited men and women found their seats on the plane, sending the occasional querulous look our way. I wondered who these people were — who could leave the country, and why were they returning? It was our first sight of the lapel badges of the two Kims, which most of the passengers were wearing. We were to see a lot of these.

Peter and I were mostly silent on the three-hour flight, holding hands occasionally, especially for landing.

'Welcome to Pyongyang.'

The plane taxied up to an enormous, gleaming modern airport and we dismounted into a large entrance hall. It had a two-to-one ratio of military to passengers. The soldiers were glaring at us. Both of us were struck by how very short and thin they all were, and how grim. Their faces were gaunt.

Getting through immigration was tense. We had to unpack our bags and show them everything. And then they separated Peter and me (the worst moment of our whole trip) while they flicked through every book and looked in every small bag we had. They made Peter turn on every piece of electronic equipment, and they looked at the films we had

Outside the United Nations Population Fund office in Pyongyang, North Korea, with Ji Ah, our translator, Dr Chang, our minder from the Ministry of Public Health, and Mr Kim, our driver.

brought in to watch, and everything on the external hard drive we had. There was not a word spoken to us.

In reflecting on this later, we surmised that this behaviour was probably an exercise in intimidation. There was no way they could understand anything that they saw. It was all just too speedy. But at the time, we were suitably impressed. It was impossible to know what anybody was feeling, as all the usual cues we might pick up were missing. It felt surreal, as did most of the rest of our stay.

—o—

We were met at the airport by our minders. Ji Ah was a fourth-year medical student with perfect English and a warm welcoming smile that instantly released a lot of our tension. She was to be our interpreter and guide. She introduced us to Dr Chang, an older woman who was a director for public health; she had no English and remained shyly inexpressive for our whole visit. I assumed that her role was to represent the ministry and maybe to keep an eye on Ji Ah. Mr Kim was our van driver. These three were to be our constant companions for the next two weeks. Ji Ah and Dr Chang even stayed in the hotel with us.

Driving from the airport into Pyongyang was eye-opening. It had just rained, which it shouldn't have done so early, Ji Ah told us, because the rice had not been harvested. The fields on either side of the road were damp and desolate. A wide concrete road led to the city and there was not another vehicle in sight. We passed a small, bedraggled battalion of soldiers marching, shuffling really, by the side of the road. Their uniforms were poorly fitting and tatty and looked like they were out of World War II. Some had hats, but most didn't. The men were tiny, with hollowed-out faces. Their heads were all bent down, and their faces looked strained with despair and exhaustion. The army had all been called out to harvest as much rice as possible before it rotted. We sped on.

Pyongyang emerged out of the fields. It is a huge, spacious city, but it was hard to decide whether it was a hallucination or an oasis. There were wide, tree-lined boulevards with multi-storey apartment blocks. It was pristine. The whole city was painted light green or pink, with the occasional bit of blue. The colours were all the same shade, as if there had been a huge bulk buy. Ji Ah pointed out gymnasiums, skating rinks, concert halls, all of which would be totally in place in a rich Western city. We saw an excess of memorials, one for the million Chinese soldiers who had died in the Korean War, and a large number of Kim statues. Ji Ah also told us that the city had been completely flattened by the Americans during the war of the 1950s.

But it seemed like a ghost town. There were hardly any cars, and most people we saw were in sombre lines waiting at bus stops. It was such a contrast to the intensity of every Asian city I had been to before.

Our hotel looked like any three-star hotel. There were shiny marble halls and wide spaces, but very few people. The staff noticed my walking stick and offered to find a room closer to the dining room. They were very kind and concerned about me for my entire stay. We had to pay up front and in Euros. No US dollars in this country. And we were not allowed to have any won, the currency of the DPRK (Democratic People's Republic of Korea, as we were to know it from then on). Our room had a little sitting room and a desk which would come in very handy. But all the windows had been painted over so there was no view.

The dining room was also poorly populated. Over the two weeks of our stay, Peter and I worked our way through the sparse menu. There was plenty of kimchi for those who liked it. Propaganda blared from the screens in the dining room (and wherever else we were), alternating between missiles, marching, Kim's speeches and chubby little children in fields of flowers. Sometimes after a full day of workshops or visits I would be exhausted, and Peter would bring my meal to our room. The kitchen and waiting staff were reticent and worried about this, but Peter's persuasiveness won them over. Doing something that was not allowed seemed to require a flexibility that was unusual. They would become very worried if we kept a spoon or plate in our room. Every evening and morning there was loud propaganda blaring out over the city. It reminded me of the Muslim call to prayer, which I had loved in Afghanistan and Bangladesh. But this felt sinister.

The first morning I had a briefing at the UNFPA office, meeting first with the director. Then we were joined by the heads of the WHO (a doctor from Nepal), UNICEF (a doctor from Uzbekistan) and FAO (a nutritionist from Uganda). I had never had a briefing at this level before, but it was the DPRK, after all. Each office had only two or three expat staff. They have very short stints in this country and long periods of leave. It occurred

266

Outside the Women's Hospital in Pyongyang, after a tour of the hospital.
It was one of the weirdest, most surreal experiences of my life.

to me that there would be very little institutional memory, and it did seem like it. The data they had provided me on maternal and neonatal outcomes was, they warned me, unverifiable. I had assumed that this would be the case. In reading their briefing documents before I arrived, I had noticed that over 98 per cent of births were attended by a skilled birth attendant and maternal mortality was 23 per 100,000. If this had been accurate, there would be no need for me to be there.

Kamala, the country rep, explained things to me: 'The whole time I have been here, I have never seen anything real. Everything is staged for us. It would be great if you could try and help, as we have no idea what is happening out there. We are not allowed access to any part of the country without permission, and we have to apply a month ahead.'

'But we do know that there is severe malnutrition, especially among the women and children,' the FAO man added. 'We would like you to put a good amount of information on nutrition into the curriculum if you are reviewing that.' They spent some time chatting among themselves, mostly about who was still 'in country' and who was heading out soon. It seemed that they didn't get much time together. I was aware that the room might have been bugged, and wondered how they ever managed to have meaningful discussions. In the garden, as it turned out.

—◦—

The first visit, later that day, was to the university, where we were taken to the office and shown the midwifery curriculum and various other documents. There were no student assignments to see, and no detailed teaching plans. I was not able to see a classroom, as they were 'busy with other students'. The library was locked and the person with the key was away. I couldn't see any midwifery students or teachers, as they were all 'working at the hospital'. I asked to see the skills lab, the first and only time, I think, that I might have caught them unprepared. They showed me a room that was clearly not a skills lab. There was no way I was going to comment. I smiled and thanked them for the visit.

When we arrived at the hospital, there was an entourage of 10 people to accompany me. It was clear from the outset that I was not going to get to explore. They had a wheelchair for me, and we all had to don white coats and paper shoe-covers. The first place we went was called the visitors' area. There was one telephone booth for each of the six floors. Anyone wanting to talk to a patient would have to ring the ward from the booth and ask for the patient to come to the phone. At this point, we were the only people to be seen anywhere; there were no staff or visitors apparent in a hospital which, according to their data, was having hundreds of births a day.

'Where are all the visitors?' I asked.

'They do not come at this time of day.'

I was suspicious. Any hospital I have visited, anywhere in the world, which has had anywhere near that many births has always been heaving with people, inside and out, including staff and visitors.

We went to the next room and looked through a glass panel at rows of cots and incubators, all of which seemed to contain large, podgy, sleeping babies. There were no staff in the room and all the babies were asleep. Apparently, this was the whole country's population of twins and triplets. It seemed bizarre and sinister. (When we got to Seattle a month later to be with the boys for Christmas, Tim looked this up online. The website stated that Korean culture places a special spiritual value on twins and triplets. They are said to portend great power. It also said that the decision to separate them from their parents is part of Kim Jong-un's rulings and is seen by outsiders as part of his need for ultimate control. There is some thought that he feels threatened by them and that they have an uncertain future. When I went to look at the website a couple of years later, there was no sign of it.)

'Where are their mothers?' I asked.

'They are all back home in the villages. We keep the babies here until they are four kilograms. Then the mothers come and get them.' It didn't seem right to me.

Our entourage proceeded through the rest of the hospital, along vast, empty, dimly lit marble corridors, with occasional floor-to-ceiling doors on either side. The noise of the footsteps and my wheelchair wheels on the shiny marble floors reverberated along the walls. It was the sound that empty makes. I wondered what the delivery unit and the postnatal wards could possibly be like, or, more likely, how they would construct them to be. We paused at one of the floor-to-ceiling doors, and it was opened slowly to reveal a small room with two beds. Each bed had a woman in it, both sitting in identical positions holding babies wrapped in identical blankets. Both smiled at me with their faces, not their eyes. There were no cribs, no personal possessions, no handbasin, no toilet. It was so obviously a set-up.

'You must have a lot more mothers than this. Where are they all?' I asked, very politely.

'We have many wards. They are spread throughout the hospital.'

According to my calculations, if they were having hundreds of births a day and all the mothers stayed for five days, as I had been told, they should have over a thousand postnatal beds.

'Where are the student midwives working? I am very keen to meet them.'

'You will see them later.'

They always had an answer.

The same process was followed at the delivery unit. Another door, behind which was a large, windowless room. It was completely empty but for a high, narrow bed in which a woman and a baby lay covered by a colourful blanket. A person beside her in a white coat looked at us and smiled, again not with the eyes. 'Here is a new mother having skin-to-skin contact with her baby.' Then the same question from me, and the same answer from my companion: 'The births are spread out right through the hospital.' There was no way this could have been a delivery room.

'I would very much like to see more of your birth rooms, especially if there are any student midwives there,' I said.

'Yes, of course. If we get time.'

The rest of the visit followed in a similar vein. We were shown rooms packed with the latest scanners and monitors, but no patients or staff members anywhere — until we passed a side corridor where there were half a dozen women who, we were told, were waiting for mammograms. As we were shown around, I asked repeatedly, but politely, where the student midwives were, as I had been told in the university that they were all in the hospital. Eventually, at the end of the visit, they said, 'Oh, I am sorry, but they have all gone home for the day.'

They were very good at this charade. And there was no way I was going to push back, not out of fear for my own safety, but out of fear for the safety of anyone who might let anything slip in front of me. Their livelihoods, their homes, their families — and their lives — could be in danger. I was very aware of the minders in the group.

As we finished the visit and reached the door of the hospital on our way out, we started to say our thanks and farewells — politely, always politely.

'Oh, wait!' said Peter, getting his camera out. 'Let's group together and have our photo taken in front of the boys.' 'The boys' he was referring to were the framed photos of Kim Jong-un and his father Kim Jong-il. From the back of the group, a startled and very worried man rushed at Peter, arms waving.

'No, no. You cannot do that!'

'Sorry, sorry. Very sorry.' Peter, chagrined and a little scared, put his cellphone back in his pocket. We subsequently discovered that images of the two Kims are sacred. No one is permitted to take pictures with photos of them in the background, and they must never be partly photographed. Framed pictures of them must also be in every home and public place. There are complex and detailed rules about how and where they are to be displayed. Any deviation of the rules results in severe punishment. At any time, officials can call to check. It was folding the image of Kim Jong-un in his luggage, rather than the stealing of it, which was the primary insult that led to the death of the American visiting student earlier that year.

Such is the level of fear and control in this country. It is extreme. Everyone has their work and accommodation allocated. There is no private enterprise of any kind, or so we were told. Everyone is watched closely, and the slightest deviation means, at best, the loss of home and work. At worst, it means being dispatched to an internment or re-education prison camp.

We did not share the camera incident with the family till we got home.

Then it was the weekend. We did not leave the hotel. I worked, we went to meals, we played cards. Peter was knitting a jersey for Maxime, and he wanted to get it finished before we arrived in Seattle on our way home. The staff who cleaned our rooms were delighted to see him knitting. Peter seized the opportunity to 'chat' with them. It was to be our only unmanaged contact with anyone in the country during our whole visit. There was a lot of smiling and gesticulating and showing of photos. Every day they watched the progress of the jersey with delight, especially on the last day when it was completed. It was the highlight of Peter's trip.

Peter's job on our adventure was twofold. The first part was to take care of all my physical needs and make sure I got enough rest. He was to organise everything, which wasn't difficult as everything was already organised. His other job was as scribe at all my meetings and during the workshop. There was no way I was going to be able to tape-record anything, so it was invaluable to have someone taking notes and taking notice. His experience and his perspectives were very helpful, except during the first hour or so of the workshop when he whispered to me 'This isn't going to work, Joan.'

We had a huge fight later about that.

Peter was also in charge of sending emails home, being careful to be reassuring for the family and aware that they could be read by the authorities. On our daily visits to the UNFPA office, he would send the emails to Matthew via one of the UNFPA expat staff, as we had no internet access at all. Matt's job was to send them on to the family. He only made one slip-up, an offhand comment in an email: 'Stenly gave us the rules for photos, which we may not have fully complied with!' It caused a major attack of terror among the family back home and in Seattle. Kena completely flipped. 'DO NOT SEND ON ANY MORE OF THOSE FUCKING EMAILS,' she shouted at her brother across the Pacific Ocean. Peter's sisters both sent discrete emails of caution. We were told all this later. Emails, texts and online chats had buzzed around and around. Everybody fretted: 'What do they think they are doing?'

I later rebuked Peter. 'What did you think you were doing?'

Peter is an off-the-scale extrovert, while I am an introvert. In previous trips I had relished having a little time without him. I could engage at my level. It was good for me to have time alone, and it was very good for our relationship. This was the first time he would see me 'in action', and the first time I would have to share my time with him. I noticed it as another loss for me, and filed it away. I knew I needed his help. He is, though, the best travelling companion anyone could have. He is relentlessly positive, curious, engaging and flexible. It was, in the end, good to be able to share such an inexplicable experience with him. And he was mostly well behaved.

—o—

Monday was to be our day out in the field, finding out (or trying to) what was going on. I had a little sliver of hope that outside of Pyongyang I might be able to get a better look at things as they really were. We headed out in the van about an hour north, to the city of Pyongsong. We met with two of the teachers and I discussed the curriculum they were using. This felt like a very different sort of meeting. The director of the school, a woman who had been teaching there for over 15 years, seemed confident and relaxed with me, and quite ready to discuss the shortcomings of the curriculum and what she felt was needed. She asked me to sign the visitors' book, and proudly showed me the signature of President Carter, who had visited North Korea on a peace mission in 1994 and had remained active in a food programme ever since. Apparently, he had offered to help broker peace earlier in the year when Trump was losing it. What a contrast!

However, Carter's connection with this particular school made me suspicious that it was one of those places where visitors were taken to show how well things were going. Indeed, my suspicions were correct (I think). I was taken to watch the student midwives having a lesson. There were about 30 young women all dressed exactly alike, with identical haircuts. They were all sitting on the edge of their chairs, hands in laps, identical books open at identical pages with identical pencils on the page. Identical bags were placed in identical positions on the floor. Their faces were blank, eyes fixed to the front where the teacher was giving a lecture using a computer (with a photo of an MRI machine). Then I went to the skills lab, where another group of very young students in white uniforms and caps were practising palpating an abdomen using instructions from a manual. It looked to me like it was the first time some of them had done it, and it seemed contrived. Every meeting we had everywhere we went, and every question we asked, was in the presence of a representative of the Provincial People's Committee.

In the afternoon we headed south, about 50 kilometres north of the demilitarised zone, to visit a provincial hospital. We did not see another vehicle the whole time, but passed huge fields of rice and vegetables. There were no trees anywhere, and there seemed to be no towns. We drove fast on a straight, wide concrete road. Ji Ah told us that the road had been built in two weeks and that everybody in the country had been recruited to help. There were no curves on the road but a lot of bumps, and by the time we got to the hospital I was feeling very nauseous. We were again taken through abandoned corridors and into a room which was to be, as it turned out, the only room we would see. There was a group of five young women in uniform who, we were told, were the students. There was a single bed containing a woman holding a silent baby.

'I'm going to be sick,' I told Peter. He was really going to be earning his

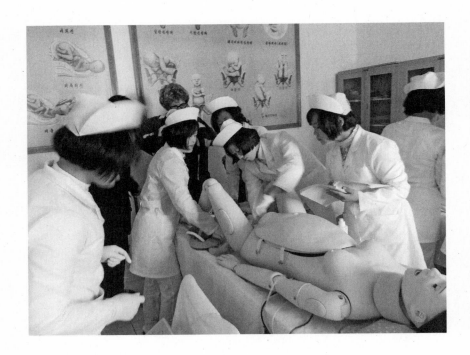

Student midwives in the skills laboratory at the Pyongsong nursing school demonstrating how to deliver a baby. It seemed completely staged and the students (or actors) seemed terrified.

keep now. It caused a huge stir. Anxious conversations followed. They seemed not to know what to do. 'It's a hospital. They must have somewhere for you to be sick!' Peter commented, slightly panicky. But apparently not. Eventually I was taken to the next room. There was a shower box there and they found a very small plastic bag. I did some very serious breathing, and thankfully kept my stomach contents in. I got them to take me back. I said to Peter, 'You'll have to ask the questions. I'm trying to keep everything down.'

'What?' he replied. He was clearly stunned, but proceeded valiantly to ask them about their training and then ask the woman with the baby about her birth. I could see he was valiantly trying to remember some of the questions I had asked at the Pyongyang hospital.

'Where do you do your training?' he asked a student. She looked terrified, and glanced hesitatingly at the two men on the other side of the room. They nodded, translated, and she replied quietly and with her head down. All the actors in this room, as they surely were, looked terrified to me. The woman in the bed holding the baby glanced anxiously at me, and replied in a monotone to Peter when he asked 'Is your baby a boy or a girl?' Peter's questions carried on valiantly in this vein. It didn't matter. By that stage we both knew we were in a charade. We only needed to spend enough time there to enable the actors to escape safely. We had no idea how dangerous for any of them this interaction could have been, but there was no point in pushing it anywhere. We smiled, we thanked and we left.

Driving back to Pyongyang a couple of hours later, my stomach having settled in the comfy UNFPA four-wheel-drive, we laughed and laughed.

'You didn't do a half bad job, but that was so funny,' I said.

'I can't believe you got me to do that. I had no idea what I was doing.'

We did reflect, of course, on how dangerous it could have been for the participants — and possibly for ourselves — if I had insisted on seeing the real thing. I felt like saying to them 'Come on, guys. This is all an act. I know you're hiding what is really happening from me.' Unsurprisingly, I never did.

—o—

Then there were three days of workshop for me to coordinate. Having no idea what any of the issues might really be made planning almost impossible. The only thing I could do was draw on my previous evaluations of what needed doing in any country to make a healthy midwifery workforce and go from there. The field visits had not reassured me that the workshop participants would be allowed to talk freely.

I was tense and worried the first morning. This is not an abnormal response for me, as even taking a workshop with my students in New Zealand causes me some tension. What was I going to do with three whole days? On one level I know that a little anxiety is good — it keeps my alert levels up and I perform better. On another level I know that there will be one time that finally sorts me out and I might fail big-time.

The workshop was held in the ballroom of the Diplomatic Club, and it was as grand as that sounds. There were six circular tables covered in white tablecloths, with bottled water and individually packaged mints. There were two screens and data-show presentation equipment, and several whiteboards. So far so good.

I introduced myself and asked for a round of introductions, all through a translator. There were about 40 participants, all unsurprisingly sitting with their peers. Hospital doctors, professors and teachers from the university, representatives of UN organisations, a group of nurses who were running maternity units or teaching, and last (but not least) a group from the Ministry of Health. This group included the equivalent of our deputy director-general of health and five of her staff. I was told that many more wanted to attend than were allowed. I understood that this gathering was important, and possibly unusual.

I decided not to mix the groups up, and I was to be very pleased I hadn't. I divided the three days into three main areas of interest. On the first day we talked about midwifery practice; on the second, midwifery education; and on the third day I planned to look at policy. I got the strong message from the participants that Kim Jong-un had demanded that maternity services in DPRK reach 'global standards' and that this workshop was to decide how to do this.

Peter set himself up with his computer and started to take notes. My fears about having reticent participants who were unable to speak freely were, thankfully, unfounded. The levels of engagement, enthusiasm and debate were amazingly high. It took Peter and me totally by surprise. I allowed plenty of time for the groups to talk among themselves, thinking that the table with the government people might need to be kept separate.

From the first group discussion onwards, I could tell that everyone was engaged with the issue. There was lots of talking and even laughter. They fed back enthusiastically in two languages, each group with a PowerPoint presentation. This was surely not an unfamiliar forum for them. 'It's going to work,' I thought, and relaxed into the day.

Our assumption that people who live in such a totalitarian regime could never have a voice or an opinion was unfounded, at least in this setting. It was so much more complicated than that. We did need to remember, though, that we were among the elite, who were privileged — and would remain so, provided that they did not question the regime's ultimate authority. We were also very aware that we had no contact with the majority of the North Korean people.

I managed the workshops with enough energy to keep on top of what was happening and even enjoyed them. My walking was good enough to cope, albeit with a stick. There were some highlights. One of the participants had worked for several years in London for the Family Planning Association with New Zealand's Gill Greer, and had returned to the DPRK to work among his people. He was a great scribe and was very funny, taking over the management of the group for a while. There was great consensus-making, and such goodwill among the participants. The only exception to this was when the time came to decide what policy changes needed to be made. The ministry group, headed up by the director, announced that they had decided on what policy changes were needed and no discussion was required.

That makes sense, I thought.

Our third day of deliberations ended earlier than planned and finished with a group photo, followed by our third delicious lunch — every type of Korean food we could wish for, and as much Coca-Cola and Sprite as we could drink. In the restaurant there was karaoke playing on the screen in the background. Peter spotted it and decided it would be fun to have a go. He sang 'Moon River'. The diners were all overexcited. I still can't explain what I felt. It was so extraordinary to be in North Korea, during a nuclear crisis, post-stroke, unable to walk properly, having led a workshop for the government, and to be sitting here drinking Coke and listening to Peter sing karaoke.

Peter and I had a busy weekend after that. I was keen to get the report of my work to UNFPA and the strategic plan completed for the government before we left. We were heading straight from North Korea to Seattle, and I didn't want to have to work there. We were to have Thanksgiving with Matt and his wife, Juls, our son Tim and new grandson Maxime. Matt was working for Microsoft, Juls for Google, and Tim had a postdoctoral fellowship at the US National Laboratory in Washington State.

We worked hard, although we did have time on Saturday for a little bit of tourism. Ji Ah and Dr Chang took us to the world-famous Pyongyang Circus acrobatic performance and then to SeaWorld. We felt like we had gone back to the 1960s. The acrobats' costumes were of that era, and they tumbled around and caught each other with skill but some predictability. At SeaWorld, the dolphins jumped through hoops and the seals were wearing bow ties. We cringed. What was not familiar, though, were the videos of rockets on huge screens in the background, the deafening music, the strident yet passionate announcements of the compères and the robot-like standing applause of the audience. We found it both disconcerting and fascinating. We had a drive around the city to see some of the sites, mainly memorials to various Kims and to wars. At a tourist shop (there was only us there), we bought some mementos and gifts to take home. During the drive, Peter asked 'Where does Kim Jong-un live?' Ji Ah and Dr Chang seemed too shocked at the question to answer. We never did find out.

On Monday I had my feedback meeting with UNFPA. Kamala, the country rep, suggested we take a walk around the garden, which I discovered was code for needing to get away from possible listening devices and ears. The North Korean government provides all the administrative staff for the UN and rotates them regularly and without warning. It is assumed that they give regular feedback to the government. The expat staff also assume that the office is bugged, as we did for our hotel.

I was more relaxed now that the work was almost over and was able to make some space in my brain to appreciate my surroundings more closely. We walked slowly, me with my walking stick, beside the high wall around the edge of the dry, dusty garden. It was autumn, a good time to have come to North Korea, as the intense summer heat had gone and could only be seen in the dry, cracked garden beds. The scrawny trees were beginning to drop what leaves they had managed to grow, and the shrubs were struggling. They did not look ready for snow.

'How did it go, Joan?'

'The workshop was excellent, and I am very pleased with the plan we came up with. Everybody participated except when it came to talking about policy. The ministry staff wouldn't let the whole group provide input into that bit.'

Kamala laughed. 'Nice try, Joan.'

'The next problem, of course, is how they operationalise the plan. We talked about this with the group on the last day. It was pretty much the only time they were silent. Normally I would try to at least develop a framework for implementation of a strategic plan, to help them get started. But I assume that, given the political context, the ministry might have a go at doing that. I am not sure how closely the "Dear Leader" monitors all this work.'

'We don't really know either,' Kamala replied. 'But you are right that any action that comes out of this plan will not be worked out collectively. By the way, my staff who attended were very impressed with the workshop. None of them had ever seen discussion at that level in this country before.'

I didn't realise it was that unusual. I was surprised at how engaged and enthusiastic they were. It's funny, the assumptions we make about people.

When I had been planning the workshop back in New Zealand, I had decided to structure it so that it would be as participatory as possible, not knowing if this would work. It had worked everywhere else I had done it. It did work, actually — thank God, as I didn't have a plan B.

'You know they'll need more funding from you to put that plan into action, so then you might at least be able to see what they are thinking. Or possibly not?' I asked.

'Probably not,' she replied. 'How did it go out in the field? Did you see anything real?'

I proceeded to describe my visits to the schools and hospitals.

'The only thing that was not staged was one moment at Pyongyang University. I didn't see any students there, as I was told they were in the hospital that day. But I asked to see the skills laboratory, which seemed to take them a little by surprise. They took me to a room where there were some books and a blood pressure machine in a locked cupboard. There was no way this was a skills laboratory. Other than that, I would say that everything else I saw had been perfectly staged. It was very impressive. I have never seen anything remotely like it.'

Handing a USB stick with the completed Midwifery Strategic Plan to the North Korean Director-General of Health.

'Remember, Joan, the people in this country have perfected the art of staging. Their very lives depend on it. It's a shame you didn't arrive a few days earlier to see their parade in the square. There is no other spectacle like it anywhere on this planet.'

We walked on for a few minutes in silence.

'Joan, do you think there really is a midwifery programme? We are providing all the funding for it. As yet, we have had no concrete evidence that one exists.'

I paused to consider my response.

'Well, I didn't see anything that convinced me there was one. There is a curriculum and there is paperwork, but I didn't see any student midwives in practice or in a setting that was not very highly staged.'

The next day, I presented the strategic plan to the government. We sat around the shiny hardwood table in high-backed chairs. It was very formal. Interactions between the government and the international agencies do not happen often in the DPRK. Around the table were the director of the Ministry of Health and her secretary, two university medical professors, the chief medical officer from the base hospital, the country representative of UNFPA and her maternal health portfolio manager, along with his WHO counterpart. And Peter, of course, although he had promised to stay silent.

I was all smiles. I handed my USB stick to the technician to open my PowerPoint presentation and began to explain the structure of the strategic plan and how the workshop had developed it. I had decided to bring up the need to operationalise the plan and explained that consultants usually do not know the intricacies of the system or the resources available to do this, but I would be very happy to provide advice about how they planned to do it once everybody had been able to look at the plan. I thought that this was very unlikely to happen. It was a shame. I had so loved working in Laos and being able to guide the plan into action, and I would have loved to be part of that process here, too. I wondered then whether I would ever hear anything back from them.

I didn't.

Leaving the country would be as stressful as getting in, we thought. We were anxious about our photos, although they were all taken when we had minders so theoretically they should have been all right. We had no photos of photos of the Kims and none of the military or of any construction. We had been advised by one of the UN staff to put our photos on a SIM card and put it in another part of our luggage, and just leave innocuous photos of food and scenery on the camera. We had no idea whether that was a good idea but we did it anyway.

We went straight through security without any challenge, but both held our breath until the plane's wheels left the ground. Peter and I did a high-five.

'Fucking North Korea. I can't believe we just did that,' I laughed, feeling the tension of the last two weeks flow away.

We turned our minds to Seattle and a new grandson, and to getting into the US with fresh North Korean visas in our passports. The US was still so hostile towards that country, so in our ESTA visa waiver applications for the US we'd stated that we were coming via Korea, leaving out the North bit. We would not have got a waiver if we had put North Korea; when I'd tried, alerts immediately popped up on the online form. Now there were freshly stamped DPRK visas in our passports and we both had stories of difficult interactions at the US border. More breath-holding as we handed over our passports for examination. We had a rather pathetic plan to plead ignorance if the DPRK visa was spotted.

However, the officer's perusal through both our passports was to find a spare spot to stamp, not to look for suspicious travel. I was pleased not to be carrying my old passport with stamps from Afghanistan, Pakistan and a host of other 'difficult' countries. The officer happily stamped away. There are some advantages to being in a wheelchair at a border, and of course being white and from New Zealand. It would never have entered the guard's mind that this old crippled woman and her husband would have come from the DPRK.

—o—

It was autumn in the mountains of the American Pacific Northwest. The trees were dropping their dense, lush foliage all around us. Peter and I soaked in a hot tub overlooking Cle Elum Lake in the mountains of Washington state. The mist hung in the trees and a flurry of early snowflakes appeared, melting the instant they landed. Matt, Juls and Tim were all inside preparing the Thanksgiving meal, along with a gang of their lovely American friends. Maxime was tucked up, having his afternoon nap. As grandmother, I claimed the role of priority Maxime cuddler (after his mother, of course). There is nothing better in this life. American football was live on TV and the chatter among the friends was the backdrop for our soak.

Matt, Juls and their friends had hired a lovely big home by the lake to escape the city and to be thankful together, their families, except us, being far away in both distance and politics. Trump had complicated family dynamics in the US. Matt and Tim showed off their DPRK T-shirts and we dared them to wear them to work. Everyone loved hearing our tales of North Korea and seeing our photos. It seemed extraordinary that we'd been there, and I basked (probably falsely) in their adulation. It was great ego stuff.

We Skyped the family in New Zealand, and they were relieved and delighted to see us. Thankfulness was uppermost in my mind that day. Before dinner, I grabbed my walking stick, put on a warm coat and gloves, and wandered down to the lakeside to have a moment to myself. There was a small flat piece of grass under a huge redwood tree — the perfect spot for tai chi, which had been a mainstay of my wellbeing over the past few years. I laid my stick on the ground, paused, breathed, felt my feet on the earth, and moved into Parting the Wild Horse's Mane, White Crane Spreads Its Wings and Wave Hands Like Clouds. I was brought back into myself. I felt my breath, I heard the wind in the trees, the lake was deep green and still. I had only the present moment.

It felt momentous and I felt done, in the best possible way. There was no longer a need to prove anything to myself or to anyone else. I could let it all go.

I could hardly believe I was that same woman who, 40 years ago, had watched another woman give birth for the first time. It felt like there was nothing I hadn't done or still needed to do. I was eternally blessed. I was enough.

'Mum! Come inside. You must be freezing. Dinner's ready!'

Epilogue

August 2022

It's been pouring for days, the wettest winter in living memory. We can't wait any longer. Four of us, all Hutt girls, umbrellas, gumboots and measuring tapes in hand, are sizing up the perimeter of the land at the front of Wesley Rātā Village in Naenae. There is mist in the hills that tuck around the village and tūī in the thick native bush are calling out, seeming to ask each other 'What are these crazy women doing?'

'We are going to put a birth centre here,' I tell them.

Vida is striding out in metre-long steps, counting out loud. Drenched, she has taken off towards the stream, treading her wishes into the earth.

'How far should we go down here? It's pretty boggy,' she yells back to us through the rain.

'David thought we could put it further up this way, more on that slope so we could put car parks underneath,' Emily, the village community worker points out. 'The gardening group has started a vege patch down there.'

'We could incorporate it into the birth centre space. Imagine wandering about the cabbages in labour.' This from Susan, my precious midwife friend of 'trying to sleep under the table' fame.

Vida is a consumer champion and birth activist. Between the four of us, we have accumulated over a hundred years of trying to get a birth centre going in the Hutt Valley. I'm not sure we should be proud of such a significant failure.

But our imaginations have taken off. We are excited. We are crystal-clear. We have decided that this will be a joyful experience. Local health authorities, having failed childbearing women and midwives of the valley, will not wear us down. Measurements in hand, we retreat to one of the village's community spaces. Leaving our coats and boots at the door, we make strong coffee, pull the whiteboard closer and start articulating the vision.

This land is owned by Wesley Community Action, a radical social-service agency committed to community-led development. It has started up so many creative endeavours, working with vulnerable children, families, gangs and isolated older people, many of whom live in social housing built on this land. There are preschool play groups; cooking, gardening and art classes. It is a formidable and visionary organisation. Peter happens to be the chair and my daughter Kena is the community innovation lead. David, the CEO, is the father of Hana, a baby I helped to birth at home. Having a birth space here would have the agency covered from cradle to grave.

It was Peter who first suggested to me that we could put a birth centre here. He has always been great at imagining the possible. And sometimes the impossible. He'd arrived home from a meeting at the village where they had been talking with Kura Moeahu, the chair of the Te Āti Awa rūnanga, about developing closer partnerships. Peter mentioned to him that they were thinking of supporting a birthing place on the land. As Peter relates it, Kura became animated about the idea because the stream that runs through the village forms the headwaters of the Waiwhetu stream which runs off these hills and down towards their marae, flowing in a big bend around the marae as if wrapping it up in its embrace. According to the traditional birthing tikanga of Te Āti Awa, newborn babies should be blessed at the headwaters of their awa. And this is exactly where we are today.

'That is a very exciting prospect, and we will want to be involved. Make sure you keep in touch on this one,' he told Peter.

I immediately told the others and it gave us shivers. It felt like a sign. We were so going to try to make this work.

—◦—

But midwifery has not been working well recently in New Zealand. On the day I began writing this epilogue, midwives again took the Ministry of Health to court. The mediation that followed the first court action in 2015 had apparently progressed, and within a year and a half it was reported to us that the new contract structure and salary scales had been settled. But we were never to find out what they were, because in late 2017 there was a change of government and part of its election promise was to reform the entire health system. They would not agree to honour the two settlements because, I presume, they wanted to restructure the whole maternity service too.

Five years later, there had been no substantial action on maternity care. Midwives continue to earn 60 per cent of what an equivalent male worker earns. Not unexpectedly, they have abandoned the profession because of exhaustion, disenchantment and an inability to pay their bills. Student midwives do not, or cannot afford to, complete their training.

The shortage of midwives and the distress of the remaining workforce moved the situation from serious to critical. And that was even before the Covid-19 pandemic. Maternity care in the Hutt Valley is a good example of what is happening in other parts of the country. The shortage of midwives in the hospital became extreme, but instead of providing as much assistance as possible, the District Health Board seemed to lack any interest in maternity care. Despite the huge savings they made in not having to pay the missing midwives, they continued to impose punishing spending cuts. I had attended a public meeting late in 2019 to address concerns from the community about the service. Midwives who had been instructed not to comment publicly wept as they talked of the horrible 'care' they were able to provide.

'I am so tired of apologising to women,' one said. 'The care I am giving is just crap.'

Another commented: 'I'm terrified every time I go to work. I wonder whether this is the day someone will die on my shift.'

'The place is disgusting. There are chairs falling to bits. There are only two sphygmos [sphygmomanometers, for measuring blood pressure] on my ward. How am I expected to care for someone when I have to spend half an hour just trying to find the equipment?'

The mothers joined in, describing how frightened they were at being left alone for hours even when they rang their call bell, and at getting little or no help to breastfeed their baby. It was extraordinary. I had never heard anything like it before.

The shortage of midwives in the hospital was mirrored by the shortage of midwives in the community. Their numbers halved, even before the pandemic. And when the pandemic arrived, midwives' lives became excruciating. Unlike many others in healthcare, they were mostly unable to move their care into the virtual space. They pressed on, trying to find creative ways to still be able to 'be with women', risking their own health and the health of their own families. The response in the media was to criticise those few midwives who chose not to be immunised.

For women now who cannot find a midwife (there are a lot) and who can afford it (there are many fewer), their only option, if they want any sort of continuity of care, is to pay thousands of dollars to a private obstetrician. This is a worse outcome than even before we got midwifery autonomy. At least then there was some equity of access to care.

The final blow in the Hutt Valley fell on the birth centre. In 2018, a private philanthropic trust, the Wright Family Foundation, built a birth centre in the central Hutt Valley. They named it Te Awakairangi, after the river that flows down the valley. It had been a real relief for both mothers and midwives in the valley, and also relieved some pressure on the struggling hospital. The services remained free for all women. There was an assumption that the DHB would divert the primary maternity funding associated with each birth in the region to the centre. But the DHB refused to do this, calling the birth centre a 'privately run business' even though it never would, or could, make a profit. It appeared that primary maternity funding was too valuable an asset for the DHB for it to provide *actual* primary maternity care. This confirmed our suspicions that this funding was not ring-fenced for maternity care, but was almost certainly used to fund services in other parts of the hospital. It forced the owners of Te Awakairangi to continue funding the centre themselves, which cost them five million dollars.

In 2019 — just before, and partly triggering, the public meeting — the birthing centre had announced that it would close over the summer due to a lack of midwives in the region. By September 2021, the centre was permanently mothballed. This despite the hospital having just announced that its maternity unit was earthquake-prone and would need to be rebuilt. Even then, no relationship with Te Awakairangi as a birthing centre would be considered. The refusal to support it as a site for primary birth has occurred despite globally accepted best evidence and recommendations that healthy women and babies should not be cared for in hospitals. Supporting the service actively as the site where healthy women and babies should be cared for, and rebuilding a hospital focused on complex care only, would have made the Hutt Valley a leader in innovative and community-engaged maternity care. But there would be no long-term thinking here.

Eighteen months later, Te Whatu Ora (the old DHB — same people, different name) announced that they had taken over the centre from the Wright Family Foundation and were to repurpose it as a postnatal support service for women with premature babies so that they would not have to go into Wellington Hospital to receive care.

This approach to birthing spaces for healthy women with well babies is reflected in many places within New Zealand. In effect, Aotearoa is squandering a model of maternity care and of midwifery that is capable of supporting transformative whānau development, enhancing the power of mothering and easing inequity in healthcare. And it is a tragedy to see a new generation of midwives who may never experience — or even be able to envisage — the possibility of reviving a midwifery model where there is enough time to wait, enough space to imagine, and enough resources to thrive. The battle for the next generation of midwives and women has begun.

—o—

Writing a book about my story of birth and midwifery has been a different sort of challenge for me. The timing was terrible; I had only just started when the pandemic struck. It seemed so overwhelming and so important (and it was) that I thought no one could ever be interested in a story of the past, which was probably going to be irrelevant anyway. And then there is climate change, an overwhelming existential threat that we seem incapable of attending to. Who would seriously want to bring babies into this mess? Add to this the erosion of global democracy, the polarising and toxic division in our communities, the war in Ukraine with its threat of nuclear attack and the poverty and hardship caused by inequity.

And Afghanistan. Such horror. Is everything to be undone? What was the point in going there? The islands of Kiribati will be covered by the ocean. Why midwives then? The families of the wet and low-lying Bangladesh will all need to flee the rising sea. What will happen to the midwifery schools and the mothers they were preparing to help? The snows of the Tibetan plateau will melt, choking the countries downstream, including

Laos, Cambodia and Vietnam. How will all those midwives and mothers survive?

Our world today feels like a cauldron. The fumes and lava disgorged from it are truly terrifying, and appear terminal. I only hope that we can activate ourselves to control it before humanity is destroyed. I try to look at the big picture. As often as I think of it, I look at the stars. They confirm the insignificance of us all. One of my best moments was looking at the photos taken by the Webb telescope, seeing the pillars of all creation. And I look to the philosophers. When I did my PhD, reading Ulrich Beck helped me to understand the place of risk and fear in our society, the impact of failing modernism in the light of climate degradation, and the growing acceptance of the certainty of uncertainty. I could see their impacts on how we give birth. Beck seemed hopeful that humankind might find a more reconnected way of inhabiting the Earth. The Buddhist and the midwife in me hope that too.

My latest favourite philosopher is William MacAskill. He supports my cauldron theory and is a very big-picture person. He looks right back to the beginning of humankind and then forward, not only into the next century but right to when we cease to exist as a species. MacAskill has coined the word 'longtermism'. He points out that, barring catastrophe, the vast majority of people who will ever live have yet to be born, and he proposes that our current state of development as a species is in an unprecedented state of rapid change. He thinks that in the next hundred years we will make values-based decisions that will impact on humankind for the rest of our existence. We must look to the long term.

I am mostly not as bleak as might be supposed from what I have written thus far. I take hope from all the amazing progress that humanity is making. It is mostly hidden beneath the horror stories, so is sometimes hard to see. Apart from extraordinary technological progress, we are also beginning to make the most of our human ability to be reflective of the past and to learn from it, to look longer-term into the future and prepare for it. The United Nations' Sustainable Development Goals remain a call to hope and to hard work, despite the fact that they are going backwards now. It is hard stuff. We have a growing understanding, as a species, of our innate drives and how to work with them. We are just beginning to examine our biases and why and how they appear, to come to terms with and to welcome diversity. Sometimes it is through recognising our dark side that redemption arises. Most importantly, we are coming to reclaim our connectivity with each other, with the Earth and with the universe. And, of course, we still carry on having babies. What is hope if not that? How we support those babies to come to life, the women to motherhood and the whānau to strength is, and will always be, important. Midwives have a crucial role in this.

—◦—

Back at Wesley Rātā Village, the whiteboard fills up fast; my hand is barely able to keep up as the ideas flow. It's a poem. We will have a space here for women to come to birth and to motherhood. A space for infants to be welcomed to their land, whatever their lifelines. A space for whānau to become what they can. A space to weave the generations back together.

Bringing the community back to birth
Wandering around the garden in labour
If it ever dries out.
We need a big space for groups to gather.
Maybe the cooking group can do some meals. I love that there
    is a café on site.
What will the neighbours think?

Yes, I can just see the word going out across the village about
    someone in labour.
Muffins might be baked
Booties knitted
It's got to be better than that pink or blue neon light.

Celebrations and blessings
Hope joy peace
We'll have to make a lovely path down to the stream.

Mothers should be able to stay postnatally for at least a day.
We'll call it a blessing day or a welcome day.
I'm sure there will be a perfect te reo Māori phrase for that.
It will be great

when we can sit down with Te Āti Awa and share
the visioning.

Weaving whānau across the generations
Mana oreti

The space should be a haven with nature close,
Peaceful and soft
Women will thrive at birthing here
It should be safe here
physically spiritually socially culturally
The vulnerable feel welcome, and the strong will contribute

Where are we going to get the money?
Agghh, let's save that for later
Midwives are honoured for their mahi
And they love their workspace
Yes, and we help them and hear them

We wonder how many babies will come to breathe on this land.

Tihei mauri ora

About the author

Joan Skinner has been a midwife since gaining her registration at St Helens Hospital Wellington in 1976. She has worked in small birth units and hospitals; been a homebirth midwife and a lead maternity carer; managed a major hospital tertiary delivery unit and a postnatal ward; and worked in a community-owned health service in a high-needs community and in an iwi health service.

After gaining her PhD in midwifery in 2005 she was a senior lecturer at the Graduate School of Nursing, Midwifery and Health at Te Herenga Waka Victoria University of Wellington.

Within Aotearoa New Zealand she has provided consultancy services for the Accident Compensation Corporation, the Health and Disability Commissioner, several district health boards, the Ministry of Health and the coroner. Internationally she has had been a consultant for the World Health Organization, the United Nations Population Fund and the United States Agency for International Development, mainly in the Asia Pacific region.

In 2020 she completed a master's degree in creative writing from the International Institute of Modern Letters at Te Herenga Waka Victoria University of Wellington.

Joan lives in Korokoro, Wellington, with her husband Peter Glensor. They have a merged family of six children and eleven grandchildren.

Acknowledgements

I am so grateful to all those who helped me to write and produce this story.

As a tentative creative writer, I ventured out by night to Wellington High School's Community Education Centre's creative writing course and the following year to Victoria University of Wellington's community night class on memoir writing. They were both joyous experiences. For the first time ever, I attempted writing in some sort of creative way and people listened. The encouragement from the tutors, Jess Richards and Diane Comer, and my co-writers was transformative. Do not underestimate the power of community night classes.

This experience gave me the courage to apply to the International Institute of Modern Letters at Victoria University of Wellington to do a master's degree in creative writing. It was crazy that I got in. I acknowledge the support and guidance from the tutors James Brown and Anahera Gildea, and the generosity and love from my student buddies Safia Archer, Areez Katki, Fergus Porteous, Sarah Catherall, Ethan Te Ora, Justine Whitfield, Barbara Sumner and Joanna Cho. I was blown away to be in the company of such extraordinary writers. We were in lockdown for a significant part of the course yet managed to remain connected and committed. Thank you, Zoom.

To Massey University Press, who have taken the book to publication. Tracey Borgfeldt, Teresa McIntyre and Anna Bowbyes helped me polish the manuscript to completion. They were such a great help.

To all those midwives I talked with about our shared midwifery story, especially Susan Lennox, Jeannie Douché, Robyn Maude, Pamela Messervy, Jane Stojanovic, Bronwen Pelvin and Norma Campbell.

A special thanks to my sister-in-law and midwifery partner, Judith Stehr. We were a great working duo. Thanks for being so excited that the book was coming.

My sister Catherine was a marvellous editor and commentator. It was wonderful to share talk of our family. My brother Lew said I was a fabulous writer and reported having wept through the first chapter. It took me a year to write that chapter.

To my friends Anna Leydon, Mary Wilson, Jane Howley and Susan Moore. They contributed in so many ways, not least of which was wanting me with them as they gave birth. They all had bits of the book to look at and gave me such affirmation that it was worth persisting in telling the story.

To Pat Duignan, Sally Munro, Karen Skinner and John Schrooten, who over the years have lent me their beach houses in Waikanae for some focused writing. Blessings to the Olde Beach Bakery.

To my niece Kate Duignan who provided guidance and advice in moving the manuscript from first draft to preparation for submission to a publisher. It was invaluable help.

Our children and their families have stayed close as I put this story together. Matthew, Kena and Timothy Duignan, Sarah, Ben and Kim Glensor, and their partners Tavis Milner, Julie Anne Seguin, Lisa Cliff, Richard Best, Felicity Glensor and Fia Logologo. They loved me, encouraged me and kept me on my toes, providing some useful critique and input. They also produced 11 mokopuna who I hope will want to read the book one day.

My husband Peter has been my mainstay as I wrote this story. He has provided the space, the encouragement and the freedom for me to write and has been unwavering in his belief that I would produce a great book. He has revelled in the adventure of it all and has been and will always be my greatest fan. I got lucky there.

First published in 2023 by Massey University Press
Private Bag 102904, North Shore Mail Centre
Auckland 0745, New Zealand
www.masseypress.ac.nz

A catalogue record for this book is available from the National
Library of New Zealand

Printed and bound in Singapore by Markono Print Media

ISBN: 978-1-99-101642-3
eISBN: 978-1-99-101643-0